SAY IT ONE TIME FOR THE BROKENHEARTED

Country Soul in the American South

REVISED AND EXPANDED
30th ANNIVERSARY EDITION
with photographs by **MUIR MACKEAN**

BARNEY HOSKYNS
foreword by William Bell

My mother bore me in the southern wild
And: I am black, but O! my soul is white.
White as an angel is the English child:
But I am black as if bereav'd of light.
—William Blake

There's a redneck in the soul band,
He's gettin' down . . .
—Benny Latimore

Contents

Acknowledgments

Thanks first and foremost to Muir MacKean for venturing into the unknown with me all those years ago, and for taking such sensitive pictures of my Southern heroes. Then to Tony Peake and Michael Fishwick for getting this baby into print in the first place, and to Matthew Hamilton, Mike Jones, and Julian Alexander for bringing it back to life. And now to Scott B. Bomar at BMG and Matthew Elblonk at DeFiore & Co. for saying it one *more* time.

Thanks to the following (many no longer with us) for sharing their memories of the great country-soul era: Johnny Adams, Arthur Alexander, Gregg Allman, Estelle Axton, Barry Beckett, William Bell, Bobby "Blue" Bland, David Briggs, Mickey Buckins, Jerry Carrigan, Clarence Carter, Quinton Claunch, J.R. Cobb, Tommy Couch, Steve Cropper, Jim Dickinson, Hollis Dixon, Big Al Downing, Billy Earheart, Fred Foster, Donnie Fritts, John Fry, Mac Gayden, Dobie Gray, Rick Hall, Eddie Hinton, Paul Hornsby, Quin Ivy, Etta James, Roosevelt Jamison, Roland Janes, Ted Jarrett, David Johnson, Jimmy Johnson, James Joiner, Stan Kesler, Buddy Killen, Stan Lewis, Stewart Madison, Cosimo Matassa, Mighty Sam McClain, Willie Mitchell, Chips Moman, Don Nix, Ollie Nightingale, Spooner Oldham, Ann Peebles, Dan Penn, David Porter, Sandy Posey, Wardell Quezergue, Mac Rebennack, John Richbourg, Forrest Riley, Troy Seals, Marshall Sehorn, Roscoe Shelton, Shelby Singleton, Percy Sledge, George Soulé, Candi Staton, Wolf Stephenson, James Stroud, Swamp Dogg,

Rufus Thomas, Johnny Vincent, Phil Walden, Travis Wammack, Jerry Wexler, Bobby Womack, and Reggie Young.

In addition, my gratitude goes out to the following for invaluable help, suggestions and hospitality along the way: Steve Armitage, Bill Millar, Charlie Gillett, Nick Kimberley, Peter McKernan, Fred Dellar, Trevor Swaine, Cynthia Leu, John Lomax III, Roy Carr, Cliff White, Elvis Costello, Bob Merlis, Dick Cooper, Peter Thompson, Pete Nickols, Tex Davis, Mary Ledbetter, Bob Taylor, John Abbey, Ronnie Pugh, Alan Stoker, Doug and Terri Bonds, Richard and Cathy Dichtel, Bill and Nina Marden, and Billy Gibbons.

Finally, many thanks to my mother and my late father for their considerable support during the writing of this book.

Foreword

I made my first record back in 1956 when I was part of a singing group called the Del Rios in Memphis, Tennessee. I was still just a teenager, but I was already writing songs and trying to figure out how the music business worked. Released on the Meteor label, we were backed up by Rufus Thomas's band, the Bear Cats. Rufus was already an important figure on the Memphis music scene, so it was no surprise that his daughter Carla turned out to be a great singer. The father-daughter duo recorded a single for a local label called Satellite Records in 1960. Shortly after, Carla made her first solo record for Satellite. It was called "Gee Whiz," and my group was brought in to handle the background vocals. That was my first association with Satellite Records, which would be renamed Stax the following year.

Stax Records was founded by siblings Jim Stewart and Estelle Axton. Jim was a white guy from rural Tennessee who fell in love with music and started playing fiddle with a country band on the weekends. I, of course, was a black kid raised in the city who cut his teeth on gospel music. You would think our worlds couldn't be any more different, but the story of the music of the South is much more complicated than that. It's made up of a series of roots and branches that are often tangled and intertwined.

Early on, Jim Stewart hired Chips Moman as a staff producer at Stax. Chips was a white boy from Georgia who started out playing country and rockabilly, ended up as a session guitarist in Los Angeles, and found his way back down South while he was still in his early 20s.

Chips was the leader of a band called the Triumphs, which was one of the first racially integrated groups in Memphis. He was always after me to record a solo record for Stax, but I didn't really have any material and wasn't even sure that was the route I wanted to go.

Around that time I was performing on the road with a traveling group. We had a couple of days off, and I was stuck in this hotel up in New York City where it was raining like crazy. I had a girlfriend back in Memphis, and I was feeling a little homesick. I wrote this song called "You Don't Miss Your Water," which was really just personal therapy for my loneliness. I didn't really think much about it, but when I got home, I ran into Chips. He asked me again about doing a solo project, so I finally said I'd come over and sing some songs for him. He loved "You Don't Miss Your Water," so we recorded it with a racially mixed band that included members of the all-white group the Mar-Keys, along with black musicians Lewie Steinberg (bass), Marvell Thomas (piano), Howard Grimes (drums), and my buddy Booker T. Jones (organ), who I knew from the neighborhood.

"You Don't Miss Your Water" became my first hit, but it's a difficult song to categorize. Author Robert Gordon once described it as "a country music ballad that had been baptized in a black church feel." Today many people think of country music as "white" music and soul as "black" music, but it was never that simple in the South. If America is a melting pot, the unique environment below the Mason-Dixon Line is a perfect microcosm of how cultures collide, intersect, and create something fresh and new. Nowhere is that more evident than in our music.

My first musical influences came from the black church, but growing up in Memphis, I heard blues to country to jazz to rockabilly, which was a hybrid of soul, R&B, and country. We heard everything. Sam Cooke certainly inspired me, but I also thought Eddy Arnold was a great ballad singer. A lot of those country sounds stayed with me as I grew older. When I was working with the Del Rios, we were an in-demand vocal group. A lot of country singers hired us to perform on demo recordings around town, and I was well acquainted with Sam Phillips, who was mixing country and blues at his little studio over on Union Avenue. From there he introduced the world to Elvis

Presley, Jerry Lee Lewis, and Johnny Cash. Memphis is a place where I recorded backing vocals with Charlie Rich and jammed with Ronnie Milsap. We're all a product of our environment, and some of those country influences really resonated with me. And those influences ran both ways. If you listen to an early Hank Williams song, you know that he absorbed some blues and gospel when he was growing up down in Alabama. What some folks don't understand is that it all comes from the same place. Country and gospel and soul and blues are cousins. There are a lot of similarities in how these songs are written to tell a story. They often have similar subject matter, and they appeal to the realities of the everyday human experience.

"You Don't Miss Your Water" has been recorded by everyone from my friend Otis Redding, who gave it a pleadingly soulful blues feel, to the Byrds, who performed it as a stone-cold country ballad on their groundbreaking *Sweetheart of the Rodeo* album. The fact that the song can be interpreted in various ways is evidence of those deep and varied influences that came together inside that Stax studio where whites and blacks collaborated in a family atmosphere—even as segregation, intolerance, and racial injustice raged in the world outside its walls. We didn't care about race, creed, nationality, or gender. All we cared about was what you brought to the table in terms of creativity and musical ability.

I spent many great years at Stax, where I worked closely with my good friend and songwriting partner Booker T. Jones. He and I grew up in the same church, where he played the organ. Later, when he was in the MGs with Steve Cropper and Duck Dunn, we mixed it all together. Booker and I came out of the church, but Steve and Duck were into R&B. They'd also had a rockabilly group and listened to country. We brought it all into the creative process at Stax.

By the time I made my third album, *Wow*, I went down to Muscle Shoals to record. Just like in Memphis, whites and blacks were making music together. I really loved the sound they had going on down there. It was even a little more country influenced than Memphis, and those players had an emotional range and an authenticity that was truly special. The same is true of Nashville, which a lot of people think of as a strictly country town. Not true. Jim Stewart and Chips Moman traveled there to record Carla Thomas's first album after she hit with "Gee Whiz," and I was aware of all sorts of cross-pollination between that Memphis-Muscle Shoals-Nashville triangle. What I love about our whole region is the way the boundaries of strict categorization are repeatedly blurred.

It's hard to believe it's been more than three decades since I was first interviewed by Barney Hoskyns for *Say It One Time for the Brokenearted*. He approached his subject with love and the unique outside perspective of a British observer who recognized the important role of country music in shaping R&B in the South. Barney shared with the world what we Southern musicians sensed intuitively, giving his readers an important overview of the key movers and shakers—some well-known and some unsung heroes—of the country soul phenomenon. He was one of the first to begin to identify those influences for a wider audience, and I'm grateful for the opportunity to revisit the discussion once again.

All those years ago, Barney was on a journey to see if he could figure out where country stops and soul begins, or maybe the other way around. The threads are so interwoven, it's hard to say. I experienced that truth once again recently when I won my first Grammy in 2016. The category? Best Americana Album. My category wasn't R&B. It wasn't country. It was that uniquely American mix of roots music that blurs the divisions and celebrates our common roots. Barney was catching that wave years ago before anyone was using the word "Americana" to describe our music. I'm glad that the words and photos of his and Muir MacKean's journey are still here for us to enjoy and for future generations to treasure. Country soul is, indeed, a deep well. Fortunately, it's a well that doesn't seem to ever run dry.

William Bell
Atlanta, Georgia
February 10, 2018

Preface to this 30th anniversary edition

Named after an extemporary yelp in the fadeout of Kip Anderson's bereft 1968 single "I Went Off and Cried," *Say It One Time for the Brokenhearted* was my first book. Revisiting it for the second time in 30 years, it feels, in places, as callow and earnest as I was myself at age 26 when I wrote it. (A reissued edition, with footnotes, was published by Bloomsbury in the UK in 1998.) I'd retroactively fallen in love with a subgenre of American popular music that barely had a name, and I was close to evangelistic in my desire to turn people on to it.

The book's original 1987 subtitle was *The Country Side of Southern Soul*, its cover sporting an awkward splice of a tuxedoed Ray Charles wearing a Stetson hat. (Tuxedo = soul, Stetson = country: you get the drift.) Brother Ray had, of course, been one of the prime movers in bringing black and white music together—he followed up his groundbreaking *Modern Sounds in Country & Western Music* albums from 1962 with the even more explicitly titled *Country & Western Meets Rhythm & Blues*, aka *Together Again*, in 1965—but not even *he* used the term "country soul," which became part of the revised subtitle for *Say It*'s 1998 reissue and stays in place for this updated edition. I'm fairly sure I first encountered the phrase in Charlie Gillett's groundbreaking history *The Sound of the City* (1970).

As I now look back to the early 1980s, when I first wrote about music for the *NME*, I ask myself why "country soul" got under my skin to such a degree that I decided to write a whole book about it. Naturally I loved the music, but there was more to it than that: something poetic, something almost mystical. Learning, as a schoolboy, that Aretha Franklin had recorded her breakthrough Atlantic single "I Never Loved a Man"/"Do Right Woman, Do Right Man" in a tiny studio in (of all places) Alabama—engineered, moreover, by a local white man named Rick Hall—gave me a thrill and instilled a curiosity that led me on a long and winding journey to—well, the very studio where Franklin made that record.

The legend of Hall's FAME studio in Muscle Shoals resonated with me for two main reasons: 1) I'd spent much of my own life in the "countryside" (of Suffolk, England), and 2) I was sufficiently politicized on issues of race relations to be impressed by the notion of the Queen of Soul recording with a white Southerner—make that *several* white Southerners—in January 1967. How had that even *happened*?

It wasn't that I'd in any sense "gone off" more urban black music—I adored—and still love—the best funk and disco records made in the '70s—but that the slow, pleading, anguished ballads that emerged from Memphis, Muscle Shoals and, yes, even Nashville possessed a kind of backwoods purity, an emotional innocence that moved me more deeply than, say, Freddie Jackson's "Love Me Tonight." And if so many of those ballads were born of the unlikely collaboration of black and white Southerners, didn't that in some way offer hope for American society? Wasn't it, in fact, as much of a pop-cultural revolution as anything that happened in San Francisco's Haight-Ashbury?

In September 1985, Muir MacKean and I set off from Washington D.C. in an orange Volkswagen camper van on a three-month quest for the spirit of country soul (often in the footsteps of Peter Guralnick, who'd already met and lionized the likes of Hall and Penn for his definitive Sweet Soul Music). Armed with tapes and books, we planned to talk to as many of our Southern soul heroes—singers, songwriters, producers, session musicians—as we could before our money ran out. We ended up spending three weeks in Nashville, proceeding from there to Muscle Shoals, Atlanta, Macon, Memphis, Mississippi, New Orleans, and finally back to the East Coast. I stood in the very room where Aretha Franklin cut "I Never Loved A Man," running my fingers over the Wurlitzer electric piano that Spooner Oldham had played on it. After three months of RV camps and Dixie hospitality, I was treated to a long lunch in midtown Manhattan by Jerry Wexler, the Northern Jew who had himself fallen so deeply in love with the South.

All these decades later—so many years since the white Steve Cropper and Donald "Duck" Dunn first played in Memphis with the black Booker T. Jones and Al Jackson, Jr., or since the black Arthur Alexander first hung out in Alabama with the white Rick Hall and Dan Penn—doesn't country soul ask questions of where America is headed after the violent events surrounding the rally for white supremacy that occurred in Charlottesville, Virginia, in the summer of 2017?[1] It's hard to watch the stark racial divide that's opened up in the US in the wake of Donald Trump's election without despairing—to see the gloves coming off, to grasp the gleeful conservative contempt for liberal values of tolerance and multiethnic community that's now rampant in America. Say it another time for the brokenhearted believer in a better world.

Not long ago, as a result of the revived interest in *Say It One Time*, I stumbled on an academic review of the original 1987 book that all but accused me of racism. My book's implicit argument, the reviewer suggested, was that without the white songwriters, producers, and session musicians who contributed to their records, James Carr, Bettye Swann, Johnny Adams, Candi Staton, Percy Sledge and, yes, even Aretha Franklin and Otis Redding wouldn't have been the musical forces they were.[2] Furthermore, *Say It One Time* supposedly lamented the way Southern country soul had been superseded by the slick R&B of the late '70s and '80s, not to mention the radical street poetics of hip-hop.

I now think the reviewer wasn't entirely wrong. Indeed, I wonder if the book's central conceit wasn't a kind of projection of my own white guilt, or at least of my hopeful fantasy that black American Southerners had been able to forgive the horrors of slavery, lynching, and segregation

---

1 As I dot the *I*'s and cross the *T*'s in December 2017 in this revised edition of *Say It One Time*, the heartening news comes in that Alabama has rejected the right-wing Senate candidate Roy Moore. But one can't help wondering how many white musicians of the Muscle Shoals country-soul era voted for Moore (and, for that matter, for Trump).

2 Persuasively argued and scrupulously researched, Charles S. Hughes's *Country Soul: Making Music and Making Race* can almost be read as a book-length version of that review. Yet it felt oddly joyless and drew on a mere nine firsthand interviews. Hughes seemed incapable of believing that a single thing a white person ever did in a Southern recording studio wasn't at least subconsciously racist. Even checking my white privilege as I'm obliged to do, *Country Soul* didn't synch with what the story's *dramatis personae*—white *and* black—told me in the interviews I conducted for *Say It One Time*.

for long enough to embrace an essentially white music that seemed insep-arable from racism. When I interviewed Hall and Penn—and dozens of other white Southerners who contributed to the greatest country soul records—it was because their socially transgressive love of black music (and specifically of black voices) mirrored my own immersion in it. Their romance with rhythm and blues and soul music was *my* romance.

I still maintain that the marriage of black gospel passion and white instrumental restraint—best exemplified by the sound and feel of the various Muscle Shoals studios—produced the greatest Southern soul of all. But that doesn't mean I deem it innately superior to the best music by Marvin Gaye, Stevie Wonder, Gladys Knight, Smokey Robinson, Curtis Mayfield, Sly Stone, Donny Hathaway, Holland-Dozier-Holland, Gamble & Huff, Thom Bell, Prince, Michael Jackson, or Mary J. Blige. (Or, for that matter, Bert Berns or Burt Bacharach). Or, while we're about it, Rihanna, whose stunning "Love on the Brain" proves in any case that the tortured lovesickness of the country soul ballad is alive and well in contemporary R&B. It's simply that I find the country soul of the '60s and early '70s more heartbreakingly cathartic than any other music I know.

Some caveats, 30 years on. *Say It One Time* is more than a little obsessive in places. It's also overly scholarly in its efforts to sound authoritative, espe-cially when so much thorough work has been done in its (and Guralnick's) slipstream. We live now in a world where one can buy box sets like Ace's *The FAME Records Story* (2011), not to mention the significantly earlier *From Where I Stand: The Black Experience in Country Music* (1999), and a world where most Americana-loving readers of *MOJO* know where the FAME studio is located. Who could have predicted in 1985 that Muscle Shoals would one day be the subject of a feature-length documentary?[3]

Still, I trust that my love for the records I was able to track down in the '80s—or which had already been compiled and reissued by labels like Charly—remains infectious in these pages. Say it one *more* time.

Ithaca, Greece, September 2017

---

3   See also the country-soul compilations on Trikont (2005's *Dirty Laundry* and 2009's *More Dirty Laundry*); on Jasmine (2016's *Please Release Me: The Soulful Side of Country*); and particularly on Ace's Kent subsidiary label: *Behind Closed Doors* (Kent, 2012), *Sweet Dreams* (Kent, 2013), and *Cold Cold Heart* (Kent, 2014), along with the corresponding *Out of Left Field* (2016), a compilation of white country versions of black R&B hits, and the *FAME Recordings* (2013) of the great Dan Penn.

Introduction

"The kind of music we're doing ain't Nashville and
it ain't Memphis. I think it's a country sort of gospel
that folks've been doing for a long time."
—Delaney Bramlett, 1971

The country of *Say It One Time for the Brokenhearted* is the American South, and the book's aim is to rectify a picture of the South in which the cultures of black and white people are ineluctably segregated. Focusing on one phase of Southern music—the soul of the 1960s and early '70s—it attempts to show how a virtually indigenous sound evolved from the marriage of black and white traditions.

This sound, for want of a better term, was "country soul," so-called not because it was made out in the proverbial boondocks (it wasn't always), but because its essential flavor was rural, earthy, steeped in the country church. It was a sound forged by blacks and whites working together and dissolving the color barrier.

Of course, the particular influence of "capital C" Country music on Southern soul may, at first glance, be hard to construe. It's not easy to see the common ground between the testifying black gospel singer and the fiddling, hee-hawing hillbilly in overalls—in twentieth-century mythology they're sworn enemies. Yet the relationship is more interdependent than it appears. The common ground is simply the South itself.

A large problem is that racism is built into the very categories of popular culture. Unwittingly, we're taught to view "country" music as an exclusively white province and "soul" as an African American birthright. Our received stereotypes of country and R&B singers only perpetuate the artificial barriers between the two races. This book hopes to show how many times the mold has been broken, how the mutual influence between black and white music extends far back to the days of slavery. Perhaps it shows how protean and elastic culture can be despite the rigidity of our models.

At the same time, there *are* differences in the way whites and African Americans express themselves in music, and one wouldn't wish to eradicate, or melt down, all the pluralities of culture. Both races bring very particular ingredients to the brew of this book, and its story is as much about the tension between those ingredients as about the harmony. For the most part, African Americans neither sing nor sound like whites: there's a physical difference in the timbre of the larynx that produces the sound. Exceptions underline the rule, of course: Charley Pride sounded close to white, while Eddie Hinton might have been black. But, in the main, an African American voice is the more emotive instrument—the fuller, richer, stronger sound.

The differences between black and white music are rooted in sure foundations, and no hybrid of styles, such as occurred with Southern soul, can alter those. Three centuries ago, when African song was both antiphonal—based on a call-and-response structure—and polyrhythmic, Anglo-Celtic immigrants in Appalachia still sang folk ballads that dated back to pre-Elizabethan Britain. Between these two musical forms there was precious little connection.

The fact, however, that echoes of primitive African song combined three hundred years later with those of the old English ballad is what makes the dynamics of culture so fascinating. For "country soul" was really a black gospel foreground—with all the vocal improvisation and intensity that implies—superimposed on a white country background. It laid down a simple country arrangement, often an actual country song, but replaced the nasal whine of Nashville singers with a more powerful black vocal straight out of the church. (The interchange between country and gospel was direct and immediate: both shared not only the 8- or 16-bar form but identical chord patterns to boot.)

There's something of a conundrum to all this, of course. One abhors racism and watches with hope for signs of interracial exchange while simultaneously hoping that the unique, vital pneuma of a culture won't be sucked into the global-village mass. As Bill C. Malone wrote in the epilogue to his *Country Music USA*, "If one would preserve the rural musical styles, he must also preserve the culture that gave rise to them, a society characterized by cultural isolation, racism, poverty, ignorance, and religious fundamentalism."

In the case of Southern soul, as it happens, the differences between black and white did not collapse—soul and country did not melt into each other. In fact, "country soul" came and more or less went within fifteen years and now, in retrospect, looks like one of those quaint golden ages of an art form. On the wider pop front, black and white styles continued to influence each other, but Southern soul shook off its country-gospel roots. There was a return to hard rhythm'n'blues, but not (despite the Levi's-inspired revival of his classic "When a Man Loves a Woman") the country-soul ballad sound of a Percy Sledge. The passionate balladeer became a sophisticated urban male in the Luther Vandross/Freddie Jackson mold, not appealing hugely (as Sledge did) to rural white audiences in the South.[4]

At least a part of the reason for this was the increasing urbanization of American life, As people became less cut off from the media and entertainment centers of New York and Los Angeles, so they were more quickly exposed to the rapid changes in musical sound and image that urban life created, and less satisfied with the traditions that hitherto had sheltered them. By the end of the 20th century, there were few true enclaves of indigenous culture or art left.

The South was, of course, the most defiantly "regional" of all American regions and the white Southerner the most extreme and idiosyncratic American. Everything about his history and culture, down to the Stetson hats and drawling accents, set him off from the rest of

---

4   Even Vandross and Jackson seemed quaint in the context of '90s R&B, swingbeat, and hip-hop. On the other hand, the spate of retro-soulsters that emerged in the wake of D'Angelo—from Maxwell and Jill Scott to Rashaan Patterson and beyond—suggested there was still room for a "country-soul" balladeer on the R&B scene.

America. New Yorkers and Californians affected to despise each other, but they were closer than the Southerner was to either of them.

What was maddening about the South's pride, its very *Gone with the Wind* "romance," was its rooting in the heritage of slavery and racism. What outsiders found so hard to comprehend was that, despite all the white hate and savagery towards black people, there was a stronger bond between black and white Southerners than between Southerners (of either race) and Northerners.

In a 1966 essay from his *Farewell to the South*, Robert Coles quoted a ten-year-old Mississippi black girl who has just spent two weeks on an exchange stay in Harlem: "It's different up North. They don't have the room we do, and they don't talk to anyone no matter what his color be . . . and I think the colored and white, they're spinning in different grooves. Back home, we all go around together. We may not be very equal together, but we're around each other, and we know things about the other race. Me, I don't think I could live up North. It makes me nervous. The streets and the people do, and you get so cold, you just pull yourself into your scarf and forget everyone."

Similarly, Gerri Hirshey in *Nowhere to Run* quoted James Brown's father Joe: "I could buy me a fancy house on Long Island, and every day I'm gonna lay my head on the pillow, scared thinkin' some white man been nice to me at the gas pump gonna blow me sky-high. Northern white man sneaky. Southern white man, least he let you know where you stand. He tell you to go round to the *back* door to get your sandwich, you gonna find a sandwich. Period."

Both these testimonies posited a South where whites and African Americans, despite—or perhaps almost because of—racial prejudice, were open and honest with each other. The little girl made a common connection between this openness and the Southern climate, a climate in which people weren't insulated from each other. Joe Brown was an old man, but his need to "know where you stand" and his suspicion of the Northern white's "sneakiness" were attitudes that long prevailed among older Southern African Americans.

The South was America's rural underside. What bonded black and white below the Mason-Dixon line was that they'd historically worked the land together; the giant cities and industries of the North largely did not exist in the South. While hundreds of thousands of poor blacks and whites migrated to those cities and industries, the many who remained behind were tied together by the agricultural basis of Southern life.

The '80s revival of "downhome blues," sparked by Z.Z. Hill's huge Southern hit of that name, expressed a nostalgia for the funky simplicity and earthiness of Southern country life. Downhome meant chitlins and collard greens; it meant red clay, everything that wasn't congested, northern, uptown. It also meant a degree of acceptance of what had happened in the South, lynchings and all. It said the South was home despite everything.

White "country" music was, of course, based almost totally on a nostalgia for the rural life that veered from sentimentality to self-parody. By the hostile outsider, moreover, it was taken to be the very voice of malicious redneck bigotry, with images conveniently formed by films such as the British-directed Deliverance. Country music's first recorded star, Fiddlin' John Carson, played for the Ku Klux Klan, and the link between "hillbilly" song and white-trash racism had always hung over Nashville.

The country music popularly heard was so unequivocally white that, combined with our conditioning images, it almost *sounded* racist. What few knew was that artists such as Jimmie Rodgers and the Carter Family were profoundly influenced by black blues. And what most overlooked was that the church was the single biggest influence on the "country" music of *both* races.

God and the land: this was what Southern life always came back to. Nowhere else in America had religion and agriculture so dominated peoples' lives, and nowhere else, ironically, were the black and white experiences of life so similar.

Why did "country soul" die out, then? Why did Stax and the other companies collapse and the blacks and whites go their separate ways? Will they ever come together again, or is a black "country" soul music impossible in our techno-synthetic age?

Broadly, two paths were laid out for soul in the '60s: one was Motown, the other Stax. Motown's Northern dance-pop sound, which brought black style into the white mainstream, was ultimately the path chosen. As Jerry Wexler said, Motown made music for white middle-class teenagers where Stax made music for black proletarian adults. (Guess who had more spending power.) It's a fine irony that where Berry Gordy's Detroit company was almost entirely black-staffed, the Southern companies were almost all run by whites.

When Otis Redding's white manager Phil Walden was asked if there could ever be another Otis, he replied "No, I don't think things will ever be that rural again." The radical black identity of Motown's emergent "artists" in the late '60s—Marvin Gaye and Stevie Wonder among them—made Redding look hokey. Motown was the victory of Diana Ross over Aretha Franklin, of Lionel Richie over Al Green, of glitz 'n' glamour over grits'n'gravy. The last thing the hip kids of the beatbox generation wanted to know about was downhome Southern soul. The rural influences of blues and church were, if not lost, at least wholly subsumed.

Did "country soul" no longer exist, then? Not exactly. It lived on in, of all places, contemporary country music, albeit in airbrushed form. Gone were the high, reedy, Appalachian voices of yesteryear; the new stars had inherited the emotional delivery of the '60s soul clan. Nor was this altogether surprising when one considered that a majority of the white players and producers who'd worked in Southern soul were now based in Nashville. It might even have been said that Music City was going through something of a midlife crisis as it watched its most sacred traditions being spurned. The popularity of Ricky Skaggs and George Strait, along with the nouveau honky-tonk of Dwight Yoakam and Randy Travis, owed at least something to the fear that "real" country music was dying out.[5]

Again we saw the dichotomy of regionalism. Nashville itself centralized (and necessarily urbanized) the country recording business, becoming too big to fend off the outside influences of pop and soul. "Country" was no longer the music of farmers, and the day came came when the concept of "country," like a leaky pail, no longer held water. It was amusing to watch urban Nashvillians become neurotic

---

5   When I spent three weeks in Nashville in 1985, one of the people I interviewed was former soul session drummer James Stroud. A veteran of sides like King Floyd's "Groove Me" and Jean Knight's "Mr. Big Stuff," Stroud had just started his own production and publishing company. By 1998 he was the boss of DreamWorks Nashville.

custodians of the old hillbilly world—the *Urban Cowboy* phenomenon showed how the fetish of "country" could even be incorporated into the culture of city life.

African Americans had less to be nostalgic about. On the other hand, we saw a generation of hip-hoppers mellowing into middle age and craving a music that answered their emotional needs more fully than a claptrack. Gladys Knight's man took that midnight train from L.A. back to Georgia, "a simpler place and time," and prodigal modern souls made the same trip home.

This book runs counter to the prevailing urban trends of youth culture. It looks back to a purer kind of expression and asks whether there wasn't something more sincere and real about the music of country people in the last era before backwoods culture was finally swamped by urban psychosis.

1 Prelude

Land of a Million Churches

"To black people music is like communion. It's
bread ... in the transcendental sense."
—Jerry Wexler

The heritage of the American South is a grim one, and one that
makes the convoluted story of black and white soul music all the
more intriguing.

How an institution as odious and barbaric as slavery managed to
survive in America for over two hundred years would surely baffle
us without the genocide of the Jews and other peoples to compare it
to. How white people in the twentieth century continued to hate and
fear African Americans enough to lynch them is stupefying until we
acknowledge the prevalence of such ritual terrorizing today. What's
really amazing is that African Americans ever deigned to make music
with whites at all.

The first Africans landed in America in 1619, a year before the
Pilgrims arrived from England. They'd been wrenched into a completely alien world as though they were animals without thought or
feeling. Nineteen years later the slave trade began in New England,
and in 1661 the first of the Black Codes in Virginia gave it statutory
recognition. Condemned by the Quakers as early as 1688, the slave

1

trade flourished throughout the colonial period, especially with the demand from Southern rice and tobacco planters. (The invention of the cotton gin in 1793 only increased that demand.) Even after the trade in human lives had been abolished in 1808, the South clung stubbornly on, forcing the Civil War that finally gave slaves freedom.

The sole musical outlet slaves had for their pain was the white man's church. The working day was too long for them to do anything but collapse when it was over. In church they were let loose on the psalms and hymns Methodist missionaries had brought from England, and in the staid formality of this music found melodies they could turn and shape to their own ends. In particular, the hymns of the English minister Dr. Isaac Watts, first published in America in the "Great Awakening" of the 1730s, attracted slaves through what Tony Heilbut called their "blunt metaphors of physical trouble and spiritual transcendence." These began to replace the scriptural psalms that had hitherto been the staple fare of the Protestant church.

Slave owners were wary of their slaves being allowed to congregate in one place but bowed to missionary pressure to allow their heathen souls to be converted. The first slave was baptized and taken into the church as early as 1641. The Great Awakening, a century later, saw many others follow. Watts's *Hymns and Spiritual Songs* was published in 1739, giving slaves such stirring anthems as "That Awful Day Will Surely Come" and "Must Jesus Bear the Cross Alone," and dominating the black church for another century. What was most frustrating for the slaves was the Protestant restriction on physical expression in the church. Where African religious ritual stressed physical movement and accompaniment to music, the white church forbade it and thus forced African Americans to channel their feelings into the act of singing.

Throughout the 18th and 19th centuries, whites were impressed by the new dimensions slaves brought to the music of the Protestant church. The roots of great soul singing lay in this encounter between European melodic regularity and African vocal improvisation, with the strict long- and common-meter hymn forms setting up challenges for the more elastic black voice. "Wild," "moaning," "plaintive," and "mournful" were just some of the epithets used by white observers to describe the vocal power of slaves as they slurred and flattened tones in the major chord resolutions.

Granted that African Americans did not *choose* to sing the white man's hymns, the meeting of black and white music in the South was the more pronounced for the greater proximity that existed there between master and slave. Only in the South did comparatively poor farmers own slaves. On the smaller farms of the Southern uplands particularly—Tennessee, Kentucky, the northern parts of Georgia, Alabama and Mississippi—African traditions quickly died out and slaves began imitating the 8- and 16-bar "ballits" that were the precursors of country songs. (Even early blues songs probably followed the English ballad structure.)

A major source of black and white interchange was the "camp meeting" that characterized the Second Awakening, or Great Revival, of the early nineteenth century. These gatherings were the best example in pre–Civil War America of blacks and whites coming together to make music. Again, their breeding ground was the upland hill country where slavery was of the more domestic kind, and slaves were more exposed to the customs and songs of their masters. The camp meeting was the great communal release of the rural South, when whites and African Americans of all Protestant denominations assembled in makeshift camps to sing and hear preachers (sometimes black) for up to three or four days. The first, in July 1800, drew thousands to Logan County, Kentucky, the evangelical craze rapidly spreading through Tennessee down to the Carolinas.

The music of these meetings was rough and rural. Eighteenth-century hymns such as those of Watts and the Wesleys were adapted to the form of popular ballads and songs, spontaneous refrains being added by the spirit-crazed Revival crowds. The slaves—sometimes intermingled, sometimes sat apart—frequently drowned out the whites and continued singing long after their masters had retired. It's generally accepted that what became the later Negro spirituals had their inception in these all-night sessions.

In 1933 George Pullen Jackson wrote of "the romantic zeal of those who wish to believe that the Negro's songs are exclusively his own creations." In his *White Spirituals in the Southern Uplands,* he attempted to expand on the work of Newman I. White and others to show that many "Negro spirituals" had evolved out of stanzas borrowed from white rural "Fasola" songbooks of the antebellum period. At the same time, he conceded that "the Negroes have never been content to use the white man's tunes without various and quite radical changes" and wrote that closer examination of the spirituals would "probably show that the Negro has simplified the tunes in respect of pitch compass, loosened up the exactions of their scale intervals, and complicated their simple rhythmic thread." A roundabout way of saying, perhaps, that English hymns plus black voices equalled a primitive kind of soul music.

Purely African elements *were* retained in the context of white religion. Both at the camp meetings and on the larger plantations of the tidewater, the all-night sessions held by slaves featured the "ring shout" service, a kind of sublimated dance ritual that lasted up to five hours and was a direct throwback to African custom. Dancing being prohibited for slaves, the service took the form of a slowly moving circle in which participants clapped and stamped, working up from a trance state to a point of physical collapse. It's significant that a bishop of the black African Methodist Episcopal Church in Philadelphia condemned this practice and dismissed the "spiritual songs" of the camp meetings as "cornfield ditties." It seems there was already a greater empathy between rural Southerners of both races than existed between urban and country blacks.

Less is known of the music slaves made outside the church. Drums were banned on plantations as instruments of incitement to rebellion, thus restricting blacks to string instruments built from materials such as dried gourds. Ironically the fiddle, symbol of hillbilly music in the early twentieth century, was a principal instrument: colonists were very fond of Negro "jigs," and slaves fiddled at plantation balls as early as 1774. The church naturally decried all such music as diabolical and remained the only real center of black musical life until after emancipation. As for the work songs slaves sang in the fields, these were undoubtedly African in form and rhythm and were encouraged by slave owners because they increased productivity.

Later black forms such as ragtime, blues, and jazz developed from this secular counterpart to church music. Access to instruments removed the emphasis on the human voice, allowing other aspects of African tradition to emerge. With emancipation in 1863, the field hollers began to take structured shape as primitive blues, and many former spiritual singers must have "backslid" from the church. Exactly when the 8- and 16-bar "ballit" (which followed the same structure as the hymns) was left behind by the nascent 12-bar blues form is hard to pinpoint. One thing that's certain is that as many ex-slaves stayed in the church and stuck to the root hymnody of the white man.

What *did* change in the black church after emancipation was that the urban denominatons expanded rapidly, affecting the music in the process. Exclusively black congregations first formed in Virginia and Georgia in the 1780s, allowing greater musical freedom and perhaps a certain reincorporation of African elements. Richard Allen, one of the first African Americans to be granted a licence to preach in America, compiled a black hymnal in 1801 that added refrain lines and choruses to otherwise orthodox Protestant stanza forms (many of them Watts hymns) in a way that clearly pointed back to the antiphonal singing of Africans.

Now large trained choirs were brought in, leaving behind the primitive and spontaneous sound and European choral tradition of the country church and paving the way for the Holiness and Pentecostal churches that became the seedbed of 20th century gospel music. (The first musically important Pentecostal sect formed near Memphis in 1895.) This was a faster, more rhythmic and orchestrated music, moving on from the heavy, mournful hymns of the country Baptist church with melodies borrowed from popular Tin Pan Alley songs and eventually, in the 1920s, from blues. Above all, it was *black* music.

Pastoral Scenes of the Gallant South

Ironically, blacks and whites of the South were more distant from each other *after* emancipation than before. The 1876 "Redemption of the South" and the "Jim Crow" legislation that began in 1890 nurtured segregation in almost every area of Southern life, the church being no exception. In towns and cities it was worse, with the more visible separation of the ghettos that sprang up when African Americans moved in from the country to find jobs in the growing steel and cotton-processing industries.

In the countryside there was generally more intercourse and less suspicion between blacks and whites than in the new Southern cities. Notwithstanding a fanatical minority of racists who materialized as white supremacy groups like the Ku Klux Klan, the Pale Paces, and the Knights of the White Camelia, the majority of poor farmers and sharecroppers found themselves cast into the same lot as enfranchised African Americans and accepted it.

"I would say it was only about 15 percent of whites who were fomenting the trouble," said John Richbourg, a white disc jockey who pioneered the airplay of rhythm'n'blues in the 1940s, and who grew up in South Carolina in the second decade of the twentieth century. "The white's attitude to blacks was 'You stay in your place and you'll be my friend.' But that place was never really defined. I guess what it meant was 'You stay in the background and if I need you I'll shake your chain.' As long as blacks accepted that, there were no problems."

Of course they didn't accept it for long, but they accepted it longer in the country than in the city. As Tony Russell noted in his *Blacks, Whites, and Blues,* racial interaction was paradoxically more fertile in areas where blacks were more scattered. The two races were first brought into direct rivalry when competing for subsistence wages in the cotton fields, mines, and wharves. Since the poor white's self-esteem was based on his hitherto unquestioned superiority over the black man, this was the ultimate degradation, particularly when Southern employers could count on African Americans not striking. Political demagogues seized on white resentment as a tried-and-tested vote catcher, and disenfranchisement of blacks began taking effect in the 1890s. Yet the racial war obscured a more basic power struggle between upland farmers on one hand, and, on the other, lowland plantation owners whose black employees could be coerced into voting in the patrician-planters' interests.

Thus did the African American become one of history's most tragic scapegoats. Between the end of the Civil War in 1865 and America's entry into the Second World War in 1941, there were over 4,000 lynchings in America, mainly of blacks and mainly in the South. By far the worst period was the last thirty years of the 19th century. After 1899 the practice declined, though the proportion of lynchings in the South increased and that of whites decreased. By the 1920s, Alabama could boast of four straight years without a single lynching, North Carolina of eight.

In his wildly impressionistic *Mind of the South* (1941), Wilbur J. Cash observed that "contact between the Negro and the rural poor white has always remained peculiarly intimate after a fashion. White croppers and tenants would not infrequently sit on the black man's steps and even in his kitchen, talk with him of the hazards of the seasons and the elements which they faced in common . . ."

In Appalachia of all places, presumed stronghold of regressive hillbilly values, the Lutheran and Calvinist bent of Celtic and North European settlers had always emphasized equality and freedom of conscience, thus breeding an unusual degree of tolerance. Although mountaineers were gradually won round to slavery, and abolition societies in the region had vanished by 1840, African American historian Carter G. Woodson could write in 1916 that "in Appalachian America the races still maintain a sort of social contact, white and black men work side by side, visit each other in their homes, and often attend the same church to listen with delight to the word spoken by either a colored or a white preacher."

In the early years after emancipation, saloons served both races at the same bar (even in Mississippi, most reactionary of the old Confederate states), while in South Carolina African Americans were permitted to ride first-class on trains—a deceptive freedom that didn't last long but was nonetheless a first taste of integration. With the building of the railroads in the 1880s, stretching from the Piedmont country of the east to the Texas plains in the west, blacks and whites worked together and heard each other's music. In areas such as the Appalachian mountains, where they were outnumbered by twelve to one, African Americans were exposed to a greater proportion of white ballads and folk songs, which they in turn adapted and altered. At the same time it's likely that black railroad workers brought the first guitars and blues songs into the mountains. Thus the influence was entirely reciprocal.

A Common Stock

Tony Russell wrote that if blacks had any form of "leisure-time" music in the nineteenth century it probably belonged to a "common stock" of ballads, train songs, hymns, and fiddle/banjo tunes sung by both races. These included ballads about heroes ("John Henry") and antiheroes ("Stack O'Lee"), train songs such as "Poor Boy, Long Way From Home," and fiddle/banjo numbers such as "Sourwood Mountain" and "Buffalo Gal." They were as prevalent in the repertoires of black songsters as they were in those of hillbilly entertainers.

In *Songsters and Saints* (1984), the late Paul Oliver wrote of an "urgent need for a more searching examination of the relationship of white song traditions to those of blacks" and added that "it may be noted that many white folk singers have acknowledged their debt to black musicians; the reverse influence of whites on blacks is far less frequently stated."

Perhaps an old liberal white guilt prevented musicologists attempting anything so contentious. Certainly the post-war cult of the blues was founded on a deification of the African American—male in particular—that only propped up the barriers it purported to demolish. Through the work of Oliver and Russell we've come to see there was more to the picture, socio-historically, than the standard "story of the blues."

White obsession with blues magnified it to the point where it obscured the numerous other "vocal traditions" of early "race" records in the South. Peetie Wheatstraw, Kokomo Arnold, Son House, and Blind Willie McTell were just some of the early bluesmen Oliver listed as retaining songs from the common stock in their repertoires. They were singers who could as well have been seen in hindsight as "songsters" as bluesmen. Admittedly, Oliver noted, many of the ballads collected in the field were more often recorded by hillbilly artists, but "there is a strong possibility that ballads generally considered to be black were, in a number of instances, the work originally of white composers, remaining in the white tradition for years after they had been discarded by black songsters." Other songs, he went on, "were very likely of black origin, but continued to be popular with white songsters, the appeal of a good tune and a strong theme transcending race barriers. But the precise origin of many ballads must remain contentious. As many white and black songsters worked together in medicine shows and rural picnics and functions, they invariably picked up or exchanged the songs of their respective cultural groups."

In any case, in the 1930s John A. Lomax could still find a black Texan convict singing old English ballads like "The Farmer's Curst Wife" and "The Maid Freed from the Gallows," while African Americans in the Appalachian and Blue Ridge mountains continued to draw from the old common stock as well as from contemporary blues. In the 1960s, the Texan singer Mance Lipscomb emerged as a songster whose repertoire had barely changed in forty years.

Perhaps the most interesting area of black-white interchange in the nineteenth century centered on the peculiar institution of the minstrel show. In this uniquely American entertainment, white vaudeville performers donned blackface and acted out parodies of "darky" life on the plantation, eventually (and ironically) influencing blacks themselves. It's a measure of the appeal of blackface comedy that it was used before the American Revolution of the 1770s and still being performed by old-time banjoist Clarence Ashley in bluegrass shows around east Tennessee in 1950.

The minstrel shows first appeared around 1800. By the 1840s they were all the rage, growing in popularity even as the Abolition movement grew. As Robert C. Toll showed in his book *Blacking Up* (1974), they served as a way of alleviating white fear and guilt: by making African Americans comical, they removed any obligation to confront their suffering. Even when the predominantly Northern shows condemned slavery, implicitly or explicitly, their strictures were always balanced out by scenes of contented buffoons on the plantation. The later black minstrel companies cannily exploited this appetite for sentimentality: in the late 1870s, for example, Haverly's Colored Minstrels staged a huge plantation scene featuring over a hundred black singers, dancers, and comedians.

Musically, the minstrel show set up a complex sequence of interrelations. Whites imitated African Americans—a not altogether insincere form of flattery—only to have African Americans imitate their imitations. Establishing a distant precedent for rock'n'roll, Northern whites visited Southern plantations to obtain "Ethiopian" material for their shows, then had their minstrel songs (now jumbled up with elements of the Scottish/Irish folk ballad) repossessed by *real* African Americans. (Toll quoted a St. Louis writer of the 1870s who noted, without irony, that "a Negro can play the Negro's peculiarities much more satisfactorily than a white artist with burnt cork.") Furthermore, the songs of the African American James Bland (1854–1911) were no less sentimental or patronizing towards black people than those of the white Stephen Foster (1826–64). The difference between Foster's "My Old Kentucky Home" and Bland's "Carry Me Back to Ole Virginny" is negligible.

With African American minstrels applying blackface and enormous red lips to their faces, the grotesque blurred into the absurd. Yet they were taking the only route available to them in American show business: marketing their very blackness. It was probably by this process, too, that the ragtime craze came about. As Amiri Baraka (as LeRoi Jones) wrote in *Blues People:* "It is valid to assume that ragtime developed from the paradox of minstrelsy, insofar as it was a music the Negro came to in imitating white imitations of Negro music."

The minstrels' influence filtered through to the South in the frontier towns where black and white musicians congregated. Although there were few actual integrated performances, many minstrel troupes were mixed. Wrote Toll, "both South Carolina Negroes and white boatmen knew 'Possum Up a Gum Tree'; Negro fishermen on the Mississippi sang 'Clare de Kitchen'; and a Negro banjoist at a white frontier frolic in Tennessee in the early 1830s played 'De Old Jawbone.' Furthermore, black and white backwoodsmen both danced many of the same jigs and reels. The blend of Afro- and Euro-American musical and dance styles, which later became common in American popular culture, began on the frontier and was first given wide exposure by minstrels."

Many of the Southern black "folk songs" later collected in the first quarter of this century were found to derive from the tunes of these minstrels. In the words of Newman I. White, who collected 680 such items in his *American Negro Folk Songs* (1928), "the Negro learned them from the white man, and on request sang them back to the white man because he knew it was what the white man wanted. After a while, as in the case of all other similar borrowings, he forgot they were not originally his own."

Even this may be too simplistic; ultimately the degree of black-and-white interaction makes it impossible to know from which side of the fence a song came. By the 1920s, medicine shows went on the road in the South and promoted their dubious potions with the aid of mixed singers, dancers, and comedians. The white Jimmie Rodgers is known to have played in medicine shows in Texas and Mississippi with the black Memphis songster Frank Stokes. Again, the common stock of songs would have set up a two-way traffic in borrowings and influences. Hillbilly songs even came to be heard on Memphis's famous Beale Street: Ma Rainey recalled that one of her most requested numbers was an old Appalachian lament called "Heart Made of Stone."

White hillbilly artists like Uncle Dave Macon, Fiddlin' John Carson, Clarence Ashley, and others all got their breaks in medicine shows. Playing at the dawn of recorded country music, they showed there was never any such thing as pure white rural music, just as eclectic black songsters like Henry Thomas and Mississippi John Hurt proved how much blues was mixed up with Anglo-Celtic ballads and dance music. Whites and African Americans alike performed minstrel songs, railroad epics, country dance numbers, and blues.

The first recorded bluesmen—Ed Andrews, Daddy Stovepipe, Papa Charlie Jackson—all came out of the medicine shows. Henry Thomas recorded many songs, like "John Henry" and "The Fox and Hounds," that Uncle Dave Macon had recorded before him, while songsters such as Coley Jones were arguably more popular with whites than with blacks. An African American harmonica player named Jaybird Coleman became so successful around Birmingham, Alabama, in the late '20s that the local Ku Klux Klan stepped in to take over his management.

Musical interchange between the two races did, of course, vary from state to state, even from county to county. Blues undoubtedly developed more strongly in Mississippi because there were fewer whites in that state. In fact, Delta bluesmen were often openly hostile to anything outside their raw 12-bar structures. In his *Blues from the Delta,* William Ferris Jr. gave the example of songster Tom Dumas,

who spent most of his performing life in a county to the east of the
Mississippi Delta where comingling of black and white traditions was
the norm. When he took his fiddle and banjo square dance tunes into
the Delta, bluesmen castigated them as "trash."

Things were different in the upland or mountain country. Brownie
McGhee, raised on an Appalachian farm near Kingsport, Tennessee,
remembered "jookin" or country quilting parties where songs were
traded back and forth between blacks and whites so many times it was
hard to tell who had made them up. In his seminal 1964 article "The
Folk Music Interchange," John Cohen described the "Two-Way"
picnics Big Bill Broonzy played as a boy, when whites and African
Americans sat on either side of a stage, with musicians moving from
one to the other playing old country songs and popular tunes of the
day. "There are recordings of a Negro string band from Campaigne,
Tennessee," Cohen wrote, "that use fiddle, banjo, and guitar and sound
much like the Old Opry string bands. In this case it seems the local
style of music is dominant over any differences that would be racially
determined."[6]

Let's All Help the Cowboys Sing the Blues

Although the influence of the emergent blues form on white musicians
has been well documented, it is still not commonly registered by fans
of country music. Once again the interaction is not acknowledged
because—as one-time head of Nashville's Country Music Foundation
William Ivey pointed out—people tend to approach the music as either
blues or country fans, seldom as both. It's analogous to the position
the young Elvis Presley found himself in when country disc jockeys
thought he sounded too black and black jockeys thought he was too
country.

---

6   Hear the black and mixed-race string bands—Taylor's Kentucky Boys, the
    Georgia Yellow Hammers, the Dallas String Band and others—on the first
    CD of *From Where I Stand: The Black Experience In Country Music* (Warner
    Bros. box set, 1998). According to country music scholar Charles Wolfe,
    the Taylor's Kentucky Boys track "Gray Eagle," recorded in Indiana in May
    1927, was the first racially integrated recording session in American music
    history.

To list all the instances of African American influence on hillbilly or country artists would take too long. Suffice to say that most of the country music pioneers were bound up with the blues in one way or another. Jimmie Rodgers learned the banjo and guitar from African Americans who worked for his father Aaron on the Gulf, Mobile, and Ohio Railroad. In turn he influenced bluesmen with his patented "blue yodel" of the late '20s. (He was the improbable boyhood idol of one Chester Burnette, who claimed Rodgers nicknamed him "the Howlin' Wolf" and who only gave up yodelling when his voice proved too heavy for anything but a howl.)

If the Carter Family epitomized the mountain-ballad harmonies of Appalachia, they too relied on African American musicians for songs and instrumental techniques. Guitarist Leslie Riddles lived with them on the Virginia-Tennessee border, serving as A. P. Carter's travelling tape-recorder on song-collecting trips. It's notable how black A. P.'s strange bass warble sounded under his wife Sara's pure mountain soprano. Meanwhile, his sister-in-law Maybelle learned from Riddles her flat-pick bass-string guitar style and upstroke "church lick."

Other whites to benefit from black influence included Dr. Humphrey Bate, whose Possum Hunters were the first string band to play on the Grand Ole Opry, and who acquired many of his songs from an ex-slave he knew as a boy. Prince Albert Hunt, a fiddler who lived in the black section of Terrell, Texas, jammed with African Americans on his front porch and recorded blues with his Texas Ramblers that anticipated the bluesy sound of Western Swing.

The king of Western Swing himself, Bob Wills, picked cotton with African Americans and adored the classic blues of Bessie Smith. Sam and Kirk McGee joined Uncle Dave Macon's Fruit Jar Drinkers in 1924 and learned their famous "finger-style" guitar technique before the First World War from a pair of black railroading brothers who hung around the McGees' general store in Franklin, Tennessee. Finally, Dock Boggs picked up the two-fingers-and-thumb banjo style from an African American player in his native Norton, Virginia.

In the late '20s, blues entered country via records, especially those of Blind Lemon Jefferson on the Paramount label. "Up until then," recalled the West Virginian singer Roscoe Holcomb, "the blues were only inside me—Blind Lemon was the first to 'let out' the blues." Once Holcomb had heard the way Lemon "dwelled" on a note, there was no other way for him to sing. The increasing popularity of the guitar since the turn of the century also accounted for much of the interchange. As Douglas Green wrote, the instrument "allowed for the phenomenon of rural blues as a relatively colorblind musical form." Indeed, only five months after Jefferson had introduced slide guitar on record in 1926, the white singer Frank Hutchison played the first country steel guitar on his OKeh recordings of "Worried Blues" and "The Train That Carried My Gal from Town."

Hutchison, like many of these white country bluesmen, sang in a distinctly black style, however clearly Caucasian the timbre of his voice. With Sam McGee he is perhaps the most purely blues oriented of these early country artists. The duo of Tom Darby and Jimmie Tarlton from South Carolina continued this mountain blues style with songs like "Birmingham Jail" (1927), Tarlton later claiming to have picked up his bottleneck guitar style from African American musicians when he was just ten years old.

In his *Folk Blues,* Jerry Silverman described white blues as a hybrid of black blues, Southern mountain ballad, and cowboy song. The three-line stanzas were black but accompanied by the steady, rhythmic guitar of mountain ballads and punctuated by long-held, yodelled notes from cowboy songs. That said, guitarists like Hutchison, McGee, and Tarlton came close to the black style of employing guitar as a kind of interacting second voice.

Even bluegrass, for many the quintessential music of white mountain people, had its roots in the influence of an African American guitarist and fiddler named Arnold Schultz, who played square dances around Rosine, Kentucky, with a young Bill Monroe and left an indelible blues mark on the future father of bluegrass. In John Cohen's words, "some of Monroe's earlier numbers, such as 'Honky Tonk Music,' often sound like Negro string band music such as that played by the Dallas String Band." Schultz's influence also descended through two other white Kentuckian proteges: Ike Everly, father of the famous brothers, and Mose Reger, who'd worked in the coal mines with a black "choke"-style guitarist called Jim Mason. Reger later taught

Merle Travis the complex two-finger guitar style, Travis in turn passing it on to Nashville maestro Chet Atkins.

While it was true that the generation of country and western singers spawned by Jimmie Rodgers—the Ernest Tubbs, Gene Autrys, and Hank Snows—moved on from the blue yodel, it was remarkable that the first really popular figure in country music should have recorded so many blues-derived songs. Of his 111 titles, twenty-five were blues and thirteen blue yodels. Rodgers's influence on a singer such as Jimmie Davis (future governor of Louisiana and composer of "You Are My Sunshine") was such that Davis actually recorded four RCA Victor titles in Dallas in 1932 with African American guitarists Ed Schafer and Oscar Woods, including (with Woods) the only white/black duet of its era. The other three numbers were all risqué blues with which future political opponents tried to discredit him. On "Sewing Machine Blues," he even makes an unthinkable (not to mention blasphemous) reference to interracial lust:

> *Gonna telephone to heaven*
> *To send me an angel down*
> *Gonna telephone to heaven*
> *To send me an angel down*
> *If you haven't got an angel, St. Peter*
> *Send me a high-steppin' brown . . .*
>
> (© Southern Music, 1932)

It was a rare example of an integrated recording session, to be sure. That it happened at all suggests the far reach of the country/blues interchange.

Deford Bailey

While there were several white performers recording blues, there was really only one early example of an African American performing country music. This was harmonica player Deford Bailey, who opened Nashville's WSM Barn Dance show (with a train song, "Pan American Blues") the very night George D. Hay nicknamed it the Grand Ole Opry.

Born in 1899 in rural Tennessee, not far from Nashville, Bailey claimed to have been raised on "black hillbilly music"—his father and uncle played fiddle and banjo respectively—and never saw himself as a token Opry bluesman. Tunes such as "John Henry" and "The Fox Chase" were released in 1928 on RCA Victor's Hillbilly series. As Tony Russell put it, "Who can say whether harmonica solos imitating trains or hunting scenes were first played by blacks or by whites?"

Bailey was a staple feature of the Opry until 1941, braving the perils of segregation on its frequent tours. Despite his popularity among Opryites like Uncle Dave Macon, however, it's difficult not to see him as, if not the token bluesman, certainly the show's token African American. George Hay called him "our mascot," and in over ten years his inclusion in the show never led to the recruitment of another black musician. Bailey claimed to have been treated like a "civilized slave" and remained a proud and bitter man until his death in 1982.

The Gospel in Black and White

Through all of this, the church maintained its powerful hold on the musical life of the South. When the Wall Street Crash of 1929 left the Negro South destitute, another religious revival put blues in the back seat. Many of the bigger recording companies went out of business.

According to Viv Broughton, African American church music in the '20s (when nine out of ten black churches were below the Mason-Dixon line) consisted of jubilee singing groups who performed traditional spirituals; singing preachers who built large followings with sermons and hymns; and itinerant street evangelists, often self-accompanied on guitar in rural blues fashion.

Jubilee groups such as the Golden Gate Quartet sang in a sophisticated barbershop style that inspired the great male quartets of the '30s to break away from church choirs. Their smooth, close harmonies were broken up by the frantic lead-and-response overlapping of quartets such as the Dixie Hummingbirds and the Five Blind Boys of Mississippi—the real progenitors of Southern soul singing as we know it. Meanwhile the choirs themselves were transformed by the new bluesy hymns of Thomas A. Dorsey, moving ever further from the traditional sounds of the Protestant church. The Pentecostal churches, practicing a more intense, extrovert kind of worship, used the faster, more rhythmic musical accompaniment of tambourines, piano, and eventually drums. They left the slow, heavy hymns of the country Baptists behind them.

The itinerant street or "jack-leg" preachers, finally, were popular among poorer African Americans, addressing congregations in the courthouse squares of small towns and accompanying themselves on guitars and harmonicas. The blues element in their songs was such that bluesmen like Blind Lemon Jefferson and Charley Patton recorded Race sides in the jack-leg style.

If the black church was busy diverging from the Methodist and Baptist hymns it had always followed, there remained surprising links to white hymnody and gospel song. Just as the gospel songs of Thomas Dorsey found white acceptance in the '30s through artists like Red Foley and the Stamps-Baxter Quartet—with white publishers snapping up such hugely successful songs as "Peace in the Valley"—so the Dixie Hummingbirds and others included hillbilly gospel songs in their repertoires. Ira Tucker of the Hummingbirds described his native South Carolina quartet style as a mixture of country and western and black forms, and moreover had many of his country-style songs recorded by hillbilly quartets such as the Blackwood Brothers (whose junior quartet the Songfellows the young Elvis Presley nearly joined) and the Statesman Quintet.

Hillbilly gospel was essentially tighter, tidier, more nasal, a complement to the wilder melisma and frenzy of the legendary black quartets. Not all African American groups appreciated the white style as much as Tucker, however. "They only wanted hillbilly style," observed the Swan Silvertones' lead singer Claude Jeter of the 45 sides they cut for King Records in the '40s. "They didn't care too much for the real gospel."

The shared heritage of black and white gospel really boiled down to the common stock of songs and hymns available in the '30s. Collections published by white companies for use in white churches were quickly taken up by black denominations, while the big gospel conventions—e.g., the National Baptist Convention—introduced new songs alike to both races. In *Songsters and Saints,* Paul Oliver noted that "blind singers, in particular, with only their ears to depend on, appear on occasion to have assimilated white mannerisms in both song and accompaniment." (For a classic example of the black "hillbilly" style, hear the Staple Singers' 1966 version of "Will the Circle Be Unbroken?" on Epic. Appropriately enough, they also performed a version on the live *George Jones and Friends* album.)

It's also worth pointing out that there were as many white Pentecostal congregations as black, as many poor whites seized in trances and speaking in tongues as poor African Americans. The alcoholic white evangelist A. A. Allen, one of the most charismatic of the "holy roller" preachers, was often accompanied by a predominantly black choir, and African Americans certainly had no monopoly on the physical hysteria of the Holiness Church. As W. J. Cash put it in *The Mind of the South,* the white holy roller congregations "went all the way with the black man."

In the '40s, black gospel star Sister Rosetta Tharpe recorded with country singer Red Foley and was asked to appear on the Grand Ole Opry. "Country music shared roots in gospel with black music," wrote Charlie Gillett, "and during the '40s probably absorbed more elements of black music than were accepted into the mainstream pop of the time." While Ernest Tubb listened to Bessie Smith and Ethel Waters, and Bob Wills performed "Troubled in Mind" and "St.. Louis Blues," future lynchpins of rockabilly Carl Perkins and Jerry Lee Lewis checked out their local black Baptist churches. "The blues didn't really go away," wrote Douglas Green. "They were simply absorbed more deeply within country music's mainstream."

Western Swing, Country Boogie, Hank Williams

The Western Swing style of the '30s and '40s was probably the most clearcut example of blues being adapted to white country music. Spawned by the Texan fiddle-breakdown style of the '20s, Western Swing developed into a hillbilly jazz dance music featuring five-to-eight-piece bands. They were the original hip country boys.

Country fiddling blended with big-band horns, bluesy vocals, and Dixieland string bass, feeding everything from waltzes to ragtime to

Mexican mariachi through this eclectic sound. It was light, airy, and wistful, different from the hard swing of the black bands, yet Bob Wills sidemen like singer Tommy Duncan gave a genuinely bluesy feel to the hybrid style.

"You listen to some Western Swing records and tell me if that isn't straight rhythm'n'blues," Atlantic Records' Jerry Wexler remarked to me. "There isn't a thing different about it except that it's played by white country boys. Western Swing had the format of rock'n'roll, one or two horns and a rhythm section playing dance music on a Saturday night." Added blues guitar legend Albert King: "It was jitterbug music. The Bob Wills band could play that stuff better than anybody I've ever heard, and they did it with fiddles."

In his *Country Music USA*, Bill Malone found that "southwestern musicians had revealed a tendency to improvise and experiment with melodic variations much earlier than their southeastern counterparts," noting that oil workers moving from Louisiana to Texas in the '20s may have brought with them the influence of New Orleans jazz. Jazz had itself by this stage fostered a reasonable degree of racial integration: Benny Goodman hired Teddy Wilson as the pianist in his touring trio of 1935, while both Louis Armstrong and Fats Waller used white musicians in the '20s. As early as 1923, Jelly Roll Morton was playing piano with the white New Orleans Rhythm Kings.

If most of the Western Swing bands broke up during the war, Wills's Texas Playboys, regrouping in various line-ups, soldiered on into the '60s. Wills followed the migrant path to California, his swing style succeeded in Texas by the less sentimental sound of the oil-town honky-tonks, whose preoccupation with alcohol and adultery was a marked contrast to the nostalgic rural music of Appalachia.

An artist who fitted in somewhere between these two poles, and who epitomized the soulful, black-influenced country singer, was Hank Williams. Born near Montgomery, Alabama, in 1923, Williams's first teacher was Rufus "Tee-Tot" Payne, an African American street singer who did odd jobs for a drug store in the local town of Greenville and taught Williams guitar while the boy shined shoes on the town's sidewalks.

Starting out at fourteen as a backwoods gospel Roy Acuff imitator, Williams gradually developed an inimitable vocal style that had all the rawness and pinched pain of Robert Johnson. Against the blithe strains of a fiddle and steel guitar, he flattened vowels and contorted consonants in his tormented tales of domestic strife and heartache. "Classic Southern country soul," Douglas Green termed it, and the many African Americans who counted him among their favorite singers were proof of his vocal power. Otis Redding worshipped Williams, while R&B artists from Dinah Washington and Ivory Joe Hunter to Esther Phillips and Al Green sang his songs.

Following the decline of Western Swing, the black influence on country music showed most clearly in the "country boogie" style of the '40s, a style that developed from Western Swing and honky-tonk—the new stepped-up dance rhythms and electric guitars of country—and led eventually to the pre-rockabilly sound of Bill Haley & His Comets. African American boogie woogie originated in the '20s with pianists Pinetop Smith and Pete Johnson; by the late '30s it had become a New York vocal style through the great Big Joe Turner.

The first white Southerner to pick up on the style successfully was South Carolinan Arthur Smith with his rolling, chugging "Guitar Boogie," although the first country boogie record was probably Johnny Barfield's "Boogie Woogie" of 1939. Veteran Grand Ole Opry duo the Delmore Brothers released their "Hillbilly Boogie" in April 1946, the title encapsulating the record's fusion of hokey country style with black rhythmic form.

The Delmores had drawn on blues influences ever since their first Columbia records in 1932, and had furthermore recorded gospel (with Grandpa Jones, Merle Travis, and Red Foley) as the Brown's Ferry Four. Now they teamed up with the bluesy Arkansas harmonica player Wayne Raney and cut such classic sides as "Freight Train Boogie" and "Mobile Boogie." They were still hitting—with the Jimmy Yancey–derived "Blues Stay Away from Me"—in 1949.

Most of these sides sounded like a milder, more relaxed form of rockabilly. Where there were drums they were barely audible, while there was nothing of the abrasive redneck sneer so prevalent in rockabilly singing. Even so, the boogie guitar style—patented by Merle

Travis—proved to be the decisive influence on the hillbilly rock'n'roll style to come. Meanwhile, on the original boogie woogie instrument—the piano—the Texan Moon Mullican was probably the major country boogie influence. Mullican learned his blues as a boy from black sharecropper Joe Jones and became "the King of the Hillbilly Piano Players" through hits such as "Jole Blon" (1949) and "I'll Sail My Ship Alone" (1951). Through other country boogie pianists like Merrill Moore and Roy Hall, Mullican's influence was assimilated by Jerry Lee Lewis. In 1956 he ended up cutting rock'n'roll sides himself.

Rockabilly

Although country boogie continued to be recorded by Capitol, Decca, King and other companies until the mid-'50s, inevitably it was superseded by the most dynamic hybrid of black and white styles yet.

To the acoustic textural base of country music, rockabilly added the drums and biting lead guitar of rhythm'n'blues, creating a radical offspring of hillbilly sound that changed youth entertainment. Where Bill Haley's fusion of jump blues and Western Swing was ultimately safe and contained, rockabilly was loose and menacing.

It began in Memphis, long a meeting point for black and white styles, and was the South's crowning moment of musical miscegenation. The first Elvis Presley records on Sun—one side R&B, the other country—were almost too symmetrical an expression of this racial and stylistic coupling. In these powerful unleashings one heard a voice literally torn between black and white identities. Here the African American Memphis of Baptist hymns and Delta blues and the white one of Western Swing and country boogie came closer than they'd ever done before.

Memphis had been as much a regional center for hillbilly music as it had been the first urban crossroads of the blues. Hank Williams and the Delmore Brothers both broadcast on WMC, while WMC DJ Eddie Hill led a country band that included Sam Phillips's original "white man with the Negro feel," Harmonica Frank Floyd. Western Swing bands based in Memphis included the Snearly Ranch Boys, the Dixie Ramblers, the Georgia Peach Pickers, and the Garrett Snuff Boys.

No figure was more pivotal in the background to Southern soul than Phillips. He was even born in Florence, the Alabama town that gave birth to the Muscle Shoals soul sound of the '60s. Raised in the '30s on a plantation where he heard blues sung by farmhands, Phillips became a disc jockey and joined WLAY Muscle Shoals in 1942. Here he programmed country and gospel music before moving on to Decatur, Alabama, to Nashville, and finally in 1945 to Memphis, where he landed a job with WREC, engineering "remote" broadcasts by big bands on the top floor of the famous Peabody Hotel.

By 1950, Phillips had become convinced there was a serious gap in the R&B market: no one was recording the wealth of African American talent in Memphis. Converting an old radiator shop into a primitive studio, he opened his Memphis Recording Service, which—though taken up much of the time by weddings and bar mitzvahs—managed to squeeze in sessions by such future R&B legends as Howlin' Wolf, B.B. King, Rufus Thomas, and Little Milton. Initially leasing sides to companies such as Chess, which had formed in Chicago in 1948, Phillips launched his own Sun label in February 1952. A year later he produced the label's first hits, Rufus Thomas's "Bear Cat" and Little Junior's "Feelin' Good."

Chess also released Phillips's first country productions, by Harmonica Frank and his fellow Mississippian Bob Price. Frank Floyd was a medicine show stalwart who'd clearly picked up a large dose of the blues from black entertainers on the circuit. With a harmonica jammed into one side of his mouth, he sang from the other in a heavily African American style. Sides like "Swamp Root," "Howlin' Tomcat," and "The Great Medical Menagerist" were typical medicine-show fare, while "Rockin' Chair Daddy," released in 1954 three years after its recording, marked a clear precedent for Presley's rockabilly sound. Price's band was a more orthodox honky-tonk outfit, as was Red Hadley's Wranglers, produced by Phillips on Trumpet in 1952.

Neither Floyd nor Price sold enough records for Phillips to press ahead with white artists, but by the end of 1953 he was facing up to the fact that his R&B productions alone were not going to keep Sun in business. (Interestingly, though, vocal group the Prisonaires' "Just Walkin' in the Rain" made No. 10 on the country chart in June of that year.) Whether or not he really did envision a "white man with the Negro feel" (not such an unlikely brainwave, though Phillips is said to have denied it), that is what he got the day Elvis Aaron Presley— brought round to Sun to warble some insipid ballads—launched into his interpretation of Arthur Crudup's "That's All Right."

"This is what I heard in Elvis, this . . . what I guess they now call 'soul,'" said Phillips's secretary at Sun, Marion Kesker, though it's unclear whether her boss heard the same thing. What he did note was revealing: "Elvis felt so *inferior,*" he recalled. "He reminded me of a black man in that way—his insecurity was so *markedly* like that of a black man." As an observation it curiously echoes the impression that hillbilly bluesman Cliff Carlisle retained of Jimmie Rodgers: "He reminded me more of a colored person . . . than any white man I ever saw."

The historic first moments of rockabilly have been described so many times it would be redundant to go over them again. Suffice to say that in Presley's vocals on "That's All Right" and Bill Monroe's "Blue Moon of Kentucky" one heard the self-preening virtuosity and playfulness of the great R&B and jump-blues singers he heard on WDIA—men such as Roy Brown and Wynonie Harris. The breathless inventiveness of his vocals, heightened by Phillips's amazing echo technique, was like nothing "hillbilly" music had ever produced. (The next single was in fact his version of Roy Brown's "Good Rockin' Tonight.") In the five classic Sun singles (each combining one black with one white song), there was a wit and intelligence that marked a wholly new kind of pleasure in white expression.

Presley embodied the tensions and contradictions that generated rock'n'roll. In the words of Bob Oermann and Douglas Green, "he was a country boy who dressed in the flashy clothes of urban blacks, a devout Southern Baptist who seethed with sex, a softspoken, polite young man who looked like a hoodlum . . ." Above all, perhaps, he was not unique—just sexier and luckier than the many other redneck youths who'd been tuning into R&B stations and banging out blues and boogie songs on clapped-out acoustic guitars.

Carl Perkins was a typical case. Born on a tenant farm in the northwest comer of Tennessee, his family the only white sharecroppers for miles around, Perkins learned guitar from an African American who worked on the farm, got into blues when the family moved southeast to Jackson, and finally formed a band with brothers Jay and Clayton that played around the town's juke joints. "I like to do John Lee Hooker songs Bill Monroe-style," Perkins claimed; "blues with a country beat." The two forms had already coalesced in Presley's "Blue Moon of Kentucky." Perkins was soon Sun bound to get a piece of the action.

Perkins's style was probably closer to country boogie than to rockabilly. Certainly Phillips didn't hear him as anything like Presley on his first session, which was pure honky-tonk in the post–Hank Williams mode. But a month after selling Elvis's contract to RCA in November 1955, Phillips recorded Perkins on two explosive originals, "Honey Don't" and "Blue Suede Shoes." By April of the following year, "Shoes" had gone Top 5 on the country, pop, *and* R&B charts—the first major rockabilly hit—and Perkins had become the quintessential Dixie-fried rock'n'roll cat.

Rockabilly was a craze that spread quickly through the South to labels in Texas and Louisiana, continuing west to New Mexico and Los Angeles before ultimately becoming a homogenous Stateside sound. Even African Americans attempted it, despite its inescapably redneck stance and nuance. Johnny Fuller cut "All Night Long" on Chess; Houston's Jimmie Newsome transformed Hank Williams's "Long Gone Lonesome Blues" on MGM; and both G. L. Crockett's "Look Out Mabel" and Tarheel Slim's "No. 9 Train" bore a powerful rockabilly feel.

Others included Ray Sharpe, Arthur Gunter, Roy Brown (on Imperial), and bluesman Magic Sam. On Sun, the only African American artist to stray close to the form was Rosco Gordon, whose last side for the label, "Sally Jo," was allegedly cut with the post-Presley house band of guitarist Roland Janes, pianist Jimmy Wilson, and drummer James Van Eaton.

King Records

While few African Americans made rockabilly records, the black/white influences of the South continued to run both ways. The only Southern independent more successful than Sun in the '50s, King

Records of Cincinnati, boasted a roster of artists that, like Sun, included as many country singers as R&B.

The difference was that King's wily boss Syd Nathan did not drop his African American artists once he'd hit paydirt with whites, but instead traded songs back and forth between them and enjoyed hits in both markets. Although Sam Phillips had cut his rockabilly artists on songs performed earlier by Sun's R&B singers, he'd never worked the other way round. At King, by contrast, jump-blues *roué* Wynonie Harris and crooner Bullmoose Jackson both had hits with adapted country songs.

Formed in 1944 as a "folk and country" label, King rapidly built up a large country catalog by signing Hawkshaw Hawkins, Cowboy Copas, and the Delmore Brothers. In 1947, Nathan approached the Lucky Millinder band at Cincinnati's Cotton Club and persuaded both vocalist Bullmoose Jackson and arranger Henry Glover to sign with him. From this fortuitous meeting came Jackson's lugubrious "I Love You, Yes I Do" and Glover's near-ten-year stay at King as A&R director—the first such black appointment in a white-owned company.

Glover had written arrangements for Jimmie Lunceford while at Wayne University in Detroit, then played trumpet with Buddy Johnson and Tiny Bradshaw. His first successes at King were hits in 1949 for the Todd Rhodes band (featuring LaVern Baker), followed by others for his old bandleaders Bradshaw and Millinder. At the same time he was producing sessions on King's country acts, including country boogie sides by the Delmore Brothers and Wayne Raney. White duo the York Brothers recorded R&B songs in 1947 and sounded, according to Glover, like the Everly Brothers. "Sam Phillips has received great recognition because he did the novel thing of recording R&B with white boys," Glover said, "but the fact is that King was covering R&B with country singers almost from the beginning of my work with Syd Nathan."

More unusual was attempting the reverse. Ivory Joe Hunter was probably the first to do so, covering Jenny Lou Carson's "Jealous Heart" in 1949—but then Hunter had grown up with Texan country music and was a natural country stylist. Bullmoose Jackson, popular with Southern whites, followed with versions of Moon Mullican's

"Cherokee Boogie" and Wayne Raney's "Why Don't You Haul Off and Love Me." Finally, the suave and sexy Wynonie Harris transformed Louie Innis's "Good Morning Judge" and Moon Mullican's "Triflin' Woman Blues" into swaggering jump-blues numbers, hitting in 1951 with Hank Penny's Western Swing song "Bloodshot Eyes."

"I'll confess we didn't think we were doing anything remarkable," Glover admitted. "When a song happened in one field, Syd wanted it moved into the other. You couldn't sell Wynonie Harris to country folk, and black folk weren't buying Hank Penny, but black folk might buy Wynonie Harris doing a country tune."

Glover helped Nathan design King's echo chamber, produced most of the company's acts, and wrote songs such as the classic country-style blues ballad "Drown in My Own Tears," a hit for Lula Reed and Sonny Thompson before Ray Charles covered it in 1955. Before leaving the company in 1956 (only to rejoin it seven years later), Glover had worked with Hank Ballard and the Midnighters, Otis Williams and the Charms and—seminal influences on future soul singers—Roy Brown and Little Willie John. Brown was a Bing Crosby worshipper who perfected the uptown gospel sob that exerted such a hold on R&B tenors like Clyde McPhatter and Jackie Wilson, while the less mannered Willie John paved the way to Southern soul with the pleading ballad "Need Your Love So Bad" and the country song "Big Blue Diamonds."

King's experiments with the R&B country crossover were unusual but not completely isolated. Sonny Til & the Orioles scored a huge hit in 1953 with the country-gospel "Crying in the Chapel," while Ella Fitzgerald sang honky-tonker Floyd Tillman's "Gotta Have My Baby Back." Dinah Washington did Hank Williams's "Cold, Cold Heart" and Hank Snow's "I Don't Hurt Anymore." The Pearls cut Williams's "Your Cheatin' Heart" on Onyx, and Bobby Comstock did the first of many black versions of Pee Wee King and Redd Stewart's "Tennessee Waltz" in 1959. Elvis Presley's "Baby Let's Play House" was a song by Nashville R&B singer Arthur Gunter that in turn derived from Eddy Arnold's "I Want to Play House with You." Another Arnold song, "It's a Sin," was covered by both Ivory Joe Hunter and the duet of Tarheel Slim and Little Ann.

Other independents, like Savoy and Imperial, followed King's lead and added country artists to their blues, jazz, and gospel rosters. On the West Coast, Imperial's Lew Chudd signed Slim Whitman along with Fats Domino, while even Aladdin—the home of boozy jump blues—had a hillbilly outlet with the Intro label. The situation recalled the pioneer days of field scouts like Ralph Peer, Art Satherley, and William Caloway, who went South in the '20s and signed both hillbilly and blues singers to companies such as OKeh, RCA Victor, Paramount, and ARC. Only King really used the conjunction of black and white artists profitably, but the mere fact that other labels had mixed rosters was significant in itself.

Examples of African Americans covering country songs might be taken as compensation for the innumerable white pop covers of R&B that so dominated the '50s. Ironically it was Dot's Randy Wood, who'd sponsored one of the first mail-order R&B shows on Southern radio (on Nashville's WLAC), who became the prime culprit in the white-cover boom. Even on Dot—home to Pat Boone and Gale Storm—Wood's first artists were Nashville R&B combos like the Griffen Brothers. So successful, however, were Boone's covers of Fats Domino songs that Dot moved to Hollywood in 1956.

African American singers also made the crossing to pop, in the form of polished crooners such as Nat King Cole. Al Hibbler and Roy Hamilton took the uptown gospel sob into white hearts with sumptuously orchestrated versions of "Unchained Melody," while Hamilton—an idol of Elvis Presley's—had hits with the Rodgers and Hammerstein showpieces "If I Loved You" and "You'll Never Walk Alone." One of the earliest African American pop stars was Louis Jordan, whose smooth, droll jump songs drew—like the previous century's minstrel songs—on white stereotypes of black life. "Is You Is Or Is You Ain't (My Baby)," "Saturday Night Fish Fry," and "Ain't Nobody Here But Us Chickens" were typical hits. As Charlie Gillett noted in *The Sound of the City*, "nobody satisfied both audiences' tastes so effectively until Fats Domino, Chuck Berry, and Little Richard."

Fats and Chuck

Domino and Berry were perhaps the most obvious examples of black rock'n'roll stars who borrowed from white country music, thus redressing the balance upset by rockabilly's theft of R&B.

Domino's sound came straight out of New Orleans R&B and the city's rolling barrelhouse piano styles, but there was plenty of country and some church in there too. "Blueberry Hill," his most famous hit, was a song from a 1940 Gene Autry western, while "A Helping Hand" (1955) was based on Jimmie Rodgers's "Waiting for a Train," and "Jambalaya" (1961) was a wonderful cover of Hank Williams's paean to Cajun Louisiana. Other country songs Domino covered included Williams's "Your Cheatin' Heart" and Don Gibson's "Who Cares (for Me)." "We all thought of [Fats] as a country and western singer," recalled Domino's producer Dave Bartholomew. "Not real downhearted, but he always had that flavor rather than the gutbucket sound. He didn't sing from the bottom."

You can hear this melancholy Crescent City style in "I Want to Walk You Home" and "Walking to New Orleans," and it influenced a hundred South Louisiana swamp-pop balladeers both black and white. Lloyd Price's "Lawdy Miss Clawdy" had much of the same feel—"a curious blend of melancholia and seeming contentment," in the words of Clive Anderson—and sold well to whites. Also in New Orleans, Smiley Lewis recorded such country songs as "You Are My Sunshine" and "Someday You'll Want Me," while Earl King further developed the Louisiana country-ballad sound on classic Ace sides like "Those Lonely, Lonely Nights."

Chuck Berry's first Chess release, "Maybelline" (adapted from an old Bob Wills number called "Ida Red"), was an uptempo transposition with a crude blues beat and guitar that made No. 1 on the R&B chart in 1955. Berry had grown up in St. Louis hearing little but country music on the radio. That plus the humour and enunciation of a Louis Jordan gave him a vocal style that lacked the coarseness of urban blues and rock'n'roll—and an inspired wit that made him the Leiber and Stoller of America's teenage heartland.

On the sleeve of his first album, Berry was described as a "rock-a-billy troubadour." Although his style was too urban to be described as rockabilly, his classic songs—"Memphis," "Johnny B. Goode," and others—were pure countrified rock'n'roll. Country singers Marty Robbins, Buck Owens, and Freddy Weller all had hits with them, while Billy Sherrill even produced bluegrass duo Jim & Jesse on an Epic album of Berry songs called *Berry Pickin*. "If Chuck Berry was white," said bluesman Jimmy Witherspoon, "he would be the top country singer in the world." Fittingly, Berry was elected to the Country Songwriters' Hall of Fame in the '70s.

Reaction and Adaptation

One of the effects of the rockabilly revolution was to alienate the country music establishment, now epitomized by Nashville. Even the arrival of Elvis Presley at Nashville's RCA studios could in hindsight be seen as a process of taming and assimilation.

More generally, reactionary Southerners were horrified by the racial implications of the new music. White church groups claimed rock'n'roll was a plot to corrupt white youth engineered by the National Association for the Advancement of Colored Peoples. The sound exploded, moreover, just as the civil rights movement was taking off. Southern African Americans had begun to vote in cities and border states after a Supreme Court ruling in 1944. Ten years later, segregation in schools was ruled unconstitutional. In December 1955, just a month after Elvis Presley's contract was sold to RCA, the black boycott of the bus system in Montgomery, Alabama, began when Rosa Parks refused to give up her seat to a white man. Out of the boycott, which lasted over a year, emerged Martin Luther King Jr. and the principle of nonviolent resistance. As Ku Klux Klan and Citizen's Council members watched their children getting into "nigger music," it was clear the South was in for some growing pains.

"Hillbilly" music—officially renamed "Country & Western" on *Billboard*'s charts in the same year, 1949, that the "Race" charts were renamed with staff reporter Jerry Wexler's term "Rhythm & Blues"—reacted against precisely the "Western" element of the '40s. The golden age of string-band country music had ended with the war's breaking down of American regionalism; now a revival of the mountain-ballad sound—mournful, constricted, and *very* white—began. African

American dance rhythms were eliminated as singers such as Webb Pierce, Kitty Wells, and Little Jimmy Dickens emerged. The high, reedy voices of duos like the Blue Sky Boys and the Louvin Brothers were the apex of Appalachian bluegrass harmony.

With the advent of rock'n'roll, however, Nashville was faced with a dilemma. It had to retain its rural tradition and audience, but at the same time adapt to reach the pop market. Thus was created the famous, or infamous, "Nashville Sound," whose principal architects were Chet Atkins, Owen Bradley, Anita Kerr and her singers, and session men such as Floyd Cramer (piano), Grady Martin (guitar), and Buddy Harman (drums). It was a straightforward update (and to some extent urbanizing) of the rural country sound, downplaying fiddles and steel guitars and introducing clearly defined rhythm tracks, sickly backing choruses, and even the saxophone of Boots Randolph. It was also very successful, as the many hits by Jim Reeves, Patsy Cline, Faron Young, and Don Gibson attested. (The story went that when Jerry Lee Lewis, like many other rockabillies, "came home" to country, Faron Young sharply reminded him to be grateful to those who'd kept country going under rockabilly's threat.)

Arguably the first Nashville pop-crossover act was Eddy Arnold, also the first major artist to record there. He turned country weepers into vehicles for smooth MOR crooning, setting a precedent for countless armchair softies to come. But there was also room for soul and emotion in the Nashville Sound: Patsy Cline and Don Gibson both cut sides that influenced the Southern soul writers of the next generation. Cline's "She's Got You" (a Hank Cochran song) could almost be a prototype country-soul ballad, while Gibson's songs were covered by Ray Charles (the huge hit "I Can't Stop Loving You") and Mighty Sam ("Sweet Dreams").

The Nashville Sound was itself a major influence on Southern soul musicians: Floyd Cramer's "slipnote" piano style, for instance, was widely emulated on Memphis and Muscle Shoals records. Other, non-Nashville-based singers were genuinely soulful. Texan honky-tonker Lefty Frizzell had a dreamy, richly nasal voice that perfectly suited the small dance-combo songs and ballads he recorded in the early '50s and influenced not only later country singers like Merle Haggard but also the country-soul balladeers Percy Sledge and Joe Simon. "I get tired of holding high notes for a long time," Frizzell once said. "Instead of straining, I just let it roll down and it feels good to me." He was especially soulful on light, melancholy ballads like "Lonely and Blue," which combined the flavor of a Jimmie Rodgers blue yodel with the Western Swing style of Bob Wills's vocalist Tommy Duncan.

Two singers from rockabilly country who epitomized the R&B-inspired country singer were Charlie Rich and Conway Twitty. Both were raised on on Baptist hymns and the blues of African American sharecroppers—Rich in northwest Arkansas, Twitty in the Mississippi Delta. Rich started out in jazz, worshipping Stan Kenton, then in 1957 became a staff writer and arranger at Sun, where he penned hits for Jerry Lee Lewis and Johnny Cash. A first solo session in August 1958 yielded little, but 1959's "Lonely Weekends"—on Sun's subsidiary Phillips International label—was a catchy, uptempo pop-rock song in Presley's RCA style and a big hit.

The '60s found Rich alternating between country and poppy soul-blues, first with Groove/RCA, then with Mercury subsidiary Smash, sung in a voice pitched somewhere between Elvis Presley and Joe Simon. Bobby Bland recorded a great version of his "Who Will the Next Fool Be?," while Esther Phillips was singing his "No Headstone on My Grave" when Kenny Rogers found her in a Houston nightclub in 1961. The country side of Rich came to the fore on Hi in 1967, and to fruition with Billy Sherrill at Epic in the '70s, leading to an engaging tension in his music between MOR country and bluesy emotion.

It took Sherrill, who'd been with Rich at Sun, to draw out the soulful ballad style that created such huge hits as "Behind Closed Doors" and "The Most Beautiful Girl in the World." *Boss Man* (1972) contained a whole slew of country-soul gems—among them Dan Penn and Spooner Oldham's "A Woman Left Lonely," Curly Putnam's "Set Me Free" and Kenny O'Dell's "I Take It On Home"—as well as fine songs by Charlie's wife Margaret-Ann.

Sherrill, who'd been in on the beginning of the Muscle Shoals sound, was often accused of taking the Nashville sound to new extremes of blandness, but his production on Rich masterpieces such as "All Over Me," "My Elusive Dreams," and "Feel Like Going Home" was far less offensive than the work of most Nashville producers. Perhaps Rich's best album was his 1976 gospel outing *Silver Linings,* which included arrangements of such standards as "Amazing Grace," "Swing Low, Sweet Chariot," and "Will the Circle Be Unbroken?"

Along with Jerry Lee Lewis, Twitty was one of the first rockabillies to make a return crossing to country music. Having turned his Phillips County Ramblers into the Rockhousers at the onset of the Presley era, he recorded rockabilly at Sun under his real name Harold Jenkins, then gravitated to pop and scored a major 1958 hit with "It's Only Make Believe." Despite writing country songs for Ray Price and others, he only moved into the country field himself in 1965, eventually settling in Nashville and recording a string of '70s hits that included "Hello Darlin'," "How Much More Can She Stand?," and "You've Never Been This Far Before."

Twitty's duets with Loretta Lynn made him country's archetypal guilt-stricken adulterer. He could also wail with a hurt and desperation that John Morthland described as "white soul at its most searing." A song called "Grand Ole Blues" took him—lyrically *and* stylistically— from Nashville country to Memphis R&B and back, eloquently summing up his career as it shifts from "those ol' twin fiddles" to juke-joint piano and a honking saxophone.

Rich and Twitty were products of a borderline between country and R&B, blue-eyed post–Sun soulmen who only found a comfortable Nashville niche after wilderness years of searching for a style. It's worth remembering that Elvis Presley himself had no country hits between 1958 and 1971, while other R&B–influenced singers like Brenda Lee and the Everly Brothers were likewise left out in the cold.

The Blues Ballad

Nashville's reaction to the assault on its precious sense of tradition was roughly paralleled by the treatment meted out by the black gospel world to singers who'd crossed over to R&B: '60s soul was fermented in this struggle. The interesting thing is that the newly gospelized style of rhythm'n'blues brought Southern black music close, once more, to the church roots of the Southern white. It was no coincidence that two of the greatest gospel-blues singers, Ray Charles and Bobby "Blue" Bland, both recorded country albums.

Soul had its inception in the "blues ballads" of these men, songs that followed a blues form but were sung with a gospel delivery. In Arnold Shaw's words, "monotonous and repetitive as R&B tends to become as uptempo jump music, so it becomes subtly and richly chorded in the ballads, with moody inner voicing and blues-rooted harmonies . . . harking back to spirituals and the expressiveness of gospel and jazz."

The pioneers were singers such as Roy Brown. "These were the guys," said Jerry Wexler, "who'd slow the Saturday night thing down and do a ballad that tore your heart out. There would always be that soulful slow number to change the pace and build aesthetic tension. The ballad tradition, after all, existed in Negro vaudeville long before R&B."

A dual movement was occurring: while gospel singers tried out R&B, R&B singers shifted away from the old Delta blues. In Memphis, B.B. King turned his band from a standard small blues combo into a big, horn-dominated lineup modelled on the Texan bands of T-Bone Walker and others. "I like the big band sound," he said. "I guess one of the reasons is my being brought up in church. I can always hear the choir singing behind me, and that's what I hear when the horns are playing behind me." While never the singer that his friend Bland was, King steered blues decisively towards soul styles, and he too recorded a country album (*Love Me Tender*) in later years.

Bland himself sat at a kind of crossroads of blues, gospel, and country music that made him as much a godfather to Southern soul as Ray Charles or James Brown. His album *Two Steps from the Blues* was the favorite record of many Memphis and Muscle Shoals acolytes, and he was invariably quoted as a major influence by the great Southern soulmen.

Born in the country outside Memphis in 1930, Bland was exposed to the church, to the blues, and to country radio stations from the earliest age. "I had a country and western, spiritual, Baptist background," he said. "All of them are somewhat alike, it's just a different delivery. I listened on the radio every morning to people like Roy Acuff, Lefty Frizzell, Hank Williams, and I think hillbilly has more of a story than people give it credit for. We were taught that hillbilly wasn't the thing, but I guarantee you they were wrong."

From the gospel side, formative influences on Bland were Ira Tucker of the Dixie Hummingbirds, with whom he worked, and Aretha Franklin's father, the Reverend C. L., from whom he acquired his trademark back-of-the-throat squall (usually employed on the link-phrase "Woah Lord!"). Blues-wise it was the mellow sound of T-Bone Walker, together with the experience of playing in the Beale Streeters with B.B. King, Rosco Gordon, and Johnny Ace, that determined Bland's style.

After cutting Ike Turner–arranged sides at Sun, Bland was signed by Duke, a new Memphis label that had a big hand in the '50s evolution of blues-ballad styles towards Southern soul (one of its '60s compilation albums was even called *Blues That Gave America Soul*). Formed in Memphis in 1952 by white country DJ David James Mattis, its initial releases were by individual members of the Beale Streeters, Bland's being either in an uptempo Roy Brown vein or in the slow, tinkling-vibes-and-breezy-sax style of Johnny Ace.

In 1953, Duke was acquired by Houston's Peacock, a label established four years earlier by club-owner and reputed gangster Don Robey as an outlet for his protégé Clarence "Gatemouth" Brown. Prior to merging with Duke, its brightest stars were great Southern gospel groups such as the Dixie Hummingbirds, the Sensational Nightingales, and the Five Blind Boys of Mississippi. With Bland, Ace, Gordon, and Junior Parker now part of the company, the '50s saw Robey chalk up many R&B hits, the best being by Bland, whose transformation from impassioned jump-blues singer ("Woke Up Screaming," "Further Up the Road") to gospel blues-balladeer ("I'll Take Care of You," "Stormy Monday") was effected with the aid of the brilliant arranger Joe Scott.

The records Bland made from 1957 onward were unmatched as fusions of gospel and R&B—two steps from the blues, indeed, but all the better for it. It's after 1957, too, that the unexpected white influences can be made out: the clear, elegant phrasing picked up from Perry Como and Tony Bennett, the pronounced country feel of songs like "Share Your Love with Me." "I never did care for the hard blues, really," Bland later confessed, adding that his favorite songs were "Lead

Me On" and "I'll Take Care of You," "because they have more of a spiritual touch to them." When he did get around to cutting a country album *(Get On Down with Bobby Bland* in 1975), the country-soul story came full circle with his versions of songs by Conway Twitty, Billy Sherrill (an exquisite reading of Tammy Wynette's "Too Far Gone"), and Muscle Shoals R&B fanatics Dan Penn and Donnie Fritts.

Duke's first star was pianist Johnny Ace, who sang his sleepy, languorously sentimental ballads (notably the posthumous "Pledging My Love") in a deadpan, almost stilted voice that appealed greatly to country fans. "Pledging My Love" showed the influence, too, of the Nat King Cole school, which, through West Coast pianists such as Charles Brown, had refined R&B into a smoochy lounge music. As with the gospel strain in singers like Bland, this was another pressure pulling R&B away from the blues; its effect on Ray Charles was profound. (Nat King Cole himself recorded a country album, *Ramblin' Rose.)*

More gospel-based on Duke-Peacock were Jackie Verdell, Larry Davis, and Joe Hinton, who concluded his career in 1964 with a lovely big-band arrangement of Willie Nelson's "Funny How Time Slips Away."

Gatemouth Brown

More orthodox bar-blues and jump-blues styles were maintained on Robey's labels by Junior Parker ("Sweet Home Chicago," "Driving Wheel") and Clarence "Gatemouth" Brown, Peacock's first artist. Brown, however, was a more versatile and eclectic musician than his T-Bone Walker–inspired '50s sides for Robey suggested. Only at the end of the decade, on his last sessions for Robey, were his harmonica and fiddle-playing skills committed to wax. Before that, one would never have guessed his primary influence while growing up in East Texas was hillbilly music.

Brown's father, Fiddlin' Tom, played everything from bluegrass mandolin to Cajun accordion in bands on the Texas-Louisiana border. He taught his son the fiddle when the boy was ten. "We didn't play zydeco—the Negro version of Cajun," Brown told Bill Millar. "We played real Cajun and bluegrass, because Daddy was raised by a Caucasian and my mother spoke French." Exposed to Western Swing and to cowboy singers such as Roy Rogers and Gene Autry, Brown only began playing R&B when bands such as Louis Jordan's came to town. Don Robey eventually heard him in San Antonio: a meeting in 1947 led to his replacing none other than T-Bone Walker at Robey's Houston club the Bronze Peacock.

Duke-Peacock artists were notoriously badly treated by Robey; Brown probably suffered more than most. Bound by a twenty-year contract that rendered him legally powerless, he was exploited and cheated until 1964, finally escaping to record for the small Houston labels Cue and Cinderella. Robey also prevented him from recording country music, his sole outlet for that passion being a local white honky-tonk band with whom he jammed ("just to keep my nails polished") when he got off the road from tours with his twenty-three-piece orchestra.

In 1965, Brown recorded a session for Nashville R&B jock Hoss Allen, from which a cover of Little Jimmy Dickens's "May the Bird of Paradise Fly Up Your Nose" was released on the Hermitage label. It was one of the few recordings he made until demand from his European cult following brought him to the 1971 Montreux Festival and resulted in albums for the French labels Barclay and Black'n'Blue. Together with *Blackjack* (1977), these gave him the opportunity at last to mix up his innumerable black and white styles into what the country singer-songwriter John D. Loudermilk called "white-hot, red-neck, blue-grass music from a red-hot, blue-collar black man (from Orange, Texas)."

1978 saw Brown recording *Makin' Music* with *Hee Haw* country star Roy Clark and playing a major country festival in Tulsa, Oklahoma. The album was a high-spirited jam more slanted to blues and R&B than to country, but it led to appearances on *Hee Haw* and *Austin City Limits* and pushed Brown yet further into the country spotlight. Cajun albums followed as he rocked on into his mid-sixties.[7]

---

7 Brown continued recording through the '90s, both for Alligator (1991's *No Looking Back*) and Verve (1995's *The Man*). He was one of several legends to make a cameo appearance on Michelle Shocked's 1992 album *Arkansas Traveller*.

Ray Charles

Almost as eclectic as Brown was Ray Charles, the major figure in the transition from urban rhythm'n'blues to sanctified country soul. Charles had synthesized a mixture of influences into his all-absorbing style. Gospel got him at an early age; a taste for big-band jazz (both black and white) developed before he was 15. Pianists such as Earl Hines and Teddy Wilson shaped his keyboard style, while the jazz-man-gone-cocktail-hour crooner Nat King Cole was Charles's main model for ten years.

Then there was country music. "You have to understand that the South was full of country and western sounds," Charles said in his autobiography *Brother Ray,* "and I can't recall a single Saturday night in those days when I didn't listen to the Grand Ole Opry on the radio. I loved Grandpa Jones and those characters. I could hear what they were doing and appreciate the feeling behind it. Jimmie Rodgers, Roy Acuff, Hank Snow, Hank Williams, and later Eddy Arnold—these were singers I listened to all the time. I wasn't fanatical about it, but I certainly dug it and paid it some mind."

Among the early Florida gigs that Ray Charles Robinson took—small combos with which he could sing the odd Nat King Cole or Charles Brown number—was one in 1946 with hillbilly band the Florida Playboys, who covered the current country hits and needed a piano player. Charles was billed as "the Only Colored Singing Cowboy" and even learned how to yodel. Audiences didn't seem bothered by his color, perhaps treating him as a novelty but in any case appeased by his blindness: "In their minds there was no way I could be checkin' over their little ladies. My gaze couldn't offend them."

In 1948 Charles moved on to Seattle, where he formed the Maxim Trio and recorded Charles Brown/Nat Cole–derived sides for the Swingtime label. Even at this point he was aspiring to the kind of success Cole had had with whites. A stint with blues man Lowell Fulson—another transplanted Southerner—followed. On the road he encountered gospel groups such as the Hummingbirds and the Swan Silvertones, sitting in on their rehearsals and picking up ideas.

In 1952, on the strength of his Swingtime sides, Charles was signed by Atlantic Records. His first sides for the New York label were written (under pseudonyms) by label chief Ahmet Ertegun and arranger Jesse Stone, only hinting at the gospel style to come. True, Ertegun's "Mess Around" had an uptempo Pentecostal beat, and Stone's "Losing Hand" was a desolate blues ballad, but "It Should've Been Me," his first hit for the label, might have been a Coasters song.

The added gospel ingredient surfaced during a period spent in the South from 1953 to 1954. In Atlanta, a gospel song by Alex Bradford underwent a secular metamorphosis as "I've Got a Woman," a big R&B hit in 1955. Slowly the 16-bar progression and call-and-response patterns of the church fell into place as an integral part of Charles's sound. "This Little Girl of Mine," "Leave My Woman Alone," and "Talkin' 'Bout You" all came more or less direct from gospel songs. On the superb "Drown in My Own Tears," with its jazzy reeds and jaunty country-church piano, Charles's first female backing group was introduced, giving Henry Glover's blues ballad an added choral dimension. (The Raelets were later formed after being spirited away from Chuck Willis's band.)

With the blueprint for soul thus sketched, the gospel-blues fusion reached its erotic apex in the propulsive electric piano riff and chorus interjections of 1959's "What'd I Say." Yet it was only the next session for Atlantic, his last, that saw Charles cutting Hank Snow's "I'm Movin' On" and experimenting with the strings that would soon feature so prominently on his ABC-Paramount records.

Charles's groundbreaking country albums followed three LPs of rather hackneyed big-band standards. In *Brother Ray,* he said he would have tried country earlier but didn't want to scare his new label. A&R man Sid Feller was "a little bewildered" when asked by Charles to assemble "the greatest country hits of all time" but complied with the request. Using a collection of songs by Hank Williams, Eddy Arnold, Don Gibson, and '30s honky-tonk stars Ted Daffan and Floyd Tillman, Charles set about making *Modern Sounds in Country & Western* (1962). Whether or not he realized the album was actually following in the steps of Ivory Joe Hunter and others, or that Solomon Burke had hit with Wynn Stewart's "Just Out of Reach" only the year before, is unknown. His heroin habit may have cut him off from what was going on in the R&B world. In any case it was only another, very similar cover of Don Gibson's "I Can't Stop Loving You" (by movie star Tab Hunter) that prompted ABC to release Charles's version as a single.

The track was typical of *Modern Sounds:* a plaintive, stoically sad melody set to a big choral-orchestral backdrop. Charles took the Nashville Sound to new heights of kitsch, with vast choirs of obviously white singers and shimmering cascades of strings. ("I am a sentimentalist at heart," he admitted.) The Gibson song worked because it was such a soulful performance; more often, the string charts and warbling voices grated with the Southern flavor of both the songs and Charles's loose vocals. Most successful were the comparatively restrained arrangements of numbers like "Worried Mind," with its bluesy, Floyd Cramer-ish piano solo, and Hank Williams's "You Win Again."

The formula was hugely successful, with "I Can't Stop Loving You" selling two million copies (an R&B as well as pop and country No. 1) and the album a million. A second volume followed in 1963 with more songs by the same kind of writers. Country continued to figure in Charles's output, giving rise to particularly fine versions of Buck Owens's "Together Again" and "Crying Time" in the mid-'60s. 1970 saw a small soul-combo version of the *Modern Sounds* style on *Love Country Style,* while in 1983 he signed to CBS and went contemporary Nashville on *I Wish You Were Here Tonight* and *Do I Ever Cross Your Mind?:* pretty tame stuff, though an album of duets with leading country stars *(Friendship)* included the excellent "Seven Spanish Angels," featuring Willie Nelson.

"There were people—black and white—who were upset with my country songs," Charles noted. "Some thought they were an abomination. Others even called me sacrilegious. I got a lot of reaction. But this was nothing new. I heard the same bellyaching when I did my first gospel/blues songs. In both instances—with my early hits and my country hits—I just happened to hit some good timing. By chance, no one had tried these things before in quite my way."

Perhaps Peter Guralnick's conclusion in *Sweet Soul Music* wasn't so wide of the mark: "In retrospect, I think [Charles] will be seen to have possessed a genius not so much for originality as for assimilation."

The Gospel According to Country Music

Charles was one of a kind: his example isn't meant to suggest that all R&B and soul singers would have been at home singing country songs. Nonetheless, country songs appealed to African American artists precisely because they included elements that blues-based songs sometimes lacked—above all a sense of narrative.

This was a further illustration of the harmony between African and European tradition. African song didn't so much recount stories as set up circular chants. It did not share the West's preoccupation with vignettes of individual lives (the sad story of another broken heart). Blues expressed sorrow but in a subjective, fragmented way, while the structure of country songs, employing the traditional 8- and 16-bar form of hymns and gospel tunes, gave the expression of pain a more ordered regularity. It was in the play of the African American gospel voice against the constrictive form of the white country song that the Southern soul ballad came about.

There was a kind of fatalism in the classic country chord progression that went back to the Anglo-Celtic ballads, to the determinism of Calvinist theology. In the standard country song of woe, everything happened in advance: the melodic theme was introduced and resolved in the opening bar; the song came to a neatly preordained conclusion. As in the old ballads, there was little element of chance. The voice was resigned to its pain, repressing emotional display. Where gospel and blues singers cried out in expressions of release, country singers reined in and controlled their slurs and idiosyncrasies. Even such great singers as George Jones only accented *within* the beat, rarely crying out *across* it. Country worked for melancholy, not agony—which was part of its nostalgia—whereas the soul singer was hurting right *now*.

The very notion of African Americans being attracted to country music seemed perverse until one realized it was country's very restraint that appealed to them. In gospel, a singer could only go further over the top in his or her attempts to "wreck the church." What a relief, then, to find an untapped source of great, simple songs that didn't require such relentless histrionics, that permitted emotional shading. Right through the '60s and '70s, church-schooled singers in Memphis, Muscle Shoals, and Nashville (and in Georgia and Louisiana, too) used country songs, or country-style ballads, as springboards for their gospel art.

It's worth bearing in mind that, before 1950, Southern African Americans would have heard little on the radio *except* hillbilly and country and western music. Blues was virtually unexposed on radio right through the '20s and '30s, while the first all-black station, WDIA Memphis, only switched to that format in 1948. True, many African Americans owned Victrola record players rather than radios, but the sight of a rural black family listening to the Grand Ole Opry on a Saturday night in the 1940s would hardly have been unusual. Even today, the nonattendance of African Americans at country shows can't taken as evidence of their dislike for the music. As Ann Malone once wrote in an essay on Charley Pride, "Who knows how many black people listen to country music on the radio—or perhaps buy records—who would feel ill at ease among white audiences at live performances?" Robert Shelton reported in 1966 that 40 percent of one country station's listeners in Richmond, Virginia, were African American.[8]

That country music appealed to many African American singers was indisputable. Blues-soul man Little Milton, who (like his peers B.B. King and Bobby Bland) started out at Sam Phillips's Memphis Recording Service, was a big country fan. "I've always been interested in country," he said. "In fact, I played it for a good part of my career when I was living in Mississippi. We used to work the black clubs during the weekend and the white country honky-tonks during the week because the black clubs weren't paying enough . . . I might have been another Charley Pride!"

Etta James, the powerhouse belter equally at home in '50s jump-blues and '60s deep-soul ballads, always wanted to cut a country album: "Those tunes are fantastic, so real and down to earth," she said. "They're white people's blues. A lot of rock'n'roll and soul music doesn't make sense to me—the beat is there but it ain't saying nothing.

---

8   In 1994, black country artist Cleve Francis went to Nashville's Country Music Foundation to inform them that, according to a Simmons poll of radio listeners, 24 percent of the black adult radio audience was listening to country stations.

It ain't saying, 'I'm laying in this bed looking at these four walls/ Waiting to hear your footsteps coming down the hall.' I can really relate to that. I can't sing about how it feels to be on the moon, I ain't never been there. All I know about is how it feels to wallow in this mud, how it feels to be so greasy you feel you just came out of a garbage can. That's what I've got to talk about."[9]

Even Jerry Butler, hardly a Southern soulman, linked country to R&B. "They are the only two forms that are gonna be around," he stated. "They stay around because they talk about everyday realities . . . true-to-life things. They don't get hung up in fantasy-ville or on Broadway. They talk about things that happen to people."

By the late '50s, gospel itself had become streamlined into urban and "country" styles. Where the East Coast Savoy label signed stars such as the Caravans and James Cleveland, the principal Southern label— Nashboro—featured such downhome acts as the Consolers, Brother Joe May, and the Swanee Quintet, recorded poorly in primitive country styles. With crude accompaniment and hillbilly rhythms—a perfect example would be the Consolers' "May the Work I've Done Speak for Me"—Nashboro artists were the immediate predecessors of the next generation's country-soul balladeers.

Sam Cooke epitomized the transition from rural to urban gospel. As R. H. Harris, his mentor in the Soul Stirrers, said, "Sam did it in a different way. He didn't want to be that deep, *pitiful* singer." Cooke's slick, pretty-boy image and high, playful voice was a new kind of gospel: despite his influence on people like Otis Redding and the power of songs like "A Change Is Gonna Come," he was never really a Southern singer. As the subsequent pop outings showed, he was temperamentally closer to Motown than to Stax.

Harris's own influence was absorbed by such raw-voiced Southerners as O.V. Wright and Ollie Nightingale: most of the great Southern soul men paid their dues in quartets directly inspired by his Soul Stirrers. Every singer had his particular idol. James Brown was influenced by screaming Archie Brownlee of the Five Blind Boys, Wilson Pickett by

---

9 James's 1997 album *Love's Been Rough On Me,* produced by Muscle Shoals veteran Barry Beckett, featured covers of country songs like Lee Roy Parnell's "The Rock" and Hank Cochran's "Don't Touch Me."

barking Julius Cheeks of the Sensational Nightingales, and Al Green by the sweet falsetto of Claude Jeter in the Swan Silvertones. Fittingly it was Alabama, the quartet state, that became a breeding ground of "deep soul" in Muscle Shoals.

One by one, these singers made the guilty crossing over to R&B and the promise of secular blessings. When they did, they found a new generation of Southern whites ready to join them.

The Jocks

The liberation of Southern whites from redneck *mores* had much to do with radio. Along with Elvis Presley, a new generation of hillbilly cats—conditioned to despise African Americans but incurably intoxicated by their music—tuned into new stations (or old stations with new formats) and heard its first unadulterated rhythm'n'blues.

Many of the pioneer disc jockeys—Southerners like John R. (Richbourg) in Nashville, Dewey Phillips in Memphis, and Zenas "Daddy" Sears in Atlanta—were themselves white, men who'd studiously acquired their gruff hipster intonation from listening to their African American counterparts. "The breakthrough didn't come, as you might expect, in the North," Ahmet Ertegun remarked; "no, it was 'prejudiced' Southerners who began programming Fats Domino, Ivory Joe, Roy Milton . . ." Long before Alan Freed's "Moondog Rock'n'Roll Party" went on the air in Cleveland in 1951, white DJs such as Johnny Martin in Atlanta and Gene Nobles in Nashville played black music on Southern radio. When John Richbourg joined WLAC Nashville in 1941, Nobles had already been playing jazz, jump blues, and gospel for over a year.

When Richbourg came out of the navy in 1945, Bill "Hoss" Allen was playing King's R&B releases on the nearby WHIN station; it was his joining WLAC four years later that prompted them to go exclusively black. "What made us decide," Richbourg told me shortly before his death in early 1986, "was that there was practically no radio station where blacks could listen to their music. It just really caught fire, and soon as many whites were listening to my program as blacks. Young white people wanted to hear that old cornfield blues, Lightnin' Hopkins and so forth, and it became the tail that wagged the dog at

WLAC. I played black music right down the line until I retired in 1973."

Richbourg was himself a fascinating case study of the white man with a black soul, a hip R&B granddaddy the majority of whose vast mixed audience assumed for years that he was black. Born of French Huguenot descent in the country north of Charleston, South Carolina, he first heard black music on his uncle's plantation in Mount Holly. "The blacks would come in during the evening, singing on their way home, mainly spirituals. And believe me, man, I say it to this day— blacks have gotten melody in their souls and it's got to come out."

Richbourg's career began in the '30s with character parts in New York radio soap operas, but a vacation back home in 1940 landed him a job at WTMA Charleston, from where he moved to Nashville. WLAC had gone to 50,000 watts shortly before his arrival and later claimed it could reach 65 percent of African Americans. Its pioneering format was the mail-order show, whereby the DJ played records that could be ordered from a distributor. The two principal shows on WLAC were Ernie's (Ernie Young, who went on to form the Nashboro and Excello labels) and Randy's (Randy Wood, who formed Dot).

After a false start doing a country show, Richbourg took over the Ernie's slot from Gene Nobles: "I'd come on at nine and go until 9:45, then Gene would come on with the Randy's show and play the same damn records I'd played. It was just a matter of who made the strongest impact as to who got the order, and I seemed to have some sort of knack for mail-order selling."

It was Richbourg who started the Per Inquiry business, advertising a bizarre range of uniquely Southern goods and earning a percentage based on the number of inquiries they elicited: "I sold liniments and Bibles and baby chicks—anything—and everything we touched turned to gold. The secret was simply sincerity." It was basically the old medicine show transferred to the airwaves.

WLAC was the first radio station to play black gospel music. Many of Nashboro's gospel artists, for instance, started out broadcasting on Richbourg's and Hoss Allen's shows. By the mid '50s, along with Zenas Sears on WAOK Atlanta, the WLAC shows had become major "breakout" points for R&B in the South. Regular visitors at the station were

Northerners who'd come down South, men such as Leonard Chess and Jerry Wexler. In ten years, Richbourg broke everything from Chuck Berry's "Maybelline" to Otis Redding's "These Arms of Mine." His show, more than any other, was the oracle of the blue-eyed country soulboy. A 13-year-old Dan Penn would disappear under his bedclothes on a remote Alabama farm and cradle his ear to the late-night sounds of WLAC. "My folks got me a radio, you know, and I'd turn that dial to WLAC, real low, and pretend to be asleep. I was listening to black music before I heard Elvis Presley."

Penn was the original redneck soul man, the "secret hero" of Peter Guralnick's book *Sweet Soul Music*. He carried the torch for R&B in the white Muscle Shoals scene and wrote over a hundred sublime country-soul ballads. WLAC was where he and so many others first heard the Ray Charles, Bobby Bland, and James Brown records that changed their lives: "I was listening to WLAC at night and Hank Williams in the day—it was either John R. or the Grand Ole Opry!" For Penn, WLAC was the only real alternative to the country stations that dominated the air. In the '60s he was able to repay his debt to Richbourg with songs for the many acts the DJ brought down to Muscle Shoals.

The Indie Pioneers

The stage was set for the country-soul fusion not just by disc jockeys but by the many white entrepreneurs and talent scouts who'd been searching out and recording Southern African Americans since the '20s: men such as H. C. Speir, the Mississippi storeowner who discovered bluesmen like Charley Patton and Tommy Johnson; Art Satherley, the Englishman who promoted Paramount blues acts Ma Rainey and Blind Lemon Jefferson before becoming the Nashville A&R man for Columbia in the late '30s; and Ralph Peer, who created the first Race records series (on OKeh) before moving on to Victor and discovering Jimmie Rodgers.

In the rhythm and blues era, many more whites (both from the South and from outside) began to realize the rich pickings to be had through working with black singers. Among the most successful of these were immigrants, particularly Jewish, who couldn't break into the WASPy world of official arts and communications. Outside the

South they included Leonard Chess, Jerry Wexler, Ralph Bass, Art Rupe of Speciality, and Herman Lubinsky of Savoy.

In the South, the first and most important were Sam Phillips and King's Syd Nathan. "King did the most work in opening up the South," Jerry Wexler told me. "They covered so much ground, with Wynonie Harris on the one hand and Moon Mullican on the other. Along with Ralph Bass and Art Rupe and the Bihari brothers, these were the major white figures in black music before the Atlantic era. All these guys had musical fire in them. They were music people who knew how to go in there and get the music out of a record."

What picture did outsiders like Wexler have of the South? "Oh, you know, people in white sheets burning crosses and lynching people. All the clichés. I think everybody thought of it like that, north of what I call the Smith & Wesson line."

On the West Coast, Art Rupe and the three Biharis started their companies when, due to the wartime shortage of shellac, the demand for records was high and hard to meet. The Biharis began by running bars and jukeboxes in black neighborhoods of Los Angeles and were recording local R&B acts on Modern by the mid '40s. In 1948, Joe Bihari undertook the company's first Southern field-trip, in the process signing B.B. King in Memphis. Subsidiary labels, most importantly RPM, were added in the early '50s; the Flair label even began life as a country and western outlet. Hits such as John Lee Hooker's "Boogie Chillen," Rosco Gordon's "No More Doggin'," and Etta James's "Wallflower" made Modern one of the most successful R&B indies of the decade.

The brothers' main rivals in L.A. were Rupe's Specialty and Lew Chudd's Imperial. The latter concentrated most of its Southern field work in the Texas-Louisiana area, signing Fats Domino and country acts such as Slim Whitman and Adolph Hofner. According to Wexler, Chudd was less of a "music man" than Rupe, who grew up in a mixed neighborhood in Pittsburgh and moved to California in the early '40s. Failing to make it in the movie business, Rupe joined the Premier/Atlas record company and then formed his own Juke Box label. Instinctively he went for the urban R&B sound the majors were overlooking: "The black people I knew—urban blacks—looked down on country music. To them it was demeaning."

With artists such as Roy Milton and brothers Joe and Jimmy Liggins, Rupe established the Specialty label as a home of hard jump-blues. A major indie by 1950, it branched out into gospel with the Soul Stirrers and the Swan Silvertones, then followed Imperial to New Orleans. Two big hits, Lloyd Price's "Lawdy Miss Clawdy" (1952) and Guitar Slim's "The Things I Used to Do" (1954), set the scene for Little Richard's string of New Orleans–recorded classics beginning in 1956. "I had never been South until I went to New Orleans," Rupe said in a 1973 interview. "I stayed away because all my black friends said 'Man, it's out.' The only reason I went there was because I was very impressed with Fats Domino. I liked the Domino sound. Our musicians were getting a little glib and either I needed a change or they did."

After the Guitar Slim hit, a slow blues with fat horns arranged by Ray Charles, Specialty opened a New Orleans office and loaned Little Richard the money to buy back his contract from Peacock. By the time Richard quit in 1958 and Sam Cooke broke away from the Soul Stirrers to go pop, even Rupe was nibbling at country music. Like so many indie innovators before him, however, he began to tire of the record industry—and in the '60s pulled out for good.

Ralph Bass was a jive-talking Jewish-Italian hustler. For him, the cantor singing in his synagogue sounded like a bluesman: "Most people don't dig minor keys, but it was home to me," he told Michael Lydon in the latter's *Boogie Lightning*. Moving from New York to L.A., he worked for Cleveland's Black & White label, later becoming West Coast A&R man for Savoy. There he produced Johnny Otis, the Robins, and Little Esther [Phillips], touring the South with Otis's revue as an unofficial road manager. Although to his eyes the South seemed unchanged from slavery days, he moved on to King subsidiary Federal and spent time talent-scouting below "the Smith & Wesson line." After producing Billy Ward & the Dominoes and Hank Ballard & the Midnighters in Cincinnati, he found himself one night in an Atlanta club watching an unknown singer called James Brown crawl across the stage screaming "Please, Please, Please." He signed him on the spot.

Though slow to exploit the gospel root of Brown's art, Bass was a crucial figure in the buildup to the soul era and an interesting precursor to Jerry Wexler as a Jewish hipster working in black music. "You had to feel your way; it had to be kind of a natural thing," he said. In 1960, he went to Chess, signing Etta James and producing the label's legendary bluesmen.

Johnny Otis himself was the most startling example of a white man in the African American world of rhythm and blues. With a show at one time or another featuring Little Esther, Etta James, T-Bone Walker, Lowell Fulson, and Charles Brown, he was a major catalyst for West Coast R&B. Born John Veliotes of Greek-American parents in 1921, he grew up in the black community in Berkeley outside San Francisco and began drumming in black swing bands around Oakland. In the mid-'40s he moved to Los Angeles and formed a prototype R&B houseband at the Club Alabam.

With smaller combos evolving out of the old Texas/Oklahoma swing bands, Otis's group was soon a major pull with the Roy Milton/ T-Bone Walker crowd. After opening the Barrelhouse club in Watts, Otis signed to Savoy and took his first revue on the road. Featuring Little Esther, it was hugely successful. In the South it played the kind of giant tobacco warehouses only Louis Jordan could otherwise fill. For much of this time, moreover, Otis passed as a black man. "I did not become black because I was attracted to Negro music," he told Arnold Shaw. "My attitude was formed long before I moved into the music field. Nor did I become a member of the Negro community because I married a Negro girl. I became what I am because as a child I reacted to the way of life, the special vitality, the atmosphere of the black community. I cannot think of myself as white."

After a decade of writing and producing hits like "Cry Baby," "Rockin' Blues," and "Willie and the Hand Jive" (plus Little Esther's classic "Cupid's Boogie" and "Double Crossing Blues"), Otis's brand of R&B was overtaken by the various new sounds of the '60s. As a result he assumed more of a backseat role in the business. The civil rights movement inspired a renewed commitment to the black cause and a book (1968's *Listen to the Lambs*) about the Watts riots of 1965.

In the South itself, two of the formative white-run R&B companies to appear in the wake of Sun were Ace and Excello. Ace was formed in 1955 in Jackson, Mississippi, by one Vincent Imbragulio, otherwise known as Johnny Vincent, a fast-talking hustler who'd begun working as a distributor in the late '40s. Following in the footsteps of Jackson's Trumpet Records—a blues and rockabilly label founded by white furniture store owner Lillian McMurry—Vincent began cutting local blues singers (Arthur Crudup, Tommy Lee Thompson) on Champion, almost getting shot by the irate white employer of one field hand he approached. In 1952 he was hired by Art Rupe to be Specialty's Southern A&R man and moved down to New Orleans. By the time he'd broken away and formed Ace, he was hooked on the New Orleans sound, signing several of the artists—in particular Earl King and Huey "Piano" Smith—he'd produced for Specialty.

Most of the Ace sides recorded over the next decade were cut in New Orleans, though the label's first local hit—Earl King's country-swamp ballad "Those Lonely, Lonely Nights"—was cut at Trumpet's studio in Jackson. In fact, Ace was really the first local New Orleans label; everyone else was a tourist. Vincent's first national hit was 1957's novelty dancer "Rockin' Pneumonia and the Boogie Woogie Flu" by Huey Smith and the Clowns, after which he followed Sam Phillips's example and signed a bunch of young whites, most successfully Jimmy Clanton with "Just a Dream" (1958) and Frankie Ford with "Sea Cruise" (1959).

"Johnny had a real gift of the gab," recalled Mac [Dr. John] Rebennack, New Orleans's original White Negro. "He inspired musicians a lot with his cornball stuff. He didn't know anything about music but he'd say, 'Hungry, put some shit in it.' He pronounced everything so funny with his country Jackson accent that he had everybody falling about laughing."

In Nashville, a similar kind of story occurred with Excello Records. Like Vincent, Ernie Young began life as a distributor, the difference being that he based his business on the mail-order show airtime he bought on WLAC. Having established Nashboro as a predominantly gospel label in 1951, Young formed Excello the following year, initially issuing a mixture of gospel and R&B releases. 1954 brought him a local hit with Arthur Gunter's original version of "Baby, Let's Play House," quickly followed by Louis Brooks and the Hi-Toppers' "It's Love Baby (24 Hours a Day)."

Ace became best known for the various Louisiana swamp-blues men recorded in the bayou town of Crowley by a Jay D. Miller. A Texan who'd settled into the town's Cajun community, Miller played guitar and banjo in hillbilly bands before setting up the Feature and Fais Do Do labels to record local cajun and country acts. Six years later a trial blues release did well, and Miller discovered Lightnin' Slim, first of the distinctive country-bluesmen to benefit from a deal inked with Excello in 1955.

Other eccentrically named characters recorded by Miller for Excello included harmonica player Lazy Lester, the more urban-style Lonesome Sundown, and—most famously—Slim Harpo, who combined the downhome blues style of Jimmy Reed with a nasal country flavor and enjoyed various periods of success on Excello until his death in 1970. These men comprised the last enclave of a rural blues sound, giving Excello a staunchly Southern identity only slightly compromised by such vocal-group hits as the Crescendoes' "Oh Julie" and the Gladiolas's original version of "Little Darlin" (both 1957).

The swamp-blues sound tapered off, only to resurface in the late '60s in the songs of Tony Joe White. Meanwhile Miller became one of the architects of late '50s South Louisiana swamp-pop, cutting big hits by people like Rod Bernard and Bobby Charles. Country, Cajun, and rock'n'roll also continued to feature in his productions. He remained an outstanding example of the independent shoestring producer trying his hand at every available style of Southern music. (Others included Eddie Shuler at Goldband and Floyd Soileau at Jin, together with Huey P. Meaux in East Texas.) The whole southwest Louisiana/east Texas area was a melting-pot of black and white styles—of Fats Domino and honky-tonk, of Cajun and Creole. This gumbo of musics bred its own paradoxes, one being that Jay Miller, recording black bluesmen in the studio next to his home, also cut abhorrent Ku Klux Klan songs for his Rebel label.

More gospel-styled singers were signed to Excello towards the end of the '50s: Nashville locals such as Roscoe Shelton and Lattimore Brown matured into '60s soul singers under the guidance of John Richbourg. After Slim Harpo's Top 40 hit "Rainin' in My Heart" in 1961, Miller's bluesmen stopped selling. Five years later, Ernie Young handed the company over to A&R man Shannon Williams, who updated both the R&B and gospel roster and built the 16-track Woodland Studios in Nashville. On the gospel side, country groups (e.g., the Consolers) were dropped and solo stars (e.g., Alex Bradford) signed as Excello moved into the Southern soul sound with Roger Hatcher, the Kelly Brothers, and Kip Anderson. (Hear the latter's wonderful "I Went Off and Cried," from which this book's title comes.)

These, then, were some of the white companies recording R&B before the '60s. Exerting the most influence on Southern soul was Atlantic, not inappropriately given the major ambassadorial role the label was to play in the South, nor given the fact that most of its great artists—Ray Charles, Chuck Willis, and Clyde McPhatter—were themselves Southerners.

Jerry Wexler joined Atlantic in 1953, six years after its inception. He came from *Billboard* magazine, having coined the term "rhythm'n'blues." One of his earliest trips was down south to New Orleans. Label co-founders Ahmet Ertegun and Herb Abramson had first made the journey for the label in 1949; now, with Wexler, Ertegun went again for the same purpose—to record the great Professor Longhair. "We really didn't cultivate New Orleans like we might have," Wexler admitted. "Imperial and Specialty really jumped in there and latched on, whereas we didn't get anything out of the South at that time. Maybe we just weren't energetic enough."

Only a period of stagnation at the outset of the '60s prompted a deeper investigation of Southern R&B by Atlantic. And yet it was only with Atlantic's Ray Charles that the bedrock of Southern soul had been laid at all.

White Boys on Soul

Charles's songs were centerpieces in the repertoires of the thousand and one post-Elvis R&B bands formed by white boys in the South. Steve Cropper recalled that in the Mar-Keys they threw in the odd Chuck Berry number but would concentrate on covering Ray Charles and James Brown songs. The ideal was to ape the testifying gospel style; party-time rock'n'roll had been left behind.

The most fervent and obsessive of the curious new breed of farm-hand soulboys was Dan Penn, who worked himself into a frenzy onstage with groups such as the Mark Vs and earned himself the occasional monicker of "Bobby Blue" Penn for his pains. "I've said a thousand times on the air, you don't have to be black to have soul," said John Richbourg. "Soul is simply the feel that puts a song over."

Richbourg maintained that it was through the blues ballad that R&B came closest to country music—"the lyric and flow of the songs was very similar"—and Jerry Wexler elaborated: "What happened was that blues had been put into regular time. And from Ray Charles on, gospel chord changes became more important than the 12-bar blues. Now gospel and country music are both in 8- and 16-bar form, and the chord changes in any gospel song can work for any country song. You've got black gospel and white gospel, but the songs are pretty much the same."

Wexler was one of the first outsiders to detect the common ground between whites and African Americans in the South—and to initiate a personal romance with that discovery. "Everybody who knows the real South," he told me, "knows that despite the Klan and the lynchings and the brutality, the liberated Southern white is a hell of a lot closer to the Negro soul than the Northern white liberal. Black or white, anyone who comes from this environment has the same local soul. To think only blacks were brought up in that tradition would be a form of Jim Crow."

Wexler's role as unofficial godfather to the Southern soul sound in Memphis and Muscle Shoals (and later in Macon and Miami) was a rare instance of a Northerner empathizing with Southern culture. He was a country fan into the bargain, having reviewed hillbilly records for *Billboard*. By a nice twist of fate, too, it was Wexler who signed Solomon Burke, perhaps the first official "soul" singer. For Burke's second Atlantic release he selected . . . a country song.

"Just Out of Reach" and "Release Me"

"My editor at *Billboard,* Paul Ackerman, had two hunches," Wexler told me in November 1985. "One, you've gotta sign this guy Solomon Burke. Two, you've gotta cut this country song 'Just Out of Reach,' originally by Wynn Stewart on 4-Star Records. They were the only two suggestions Paul ever made, and I followed both of them."

It was a strange gamble for a New York record company: the song was a classic country ballad, already covered by Patsy Cline and Faron Young, while the Philadelphia-born Burke had little to his name except some sentimental '50s sides on Apollo. Yet the portly singer had a church background that jelled perfectly with the song. Moreover, it was a majestic performance, the voice wistful and lilting and working all the tiny gaps and possibilities that country singers overlooked.

"When Atlantic signed me, I think Jerry was so confused he didn't have any idea what to do with me," Burke recalled. "I was the first black artist to have a million-seller singing country music, but it didn't *sound* like country music. I would see the words on the paper, and my own spiritual projection would come and just say what I felt."

The record looked like a flop for several months but began to take off in the South; by October 1961 was in the National Top 30. Its success left Burke with a problem, though: "They didn't want to classify me as a country artist, because there were no black country artists at that time. And I didn't want to be put down as an R&B artist. So I asked God to give me some sign to show me what we could do or how we could do it. Then I had an interview with a DJ in Philadelphia, and he says, 'Well, you're singing from your soul and you don't want to be an R&B singer, so what kind of singer are you going to be?' And I says, 'Well, I want to be a *soul* singer.'" Although the term was already in vogue in reference to the kind of bluesy instrumental jazz Ray Charles recorded in the '50s, it had suitable religious connotations and served as an ideal shorthand for the gospel-based R&B to come. (That the soul era kicked off with a country and western song is an irony that's subsequently been rather overlooked.)

Though Burke didn't immediately follow with another country song—his next release was the seminal "Cry to Me"—his career was dotted with country performances, from Jim Reeves's "He'll Have to

Go" and Eddy Arnold's "I Really Don't Want to Know" via immaculate country-soul ballads like "Hangin' Up My Heart for You" to late '60s songs by Mickey Newbury and Tony Joe White. "Burke could connect with the white Baptist Southerner," said Wexler.

As with Joe Tex, the singer's raw, downhome preaching had the South eating out of his hand. "King of Rock'n'Soul" has a nice ring to it, but the term could only be applied to such uptempo material as "Everybody Needs Somebody to Love": despite the power of his voice, Burke's real art consisted in the restraint and tension of his ballad performances. "He had raw tone," Wexler told me, "but incredible control."

Some remain unconvinced by these early soul treatments of country material. The late Charlie Gillett remarked that "whereas when singers raised on white country music had turned to [black] R&B they combined the strengths of the two styles to create a dynamic new one; now, when gospel-styled singers used country material, they were exploiting the sweet and sentimental aspects of both musical cultures, seeking to entertain and not to express themselves." This might have applied to Ray Charles's more cloying arrangements on *Modern Sounds in Country & Western,* but it's surely wrong in the case of Solomon Burke.

Another unique black voice to be given the country treatment in the early '60s was (Little) Esther Phillips, who'd more or less quit recording after leaving King in 1953. A bad drug problem had driven her back to her home state of Texas, where—in a Houston club called Paul's Sidewalk Cafe—future pop-country superstar Kenny Rogers heard her singing one night. Rogers raved to his brother Lelan, a Southern promoter who'd produced records by Mickey Gilley, Big Al Downing, and Kenny's own group the Scholars. The brothers had grown up with African American kids in the '30s, absorbing a typically East Texan mixture of white and black influences. Now, a couple of months after Ray Charles smashed with "I Can't Stop Loving You," Lelan had the bright idea of trying Phillips out on a country song.

Signing her to his Lenox label, Rogers chose the weepy "Release Me," a country hit for both Ray Price and Kitty Wells, and brought Phillips up to Bradley's Barn studios in Nashville to record it. It was very much in the Ray Charles vein, featuring tinkling slipnote piano, Cliff Parman–arranged strings, and the faintly ludicrous strains of the Anita Kerr Singers. But Phillips attacked the song with her customary blend of melisma and abrasiveness and—like her idol Dinah Washington on her version of Hank Snow's "I Don't Hurt Anymore"—effected an extraordinary fusion of jazzy slipperiness and Nashville Sound corn.

"Release Me" made the National Top 10 (and No. 1 R&B), leading to an album of the same name that Atlantic picked up and reissued as *The Country Side of Esther Phillips*. Much of it was derivative of the basic novelty of the single—with a fairly feeble rendering of "Just Out of Reach" thrown in for good measure—but tracks such as "Am I That Easy to Forget" and Hank Williams's "Why Should We Try Anymore" worked beautifully. "I like country songs," Phillips said. "I think they tell great stories."

Of Phillips's remaining Lenox masters, only "Half a Heart" was released, after which she parted company with both Rogers and country songs, scoring only once more on Atlantic with 1965's "And I Love Him." The pair briefly teamed up again in 1969 when Phillips emerged from a spell at Santa Monica's Synanon rehab community. A nice version of Al Dexter's "Too Late to Worry, Too Blue to Cry" on Roulette made No. 35 in the R&B chart but wasn't enough to warrant further collaboration.

Atlantic was an appropriate home for these early country-soul hybrids, since Wexler and the Erteguns had started to look South again for an ingredient that eluded them in New York. The label was still having hits—with the Drifters, Ben E. King, and Bobby Darin—but the whole operation was beginning to feel stale.

"Entropy had set in," Wexler told me, "and we were winding down. Everybody was out of ideas, and musicians were out of licks. It was a terrible time, and I got out of the studio. It's an awful thing when you're sitting there with a band and you don't know what to do next. It's like rigor mortis has set in. But after I found Memphis and Muscle Shoals, I never experienced that again for the rest of my life."

2 Memphis Stew

When Atlantic signed a deal to distribute a tiny Memphis label called Satellite in 1960, the music scene in that most influential of cities was undergoing a vital change. "For a century and a half," Gerri Hirshey wrote in *Nowhere to Run,* "Memphis has turned out a variety pack of black and white musicians who mixed blues and Baptist and hillbilly idioms." Now, after Elvis Presley, these three strains were becoming more interwoven than ever. Satellite, which in 1961 changed its name to Stax, was to have a major hand in the mixture.

Sun began to decline after Jerry Lee Lewis's marriage scandal in 1958. The Killer's hit streak dried up by the end of that year, while the company's main promotion man—Sam Phillips's brother Judd— came under investigation for payola. Phillips's extraordinary success, however, led to the formation of countless other Memphis indies— among them Fernwood, Rita, and Hi, who all released rockabilly records. Satellite/Stax founder Jim Stewart joined the crowd with his first label Jaxon, though only four singles (including "Gonna Rock and Roll All Night" by Sun rockabilly artist Carl Mann) were ever issued.

Music was little more than a hobby for this fiddle-playing hick from Middleton, Tennessee. After graduating from Memphis State University, Stewart went to law school and was all set for a lifelong career in the bonds department of the First Tennessee Bank. Yet his country roots were deep, and he held down regular gigs in such

Western Swing bands as Clyde Leoppard's Snearly Ranch Boys, who were refused recording work by the Musicians' Union because they'd gigged with an African American act at West Memphis's Cotton Club.

After Jaxon, Stewart decided to start a country label based outside Memphis in Brunswick. In a primitive studio built in his garage he recorded local country DJs like Fred Bylar ("Blue Roses") and Nick Charles ("For You"). "You took a chance on disc jockeys because they might play some of your other records," Stewart's sister Estelle Axton told me. Charles's "For You" was in the late Sun style, a typical Memphis hybrid: in Clive Anderson's words, "The vocal breaks suggest rock'n'roll, the fiddle is country, while the driving drums and filigree guitar fills are essentially R&B." Neither Bylar nor Charles sold, however, and Stewart lost $10,000 before his sister mortgaged her house to buy a $2,500 Ampex recorder.

"Despite Sam Phillips's success," Axton recalled, "nobody believed that you could make any money in the recording business. I'm not a gambler, but I like to take a chance."

Chips Moman

Bona fide country artists Charles Heinz and Don Willis followed the DJs on to the Satellite roster. Heinz's touring with Gene Vincent's Bluecaps in 1959 led to the arrival at Satellite of guitarist Chips Moman, a mean-looking twenty-one-year-old from rural Georgia who'd been raised on a diet of white country and black gospel music.

"The only radio station we could pick up when I was a kid," Moman told me, "was one which played country music in the daytime and black gospel at night. I'd have the radio under the cover listening to that gospel stuff, and I can still remember the Angelic Gospel Singers singing 'Touch Me, Lord Jesus.'"

Though Moman picked up bluegrass guitar from his cousins, he became a rockabilly maniac within days of first hearing Presley. At fourteen he left for Memphis, where he lied about his age and gigged with Warren Smith and Johnny & Dorsey Burnette. With the latter act he went to California in 1957: "Gold Star in Hollywood was the first real studio I ever worked in, and the first time I heard Stan Ross working on echo there, I knew this was what I wanted to do."

A car wreck had Moman recuperating in Memphis, where Heinz introduced him to Jim Stewart. "Jim had a girl called Donna Rae who he wanted me to play a session for. He also had this studio in a garage with a tape recorder and 4-channel mixer, so we became friendly. I started talking to him about black music, because out in California I'd been working with both black and white musicians. I also told him I wanted to find a better building to put the studio in."

It was Moman who located the vacant Capitol theater on East McLemore Avenue, in a run-down neighborhood of Memphis. The theater was used for country and western shows, then converted into a church, so its country and gospel roots were planted well in advance. Moman also found the Vel-Tones—Satellite's only R&B act before Rufus and Carla Thomas—in a West Memphis joint called the Plantation Inn. "I really think if Jim and I hadn't crossed paths, Satellite might have remained just a country label," Moman told me. "Which isn't to say Memphis wouldn't have happened anyway, because musicians like Tommy Cogbill and Duck Dunn were already hanging out with black bands."

Moman himself formed one of the first integrated bands in the city, the Triumphs, with a very young Booker T. Jones on keyboards and future Memphis Horns member Floyd Newman on baritone sax. "We caused a little static playing clubs around here," Moman recalled.

The dominant Memphis sound of 1959 was the instrumental, a fad started at Sun by Bill Justis's huge 1957 hit "Raunchy." Justis was an arranger who'd worked on Sun hits by Johnny Cash, Jerry Lee Lewis, and Charlie Rich, helping to soften rockabilly's raw edge for the mass audience. His dreamy alto-sax figures and the record's muted country-rock raunch sent it to No. 3 on both the pop and R&B charts and initiated a series of Memphis instrumentals that took in the Bill Black Combo's "Smokie Part 2," Ace Cannon's "Tuff," and the Mar-Keys' "Last Night," then culminated in Booker T. and the MGs' "Green Onions."

The Bill Black Combo was a link between the Memphis of Presley's Sun sides and the Memphis of the Stax sound. Fronted by Presley's original bass player, their instrumentals were repetitive but pleasantly snappy. Out of their ranks, moreover, came several of the players—Tommy Cogbill, Reggie Young, and others—who'd form the nucleus of Chips Moman's great studio band at American. By the time the Combo cut its version of "Turn On Your Lovelight" in 1964, they sounded a little like the MGs on Albert King's "Born Under a Bad Sign."

Still in plaster from his car accident, Moman set about building the McLemore Avenue studio in 1960. A partition was erected down the middle of the theater, a control room built on the stage, and an echo chamber rigged up in the toilets. It wasn't long before young African Americans from the neighborhood—including Booker T. Jones and David Porter—started nosing around.

One day a disc jockey from WDIA was brought in by trumpeter Bob Talley. It turned out to be Rufus Thomas, a veteran of Memphis music who'd recorded the first hit on Sun and had a song he wanted to cut with his 16-year-old daughter Carla. Moman and Stewart co-produced the duo on "Cause I Love You," an engagingly funky song that broke regionally and led to a distribution deal with Atlantic. In February 1961, Carla's enchanting teen rhapsody "Gee Whiz" made the National Top 10 and put Satellite on the map.

The musicians on these first hits came out of Moman's Triumphs and rival combo the Mar-Keys, who scored the label's next hit with "Last Night." The Mar-Keys had started life—with the improbable nomenclature of the Royal Spades—as a bunch of R&B-crazy white kids at Memphis's Messick High School. Guitarist Charlie Freeman was the prime mover, rounding up ex-country bassist Duck Dunn, Arkansas sharecropper's son Wayne Jackson (trumpet), piano player Smoochie Smith, baritone sax man Don Nix, and Estelle Axton's son Packy (tenor). Terry Johnson joined on drums, and the singer was Ronnie Stutes, a.k.a Ronnie Angel. "We were kind of a lounge band," remembered Don Nix, who sported a Chuck Willis-style turban. "We never did like rock'n'roll shows."

Through Packy Axton's connection with Satellite, the Royal Spades hung out at the Brunswick studio and followed Jim Stewart to East McLemore Avenue. At night they'd sneak in the back of Danny's in West Memphis and listen to Willie Mitchell's band, soaking up the riffs that formed the bedrock of the Stax sound. Accounts of the Spades' metamorphosis into the Mar-Keys are conflicting: who left and who joined at what point seem unclear. In all probability it was a loose aggregation. At some point Freeman was replaced by Missouri-born Steve Cropper, and the black horn players Andrew Love and Joe Arnold took over from Don Nix and Packy Axton.

Exactly who played on "Last Night"—the infectiously funky instrumental that launched the Stax label—is similarly uncertain. "Jim and Chips didn't think 'Last Night' would hit," recalled Estelle Axton, who operated a record store in front of the studio and sensed from the reaction of local kids to an acetate of the track that it might be a smash. "They kept stalling on putting it out, and only when I started cussing did they agree to press up 2,000 copies. In the end it was a gold record."

William Bell

Other musicians at the studio included African Americans Lewie Steinberg (bass) and Howard Grimes (drums)[10]. "We didn't know there was such a thing as integration until someone told us about it," said Jim Stewart, whose first meaningful contact with African Americans was in the studio.

Following Rufus and Carla Thomas into the Stax fold were David Porter and William Bell, who'd both grown up singing in neighborhood gospel groups as students at nearby Booker T. Washington High School. Porter had recorded as Little David for Savoy and as Kenny Cain for Hi ("they wanted me to sound like a white Clyde McPhatter!"); Bell sang on such Meteor sides as "Lizzie" and "Alone on a Rainy Night" by vocal group the Del-Rios.

"In the Del-Rios we sang Sam Cooke and Hank Ballard numbers," Bell remembered. "After we split, Chips Moman was always wanting me to record solo." Bell's 1961 single "You Don't Miss Your Water" was the first great Southern country-soul ballad, mercifully unearthed by Southern DJs on the flip side of the poppier "Formula of Love."

---

10 According to Charles Hughes, Steinberg felt his subsequent replacement by the white Duck Dunn was "racially motivated."

From its opening country-church piano figure, it pulled together Bell's beautifully restrained gospel vocal and Moman's country-ballad feel. As Robert Palmer observed, "the song itself could easily pass for country and western, but the vocal, piano arpeggios, and organ-like chords played by the horns are in a black gospel vein."

"I went over the piano intro with Marvell Thomas [Rufus's son] for hours," Moman told me. "The drums just kind of fell in, and Jerry Wexler's first comment when he heard the record was that he loved those cymbals." "You Don't Miss Your Water" was a perfect marriage of country and gospel, giving Bell an enduring musical style for some time after Moman left Stax: "I was one of the first Stax acts with that pop-country crossover flavor, which was a good thing and a bad thing, because Stax was an R&B company. They tried me on things like 'Any Other Way' to put me in a more saleable R&B market, whereas my sound was a combination of gospel, country, and blues-ballad."

Answering to that description perfectly was "Somebody Mentioned Your Name" (June 1963), which might have been a downhome version of Ray Charles's "Drown in My Own Tears." "You Don't Miss Your Water" itself became a repertoire standard among black and white artists alike, covered eventually by everyone from Otis Redding to the Gram Parsons–era Byrds. "I'll Show You" in September 1963 already bore the imprint of Otis Redding's phrasing from "These Arms of Mine," another country-soul classic of that year. By now the punchier Steve Cropper/MGs sound had superseded Moman's sparsely churchy style of production, a development with the unfortunate side-effect of making Bell a low priority on the Stax roster. The Redding-style stomp of his "Don't Stop Now" (1965) was hopelessly unsuitable ("I was never comfortable with uptempo stuff"), the Impressions lilt of "Crying All By Myself" somewhat desperate.

Only on the superb "Share What You Got" (1966) was there any kind of harmony between the Stax sound and Bell's ballad style, while 1967 saw three country-soul gems: "Everybody Loves a Winner," with Booker T.'s bluesy Floyd Cramer piano; "Do Right Woman—Do Right Man," the song Moman had written with Dan Penn for Aretha Franklin; and John D. Loudermilk's "Then You Can Tell Me

Goodbye," a hit the following year for Eddy Arnold. Bell remained on Stax until the company's bitter end, not without success (the gorgeous "Forgot to Be Your Lover" was a hit in late 1968), but his great Southern soul phase was over.

Stax and Country

When the Mar-Keys went on the road to capitalize on the success of "Last Night," they featured Steve Cropper on guitar. The only non-Memphian in the group—he hailed from the Ozark Mountains of Missouri—Cropper's background was pure country.

"My family were all country musicians," he said. "My uncle played fiddle, banjo, and guitar, and we listened every Saturday night to the Grand Ole Opry. I've always connected country music and blues because of the subject matter. To a black person, blues was country music; to a white, country and western was blues." The family tradition did not inspire Cropper, however: "I loved the bluegrass of Lester Flatt and Earl Scruggs, and I loved Patsy Cline, but I never had the desire to play country music. Once I'd heard the rhythm and blues stuff on WDIA in Memphis, I knew that was what I wanted to do."

Cropper's career began at 16 when he took a zany R&B instrumental called "Flea Circus" to Scotty Moore and had it recorded by Bill ("Raunchy") Justis on the B-side of "Cloud Nine." Four years later he was playing with the Mar-Keys, though his real dream was to make records in the studio. "I didn't like being on the road with nine guys, so I told everyone I was coming back home, and I started working in Estelle's Satellite record shop."

Another reason for Cropper's exit was a falling-out with Packy Axton, who believed he was the rightful leader of the group. Axton may have been the cause, too, of Chips Moman's departure from Stax in early 1962. A near-chronic alcoholic (he was to die at 30), Axton aggravated Moman to the point where there was little alternative but to fire him. The resulting strain between Moman and Axton's mother was too great, and his parting opened the way for Cropper. This made a profound difference to the style of production; as Estelle Axton told me, "I think they'd gotten so into R&B and gospel that there wasn't any room for country anymore. Chips had a lot of country in him and put that influence in, but after Steve came along it changed."[11]

The Stax sound moulded by Cropper with Booker T. and the MGs in the course of the next eight years was not, in the main, country soul. Southern, yes, but more black than white, looser and funkier than the rival styles of companies like FAME and Goldwax. If Stax had grown on a country foundation, now people thought of it in terms of "Knock on Wood," "In the Midnight Hour," the gritty gospel-R&B of Sam & Dave.

And yet, as Jim Stewart said at the time, Otis Redding's "These Arms of Mine" was a classic example of the "black country" sound the rest of America seemed to be leaving behind. If it had more to do with the Little Richard of "Send Me Some Lovin'" than with the Ray Charles of "I Can't Stop Loving You," the song was still rooted in a downhome country-gospel base and—broken by John R. at WLAC—a pivotal moment in the evolution of Southern soul. The record's plaintive piano-triplet style was used to great effect on such Redding sides as "Pain in My Heart" (1963) and "Chained and Bound" (1964).

Carla Thomas was also a natural ballad stylist, so much so that the 1966 *Carla* album included versions of Patsy Cline's "I Fall to Pieces" and Hank Williams's "I'm So Lonesome I Could Cry." Country music had always been a part of the Thomas household ("My family and I were raised on the Grand Ole Opry," Rufus told me) and Carla was encouraged to sing country songs long before the release of Ray Charles's *Modern Sounds*. This side of her was heard as late as 1967, on *The Queen Alone* album, with its beautiful ballads "I'll Always Have Faith in You," "Unchanging Love," and "Lie to Keep from Crying."

Isaac Hayes and David Porter, who produced *The Queen Alone,* are usually associated with such funky Sam & Dave classics as "Soul Man" and "Hold On I'm Coming," yet they too had absorbed the influence of country music. "Where I grew up in Tennessee," Hayes said, "that was about all you heard on the radio." Hard though it might have been to connect the gold-chained Superbad dude of "Theme from *Shaft*" and *Wattstax* with the cottonfields of Covington, Tennessee, one could nevertheless detect a strong country-gospel influence in the many ballads he and Porter wrote.

---

11 Sam Moore of Sam & Dave claimed in the early '80s that Cropper "didn't have that much love for blacks, but he saw that he could make money."

"Hayes and I studied country and western tunes because we discovered that some of the greatest lyrics in the world came from these," Porter said. "We might take a country line and put it into an R&B bag, but we got our definition out of the line. Hank Williams was someone whose stuff I studied and whose emotionalism was a great inspiration for me."

One of Hayes and Porter's greatest productions was Ruby Johnson's "I'll Run Your Hurt Away," a thrillingly tortured performance whose choppy country rhythm set up a superb tension with the haunting tune and with Johnson's agonized, Betty Harris–style vocal.

"'I'll Run Your Hurt Away' was the only record I can ever remember crying for," says David Porter, "and it hurt me so very bad that most people didn't understand where it was coming from. I feel that was the most powerful lick, lyrically, that I've ever come up with in my life, and there was a strong country twist to it. I can't remember 'Soul Man,' but I can remember 'More than the cold winds have ever made you cry/And someone has taken away the warm glow that used to be in your eye.'"

Hi Records

The country roots of the Hi label were more far-reaching. They went back to the early '40s, when a honky-tonk band comprising Bill Cantrell (fiddle), Quinton Claunch (guitar), and Dexter Johnson (bass) formed in Tishomingo in northern Mississippi.

Sponsored by the Blue Seal Flour Company of Columbia, Tennessee, the band became the Blue Seal Pals and began playing radio shows around Tennessee, Mississippi, and Alabama to promote the company's products. One of the shows they played regularly was Sam Phillips's Saturday afternoon spot on WLAY Muscle Shoals.

Ten years later, in 1952, Phillips hired Cantrell as a sessionman and talent scout for Sun in Memphis. Out of this came a staff band that included Claunch on guitar, Stan Kesler on steel, and (initially) Johnson on bass—the lineup that played on country sides by Charlie Feathers, Carl Perkins, and the Miller Sisters, developing a "hillbilly" sound like that of Hank Williams's Drifting Cowboys. Claunch recalled that he'd never heard black music before moving to Memphis: "I got to love R&B, because Sam would follow a country session with an R&B session. It was impossible not to hear it."

In 1956, after four years at Sun, Claunch and Cantrell teamed up with Ray Harris—one of many post-Presley Sun rockabilly singers—and formed Hi Records. Securing $15,000 backing from Memphis record store owner Joe Cuoghi, they began producing country and rockabilly records by singers such as Carl McVoy, Jay B. Lloyd, and Tommy Tucker. Only with the arrival of the Bill Black Combo in 1958, however, did they attain any real success. Both Black and Scotty Moore had quit Presley's band in 1957 in a dispute over pay, Moore buying into the Fernwood label and producing Thomas Wayne's hit "Tragedy" before moving to Nashville, Justis forming his instrumental group with Reggie Young (guitar), Jerry Arnold (drums), Carl McVoy (piano), and John "Ace" Cannon on sax.

Another arrival was Willie Mitchell, the first African American artist on Hi. At 31, he was a trumpeter who'd worked in Memphis swing bands—Tuff Green's and Al Jackson Sr.'s—and who led the house band at Danny's in West Memphis. "When a girl got killed at Danny's," Mitchell recalled, "they closed down all the clubs in West Memphis, so we moved back to Memphis and got a gig at the Manhattan Club. It would be loaded every night, and when the white musicians got off at one o'clock, they'd come over and jam until three or four in the morning. The guys from Hi would come to see what they could do with the Bill Black Combo. They even got my pianist Joe Hall to play on 'Smokie Pt 2,' and that was the beginning of my association with them."

Mitchell became the arranger at Hi, working on further records by the Combo and on Ace Cannon's many solo sides. "Bill Black's music was kind of strange," Mitchell told me. "It was a hybrid form that seemed to appeal to all markets, pop, R&B, and country. I suppose it was a kind of country R&B. There were whites and blacks on most of the records, and I suppose they just kind of fused their music together."

Mitchell's own combo played in a very similar style, making the Top 50 in August 1964 with "20–75" before sliding into the same stylistic rut as Black's Combo. Better was the work he did for Reuben Cherry's Home of the Blues label at the beginning of the '60s, when he produced sides by '50s stars Roy Brown and the 5 Royales (including a version of "Please Please Please" that paid James Brown back for his cover of their "Think"). Best of all were his productions of classic records by Bobby "Blue" Bland *(Two Steps from the Blues)* and O.V. Wright *(Eight Men, Four Women* and *Nucleus of Soul).*

Goldwax

In 1960, Quinton Claunch sold his interest in Hi, possibly frustrated by the label's formulaic instrumental sound. R&B had been attempted with local boys Donald Hines and Kenny Cain (aka David Porter) but wasn't pursued.

Continuing in his regular job as a salesman for the Three States Supply Company, Claunch began to dream of an R&B label along the lines of Stax or FAME in Muscle Shoals. At the tail end of 1963 he formed Goldwax in partnership with local pharmacist Rudolph "Doc" Russell. "Otis Redding just amazed me," Claunch said. "I loved that sound, and I wanted to record that kind of music."

The records Claunch produced and often wrote on Goldwax— particularly those by James Carr—were arguably the greatest country-soul sides of all. "Quinton was really too country to cut rhythm and blues," said Estelle Axton—but that depends what one means by rhythm and blues. Claunch's country feel was indeed pronounced in some of Carr's songs, but balanced against the singer's intense gospel baritone, it worked perfectly. As with Muscle Shoals, the Goldwax sound fused black and white in a brilliant harmony.

Claunch owed the discovery of James Carr to one Roosevelt Jamison, who found both Carr and O.V. Wright singing in Memphis gospel groups and encouraged them to try soul music. "I remember the way I met James and O.V.," Claunch recalled. "It was right here on my doorstep in 1963, when I heard a knock on my door at about ten o'clock one night and found Roosevelt, James, and O.V. standing there. They had this little portable recorder, so we sat right down here on this floor and listened to some tapes. Both of them just knocked me out, and I made moves to sign them on the spot."

Jamison had grown up singing in the Baptist church but chose to concentrate on writing "because my timing wasn't very good." At 19 he began working as "a kind of manager" for various gospel quartets, running into Carr singing with the Harmony Echoes. "The way this guy sang really made goose pimples break out all over me," he told me. "His voice was a voice of humbleness and yet power. I guess subconsciously I was putting myself in him, expressing myself through him. We learned the feeling of soul through our striving for God in church, and that feeling had become a part of him."

"I grew up with spirituals," Carr told British radio broadcaster Andy Kershaw in 1987. "I started singing in a gospel group when I was nine years old and we sung in [the Harmony Echoes] about three or four years. I sang in about three groups, but it wasn't like singing solos. I had to produce different songs for them to sing them. I had to arrange them . . . I'm a beautiful arranger, you know?"

Later, Jamison found Overten Vertis Wright in a quartet called the Sunset Travellers. Wright possessed a raw, gravelly tenor of the R. H. Harris type; in Jamison's words, "all the emotion of the old hymns and spirituals. I'd taken 'That's How Strong My Love Is' down to Stax," Jamison said. "I didn't know Otis Redding had looked at the song, so I began to scout around elsewhere. Quinton Claunch heard it but didn't particularly like it—the song he liked was 'There Goes My Used to Be,' and that was the side they tried to push on Goldwax."

Wright's version of "That's How Strong" was the sixth release on Claunch's label. Barely had it come out when Redding covered it on the flipside of "Mr. Pitiful." On top of this setback, it turned out that Wright was already under contract to Duke-Peacock as a member of the Sunset Travellers (you can hear him on such Peacock sides as "On Jesus" Program). Don Robey quickly put out an injunction to stop the release. Wright never again recorded for Goldwax.

Carr's first release, the eighth Goldwax single, was "You Don't Want Me," a routine Bobby Bland-style blues written by Jamison. The follow-up, "I Can't Make It," was even less exciting. Only with "She's Better Than You," written by future (black) country singer O.B. McClinton, did Carr get a decent Southern ballad to work with. The song gave him a basic Redding-derived style (to which he added shades of Wilson Pickett and Joe Simon) and "You've Got My Mind Messed Up" consolidated it. Carr was an even more powerful and skillful singer than Redding, however—perhaps the greatest "deep" Southern voice of all.

If the entire sound and construction of "You've Got My Mind Messed Up" were pure Stax (though deriving from "That's How Strong My Love Is"), Carr's voice was richer and subtler than Redding's, building from an immaculately controlled Joe Simon style to the frantic, almost frightening shrieks that closed the record. Claunch's own "Love Attack" was even better—it's surely one of the most intense performances in all of soul music, every line delivered with a burning hurt, every word perfectly placed and wrenched from his throat. The sound, too, was perfect, with a fluidity Stax never had. A cover of Percy Sledge's "Pouring Water on a Drowning Man" followed, not a patch on Otis Clay's later version but a strong reading of a song whose title Nick Kimberley saw as a possible "image of amniotic submersion by Southern soul's archetypal *femme fatale.*" The flip's "Forgetting You" (another O.B. McClinton song) was perhaps the closest Carr came to pure country. "He was all for this kind of country-style soul music," Claunch recalled. "He tried anything we wanted to try, and we just let him inject his feel."

Most of Carr's sides were recorded at the Sam Phillips Studio on Memphis's Madison Avenue, the larger complex Phillips had built in 1959 when Sun's golden age was over. Engineered by Phillips's old steel guitarist Stan Kesler, the band was drawn from a pool of musicians assembled at the American studio by Chips Moman.

"I'd left Stax in '62," Moman recalled, "and I'd gone to Nashville with the intention of making records on Buddy Killen's Dial label. But when I got there all I did was play guitar on country demos. I was supposedly going to help Buddy break into the R&B field, but I was so depressed and down and out and broke—with my guitar in hock—that I came back to Memphis and tried to get the American studio started. By that time I'd become a drunk, depressed because I never got paid anything by Stax, and I made quite a few of the Goldwax records for twenty bucks and a bottle of whiskey. One day a country singer friend of mine came by and said he'd heard about this guy who'd give him a hit record for $20 and a bottle of whiskey, and that made me quit drinking. The next time Goldwax wanted me to cut James Carr, I said it would cost them $5,000. What's more, they paid it. And that was 'Dark End of the Street.'"

"Dark End" was a masterpiece of guilty country-soul adultery. Carr's vocal style, closer now to Joe Simon's mellow restraint than to Otis Redding's barking passion, gave the song a somber, doom-laden power:

> *I know time's gonna take its toll*
> *We have to pay for the love we stole*
> *It's a sin and we know it's wrong*
> *Oh, but our love keeps comin' on strong . . .*
> (© 1967 Screen Gems EMI Music Inc, USA.
> Reproduced by permission of Screen Gems EMI
> Music Ltd and International Music Publications)

"'Dark End of the Street' came about at a DJ convention in Nashville," Quinton Claunch told me. "Chips and Dan Penn had come up to my room—popping pills and playing poker—and they sat down and started to write a song. So I said, 'Boys, you can use my room on one condition, that you give me that song for James Carr.' They said I'd got me a deal, and they kept their word."

"We were only in there for about thirty minutes," Penn said. "I guess 'Dark End' was the culmination of two or three years of thinking about cheating. When James sang it, he did it exactly how Chips and I heard it in our minds." On *Moments From This Theater*, a 1999 live album made with Spooner Oldham, Penn prefaced the song with these words: "People ask me what my favorite version is, as if there were any version other than James Carr's."

"James had an emotional power that really stirred me up," said Moman, who engineered the session at Hi's studio. "I could have sat and listened to him all day. He never got anywhere near what he should have been, which was an all-time great."

Further Carr sides included Penn and Oldham's "Let It Happen," country writer Harlan Howard's "Life Turned Her That Way" (covered by country singer Johnny Bush), and the almost unbearably painful "That's the Way Love Turned Out for Me." Like so many great singers, Carr was unstable and disturbed; by the late '60s he was abusing various kinds of drugs. "He was very reserved," Quinton Claunch remembered. "It was hard to get a conversation out of him. He was a real religious-type person, but I think maybe the guy that used to drive him around got him into drugs." When Carr became catatonic in the studio, Moman was forced to ask Penn to sing in hopes of motivating him.

In the end, Claunch had to give up: "After Goldwax folded in 1970, I had a deal with Capitol that would have retired James and me both. They waited on me eight months for him to get straightened out, but he ended up in jail down in Florida. It was a crying shame to see that much talent go down the drain."

Atlantic had Carr for one good single ("I'll Put It to You"/"Hold On") in 1971. Recalled Claunch: "I was still acting as his manager, and when Atlantic flew James down to the Malaco studio in Mississippi, he wanted to know where I was. He wouldn't go in the studio without me. So they had to talk to Jerry Wexler, and Jerry had to call me, and my wife and I had to set off in our little Volkswagen and drive to Jackson. Well, we were up all night and James just sang like a bird."[12]

Roosevelt Jamison, who'd dropped out of the Goldwax picture after putting together vocal group the Ovations, recalled Carr's troubles: "Phil Walden and Larry Utall wanted to manage him, but they didn't realize he needed a friend, a big brother, as well. He was very quiet, and after he got on the drugs he became even more of a loner. He began to call me occasionally saying there were people following him at the airport."

Jamison is not even convinced Carr found his true style on record: "Quinton saw a country song with a good picture and wondered how James would sound on it. I'm not sure he was as concerned with James developing a style as he was with jumping on the track of something that was already making money. The whites put their feel under the black man's feel and it seemed to work, but I don't think James ever really found himself. Plus he jumped from working for a lumber company one minute to making money the next and couldn't handle it. He never stabilized."

---

12 Among the other tracks Carr cut at Malaco was a stunning version of George Jones' Top 20 country hit "Tell Me My Lying Eyes Are Wrong" (1970). Included on the Kent *Sweet Dreams* anthology, it remained unheard until 1995.

When Andy Kershaw tracked him down in 1987, Carr couldn't account for the years between 1971 and 1977 (when Jamison again took him under his wing). "I can't recall," the singer said. "I think I was traveling . . . it's hard to say what . . . I can't think, I just can't think of it."

Jamison tried to help a sick and destitute Carr in 1977 by recording tracks for the little River City label he'd formed with his friend Earl Cage. Out of the session came the sadly ordinary "Let Me Be Right"/"Bring Her Back," which had little success. In 1979, Jamison accompanied Carr on a short tour of Japan where—like many Southern soulers—he was the object of an obsessive cult following. On the last night of his Tokyo shows, Carr took an overdose of his antidepressant pills and became spellbound onstage.

More lost years followed in the '80s. Kershaw found him all but retired from music and living with his sisters in a South Memphis housing project. "I didn't want to do any more concerts," he told Kershaw. "I stopped to be around the city, talking to my sisters and helping them out, you know, because they have financial problems. So I just stayed off and tried to spend a little time with them."

Things began to go wrong following the diagnosis of lung cancer and subsequent removal of a lung in 1997. When Carr stopped taking his antidepressants and started acting strangely, his sister had him committed to the West Tennessee Mental Hospital. "He was in and out of the local psychiatric ward here in town," Quinton Claunch told me. "He'd stop taking his medication and they'd put him back in. He'd grin and you couldn't get anything out of him and he was just contrary. For three or four years I was picking him up and taking him to the doctor's to give him his shot, and long as he was taking those shots he was great. That's why I could send him up to New York to do shows. But I'd always have to arrange for somebody to look after him, because if he wanted a cigarette he'd go off in the opposite direction. He meant well, but he just didn't have the mental factor to deal with it."[13]

---

13 Carr made an unlikely return to the scene in 1991 with *Take It To The Limit*, recorded with Claunch and Jamison for the reactivated Goldwax label. Claunch then took Carr with him to the new Soultrax label for 1993's *Soul Survivor*. If neither album was a patch on his late '60s singles, Carr was still cavernous of voice—and otherworldly of presence—when I saw him play

Carr was not the only practitioner of country soul on Goldwax. For one single, 1966's "I Can Make You Happy," Claunch even had the original black country singer, Ivory Joe Hunter, on his label. Meanwhile, sides recorded as "Oboe" by O.B. McClinton anticipated the latter's forays into Merle Haggard–style country.

Carr aside, the best singer on Goldwax was Spencer Wiggins, who combined something of Carr's rich resonance with the country phrasing of Johnny Adams and a touch of Howard Tate's wavering falsetto. His opening shot was the Penn/Oldham song "(Take Me) Just As I Am" (1966), a poor-boy country plea covered a year later at American by Solomon Burke, who also covered Wiggins's churchy "Uptight Good Woman." Claunch's song "The Power of a Woman" was a classic deep-soul statement of righteous male masochism, while Wiggins's final Goldwax release was a wild version of Aretha Franklin's "I Never Loved a (Wo)man," cut at FAME in Muscle Shoals and featuring the blistering slide guitar of Duane Allman.

The most successful act on Goldwax was the Ovations, an example of that rare phenomenon the Southern vocal group. (Like country, Southern soul was performed mainly by solo artists, honorable exceptions being Atlanta's Tams, the Astors and Mad Lads on Stax/Volt, the Masqueraders at American, and the Impressions-style Van Dykes from Fort Worth, Texas.) It was Roosevelt Jamison who saw the potential in the uncannily Sam Cooke–style voice of Louis Williams, once a member of William Bell's Del-Rios. Jamison organized the group around Williams, placed them on soul package tours, and wrote their first single "Pretty Little Angel." Hits on Goldwax included "It's Wonderful to Be in Love" (1964), "I'm Living Good" (1965), and "I've Gotta Go" (1967), all derivative of Cooke's airy pop-ballad style and no less pleasant for that.

One-off soul releases on Goldwax included sides by original Satellite group the Vel-Tones, local girl Barbara Perry (the fine "Say You Need It"), and George (Jackson) & (Dan) Greer, African Americans who wrote for both James Carr and the Ovations. (Jackson subsequently

---

a small Greenwich Village blues club in June 1996. Versions of "To Love Somebody" and "Pouring Water On A Drowning Man" were chillingly intense. He died of lung cancer in 2001.

went on to FAME and wrote for Wilson Pickett, Clarence Carter, and even the Osmonds; Greer took the Ovations to MGM and produced them into the '70s.) Milwaukee-born Willie Walker released a cover of the Beatles' "Ticket To Ride" but was better represented on "You Name It, I've Had It" and "Warm to Cool to Cold," Claunch-produced sides leased to Checker in 1967.

Claunch maintained that Goldwax went bust because his partner Doc Russell turned out to have less money than was originally supposed. After the label's demise, Claunch concentrated on country acts but never cut his ties to black music: "Bill Cantrell and I produced one of Al Green's biggest-selling gospel albums, *Precious Lord*, which we did in Nashville with country pickers," he told me. "I've also done a contemporary country album on Johnny Nash that's still in the can. Contemporary country is what we called pop/R&B twenty years ago—there's a new song by Exile, 'Hang on to Your Heart,' that I'd give anything to have had for James Carr back then. The trouble with contemporary soul is that few of the singers are coming out of the church anymore. That religious element is gone."

American

Using the $3,000 settlement he eventually won from Stax, Chips Moman set up his American studio in 1964. His partner was Seymour Rosenberg, the lawyer who'd won the case. "The studio really wasn't in any shape until 1965," Moman said. "I did some early Goldwax things there, and meanwhile I was still going to Nashville to do Joe Tex sessions."

The American musicians—later known as the 827 Thomas Street Band—were veterans of the Memphis club and session scene, most having played in either the Bill Black/Ace Cannon or Willie Mitchell bands. By 1966 an established nucleus consisted of Reggie Young on guitar, Bobby Wood and Bobby Emmons on keyboards, Mike Leech and Tommy Cogbill on bass, and Gene Chrisman on drums.

Leech and Chrisman were native Memphians. The two Bobbys were from Mississippi, while the Missouri-born Young had started out playing with country star Johnny Horton on Shreveport's *Louisiana*

Hayride. "Reggie can mimic Chet Atkins, then turn around and play B.B. King," said Stan Kesler, who used the band for sessions at the Sam Phillips studio. Cogbill was a virtuoso guitarist who'd worked in jazz bands while retaining a solid country background. "Tommy had country roots," Moman recalled, "because he was originally a steel guitar player. He even played steel guitar in a jazz band." It was with Cogbill, in 1966, that Moman went to Muscle Shoals to play on a Wilson Pickett session for Atlantic. "Jerry Wexler knew me from the early days at Stax and knew I was making those records," Moman said. "That's how we ended up in Muscle Shoals."

Back in Memphis, the American studio made enough money to warrant replacing its old mono board with a three-track Universal Audio machine. Soon after it was installed, Florida disc jockey Papa Don Schroeder brought in some of the acts he'd been recording in Muscle Shoals. Big hits for James & Bobby Purify ("Shake a Tail Feather") and Oscar Toney Jr. ("For Your Precious Love") soon followed. It was the start of a glorious five-year run for the studio.

If the Purifys poppified the Sam & Dave male duo style, Toney was a pure country-soul preacher, turning the Impressions' devotional "Precious Love" into a Baptist sermon and working similar magic on the two Moman/Dan Penn gems "Dark End of the Street" and "Do Right Woman—Do Right Man." Born in 1939 in Selma, Alabama, Toney grew up in Georgia and sang in gospel groups until his Searchers recorded "Yvonne" and "Little Wonder" for the Max label in 1957. In Macon, four sides produced by Otis Redding's original mentor Bobby Smith were leased to King in 1958. Six years later, Toney replaced James Purify in Florida group the Dothan Sextet. By the time he met Don Schroeder in Pensacola, his voice was a harsh, untutored howl, conveying a backwoods sincerity that perfectly suited such country soul sides as "Until We Meet Again" and "Just for You."

If the American sound was glossier and less countrified than Goldwax's—there were more strings and choruses, while Chrisman's drum sound occasionally verged on the Spectoresque—the country was nonetheless there in Reggie Young's quicksilver fills and Bobby Wood's piano embellishments.

Toney's records came out on Bell, the New York company that since 1964 had picked up independent productions by the likes of Bob Crewe and Burt Bacharach. Like Atlantic, Bell had begun looking South, signing deals with Allen Toussaint (1965) and Goldwax (1966) that yielded hits by Lee Dorsey, James Carr, and others. Papa Don Schroeder had made his deal in Nashville with company president Larry Utall, who shared Jerry Wexler's romantic preoccupation with the South.

"Some of those independent producers are dedicated to the point where they'll go into the hills and fields to find talent," Utall said in 1969. "They're interested in bringing out the soul of the singer, not the technical perfection. They also have a unique ability to communicate with the artists. Most of them have either country music or blues backgrounds, and these two forms—in my opinion—come from a largely common source. There's not that much difference between James Carr's 'Dark End of the Street' and a country record. It's a country song done with a blues feeling. Songs such as 'Sweet Dreams' and 'Release Me'—these can go back and forth and be done well in either field."

In 1967, Moman signed a distribution deal with Bell for his American Group Productions label, among them pop sides by Merilee Rush (including "Angel of the Morning") and instrumentals by the American Group itself. The majority of the records were R&B, one of the earliest being Sam Hutchins's Joe Tex–ish cover of Roger Miller's "Dang Me." This was followed by sides on vocal group the Masqueraders, Memphis soul men Roosevelt Grier and Chuck Brooks, and even the great Roy Hamilton (with yet another reading of "Dark End of the Street").

The Masqueraders had formed in Dallas in 1958, gigging around the South before making their way up to Detroit in 1967 to record for La Beat. Signed to Ward, they were produced by Tommy Cogbill on two superbly sparse ballads, "Let's Face Facts" and "Sweet Lovin' Woman," before being recorded as Lee Jones & the Sounds of Soul on the equally fine "On the Other Side." On Bell they had a lovely, half-Southern/half-Chicago-style ballad called "I Ain't Got to Love Nobody Else," then signed to AGP itself for three less interesting singles. Another rare example of a Southern vocal group, the Masqueraders went on to Hi and to Isaac Hayes's Hot Buttered Soul label in the '70s.[14]

Moman was a magnet for talent, drawing the Muscle Shoals writers Dan Penn and Spooner Oldham away from Rick Hall and creating a hive of late '60s activity that turned American into a virtual pop factory. Another character he met in Muscle Shoals was Wilson Pickett's buddy Bobby Womack, who came to American to record his first Minit album and stayed on as a session guitarist. "Bobby and Reggie played guitar together for a couple of years there," Moman told me. "The two of them would be just magic, alternating between lead and rhythm and getting each other's playing down totally."

New York Times critic Robert Palmer (at the time a jazz saxophonist from Little Rock, Arkansas) later recalled the scene at American: "Musicians would show up for scheduled sessions to find Moman, who looked and talked like a country sheriff, and Womack, meticulously reassembling the recording machine, testing connections, and lazily talking shop. 'It oughta be ready by the middle of next week,' Moman would drawl, while Womack grinned in disbelief." 1986 saw the two men reunited on the fine *Womagic* album, recorded in Memphis with American Studio veterans.

Among the soul artists who continued to use American were Joe Tex and Joe Simon, plus other acts brought down by Nashville producers Buddy Killen and John Richbourg. Even Jerry Wexler, hurt that AGP went to Bell rather than Atlantic, brought King Curtis, the Sweet Inspirations, and Dusty Springfield to the studio.[15] Pickett, too—having cut his first smash hit "In the Midnight Hour" at Stax—returned to Memphis.

"Of course I was disappointed that AGP went to Bell," said Wexler, who'd given the studio early financial backing. "I was expecting so much love and acknowledgment, I thought they'd just offer everything

---

14 In *Memphis Boys*, her book about the American studio, Roben Jones mentions a session in which Lee Jones—the group's leader singer—became so enraged by Gene Chrisman's repeated requests to sing a line over again that he finally replied "Yassuh, massa" to him.

15 Springfield's final vocals for the much-loved *Dusty in Memphis* (1969) were eventually recorded in New York.

to me that was worth a damn. But Larry Utall was in town, and they were right to go with him. American was very much like Muscle Shoals, with a bit of Atlantic's New York sound. Of course Chips was very influenced by the musicians we brought down there, like King Curtis and Herbie Mann."

"The main thing we did at American was to get out of 'secondary chart' thinking," said keyboard man Bobby Emmons. "We decided to cut hits." And hits they cut, including smashes by Neil Diamond, Dionne Warwick, and—on his first Memphis sessions since 1955—Elvis Presley. Clearly Moman had come a long way from "You Don't Miss Your Water." "Elvis wasn't the world's greatest singer," he told me, "but he had a sound and that's all that's important." It was the meeting of two redneck hepcats reared on black music, and together they recorded versions of Chuck Jackson's "Any Day Now" and Jerry Butler's "Only the Strong Survive," together with country-soul ballads like "After Loving You" and "I'll Hold You in My Heart."

Presley was singing terribly—"when I told him he was off pitch on certain notes, his whole entourage nearly fainted," said Moman—but *From Elvis in Memphis* was his best album in years. As Charlie Gillett noted in *Making Tracks,* the recordings had a pronounced Atlantic feel to them: Moman used more echo on drums and vocals than either Stax or Muscle Shoals ever did. Coincidentally, Roy Hamilton, one of Presley's idols, recorded his very last sides the same week, and the two sat in on each other's sessions.

Although the American sound was geared to the R&B/pop crossover, Moman never entirely forsook his country roots. An experiment in 1966 involved singer Sandy Posey recording country-pop songs with a Staxy Memphis feel. Posey was a country girl from Jasper, Alabama, raised on the Opry and the Pentecostal church until her family moved to West Memphis in 1955 and she heard the first Presley records. She worked as a backing singer in Memphis and Muscle Shoals (hear the amusingly Nashville-style chorus of Percy Sledge's "Warm and Tender Love") before Moman decided to record her on the self-penned "Born a Woman."

Overlooking the fact that it set the women's liberation movement back approximately five hundred years, Moman decided the song was a hit. "Chips instinctively knew that he couldn't cut a soul record on me," Posey told me, "but at the same time he realized I shouldn't be cutting strictly hard country." What emerged was a straightforward synthesis of the two, with Sandy's deadpan little-girl voice singing over a strong rhythmic line and R&B instrumentation. "If the Shangri-Las had come from Alabama and not Brooklyn," Charlie Gillett wrote in a review of Posey's greatest hits, "this is what they would have sounded like."

"Born a Woman" made No. 12 on the Hot 100 and was followed by the even more successful "Single Girl." Other hits included John D. Loudermilk's "What a Woman in Love Won't Do," Penn and Oldham's "Are You Never Coming Home?," and Joe South's "Something I'll Remember," while the Born a Woman album included covers of "Just Out of Reach" and Otis Redding's "I've Been Loving You Too Long." The latter anticipated country superstar Barbara Mandrell's versions of soul classics at the turn of the decade: Joe Tex's "Show Me," Aretha Franklin's "Do Right Woman—Do Right Man," and the Redding song itself were all big country hits for Mandrell, while in the mid-'70s her covers of Denise LaSalle's "Married But Not to Each Other" and Shirley Brown's "Woman to Woman" were even played on black radio stations.

Moman, who went on to produce hit records by Willie Nelson, Johnny Cash, and Waylon Jennings (he even co-wrote, with Bobby Emmons, the latter's Outlaw anthem "Luckenbach, TX"), recalled his feelings about country music: "I was so into black music, but all of a sudden in 1961 Willie Nelson came along and floored me so bad that I went into the studio and tried to sing like him. I mean, I never looked at Willie as a country singer; I saw him as the South's answer to Hoagy Carmichael, and I still do. I think if he'd gone to New York or LA, he'd have been a star in 1961. Jimmie Rodgers and Hank Williams were sort of soul singers, and I guess I've always been partial to that side of country.

"I was involved with country records in the '60s, like Sandy's stuff, but they weren't just country records; they were Top 10 pop records. When I was making records, I never gave any thought to markets. The only thing I've ever thought about is amusing myself with what comes out of the speakers, and that's given me somewhat of a problem in Nashville, where people tell me this is too pop for the country market or that's too country for the pop market. I get stranded in between with a lot of good products, There's really only two kinds of music, and that's good and bad."

Posey wound up on Columbia in the early '70s, enjoying a Billy Sherrill–produced hit with another paean to female subordination called "Bring Him Safely Home to Me." In 1977 she was back with Moman and recording for Warners, where she hit with such adapted pop songs as "Born to Be With You" and a medley of "Love Love Love"/"Chapel of Love."

On the other side of town (not far from Stax), Willie Mitchell established a reputation as a producer with his work on Bobby Bland's *Two Steps from the Blues*. After Duke forced Goldwax to withdraw O.V. Wright's original version of "That's How Strong My Love Is," Don Robey passed Wright over to Mitchell, who (albeit uncredited) produced him on a string of gospel-soul beauties for Duke's Back Beat subsidiary. "Eight Men, Four Women" was one of the first, a gloriously solemn "jury of love" adultery saga that defined Wright's desperate, aching style.

Wright's voice was like Sam Cooke's, without the playful narcissism—a Cooke in terrible pain. (Willie Hightower would later achieve a similar effect.) Other superlative sides included the desolate "This Hurt Is Real" and a cover of Brook Benton's "I'll Take Care of You" (also recorded by Bland on *Two Steps*). Despite the probable presence of musicians like Reggie Young, Bobby Emmons, Mike Leech, and future Dixie Flyer Sammy Creason on drums, there was less country in these "sanctified soul ballads" than in James Carr's Goldwax sides, but hear "What About You?," "Why Not Give Me a Chance?," or "I Want Everyone to Know" for examples of songs that might easily have been recorded at country-soul oasis Muscle Shoals.

Hi itself went into a slump in the mid-'60s, despite odd hits such as "Haunted House" (1964) by ex-rockabilly man Gene Simmons. The Bill Black Combo carried on under that name even after Black's death in 1965, but never matched their earlier success. In the '70s they adopted a more country-rock sound and scored hits such as "Redneck

Rock." The company seemed to lack any real identity. Charlie Rich recorded big-band torch songs (and soul numbers such as the Porter/ Hayes/Cropper-penned "Love Is After Me"), then followed with a disastrous LP of Hank Williams songs. Rock'n'roller Jerry Jaye hit with "My Girl Josephine" the same year.

Little else was being done at Hi besides Ace Cannon's and Willie Mitchell's own soporific instrumentals. Only with president Joe Cuoghi's death at the end of the decade did the necessary changes occur for Hi to commence their most illustrious decade.

3 Muscle Soul

If Memphis boasted its share of disaffected white country boys, Muscle Shoals—a few hours' drive south of Nashville—was dominated by them. Between Memphis and Nashville lay a gulf that this small northern Alabama city fell right into.

"Memphis has more in common with its neighbors to the south and west than it does with people in middle and east Tennessee," said producer John Fry, whose Ardent studio served as a spillover for both Stax and American. "In Memphis the whites weren't hillbillies, so there was less of a country-R&B mixture than Muscle Shoals had."

The name suggested some grotesque image dreamt up by a surrealist painter. In fact, the muscles were mussels found in the shoals of the fat Tennessee River that carved this Quad Cities area into its two halves of Florence on the north side and Tuscumbia/Sheffield/Muscle Shoals on the south. Described once by writer Ritchie Yorke as "an untidy cluster of dirty gas stations, wandering wisteria, and burned-up bitumen," the area gave birth to a sound and style of rhythm and blues that became the connoisseur's brand of deep soul music. Almost exclusively it was written, arranged, and produced by whites raised on country and western: no parallel case exists of an R&B scene developing from such limited and unlikely resources. "There seems to be a strip from Meridian, Mississippi, up to Florence," said Dan Penn, greatest of the Shoals songwriters, "and a lot of white rhythm and blues people came out of that strip." Even Florence-born W. C. Handy, the "father of the blues," learned the cornet from the town's white bandmaster at the turn of the century.

White rhythm and blues people: a curious breed of Southerner, especially when—in hillbilly accents as thick as Jed Clampett's—they tell you how much they detested country music. "We weren't interested in any kind of white music, period," Penn told me, reclining in his farmhand overalls. "I did not want to fool with any country music. It did not smell good or taste good to me."

A world away at the Friars' Club in midtown Manhattan, Jerry Wexler chuckled at Penn's words: "The thing about those guys down South is that not one of them will admit to liking country music, but it's impregnated in them. You ask them for a country lick and they'll play it perfectly." Indeed, ask Penn for any of his '60s soul masterpieces and you'll get straight country songs: Percy Sledge's "It Tears Me Up," Aretha Franklin's "Do Right Woman," James Carr's "Dark End of the Street." Most of them have been covered as such.

Geographically, Muscle Shoals was perfectly placed to pick up on the different country, blues and gospel influences of Nashville, Memphis, and the deeper South. As keyboard player Barry Beckett put it: "The musicians were tied in a kind of triangle that stretched from New Orleans to Memphis to Nashville. Maybe it even stretched as far as Houston, with all the Bobby Bland stuff. Whether it was really regional music or not I don't know, but it was more popular down South. When the Shoals bands played fraternity parties, they did rock'n'roll but it had a blues connotation, it had the connotation of this regional black music, and what came out of it all was a hard form of rock'n'roll that picked up off of Ray Charles licks and Bobby Bland horn riffs."

As happened in Memphis, a generation of white males switched on to rockabilly, and from that base discovered the uniquely Southern gospel-blues of Charles, Bland, and James Brown. Party bands who'd started life as square-dance country-rockabilly outfits slowly incorporated blues and R&B songs into their repertoires. As white Southerners, their feelings for black culture were almost certainly ambivalent; full desegregation was not implemented until 1963. "Segregation was something you didn't talk about or think about," said Beckett, but singer and songwriter George Soulé admitted that as a teenager he was racially prejudiced: "Back then, if you said you weren't prejudiced, you were in trouble, so I think the prejudice was conditioned. Certainly it was a strange feeling to like black music and yet . . . appear prejudiced." (In 1973, Soulé was to record the tough black message song "Get Involved.")

"I really think all the R&B stuff cut in the South *did* make a difference to the way blacks and whites thought of each other," said Quinton Claunch, who lived in Muscle Shoals in his early twenties. African American horn player Harrison Calloway remembered his first session at Muscle Shoals's FAME studio: "I liked the fact that white people were getting involved in the music that I was raised on, even though that meant the opportunities for black musicians were lessened. When we combined, say, four white musicians and four black, man, the end results just brought everything together."

"Muscle Shoals was something to get used to, because I'd always played with black folks," remarked the blind soul singer Clarence Carter. "But the whites had a way of playing that was different, and I took it as an opportunity to learn something. And hell, they knew about watermelons too!"

According to many on the Shoals scene, race conflict in northern Alabama was less severe than in the southern part of the state. As had always been the case, relations in the uplands were generally more harmonious. In a small town such as Vernon, where Dan Penn was raised, complete segregation precluded any possibility of violence. "There wasn't any such thing talked about where I lived," Penn said. "We didn't know them and they didn't know us. I never even thought about somebody being a different color from me."

Things were different in the Shoals area itself: piano player David Briggs grew up playing basketball with African American kids, while Arthur Alexander, the town's first black star, played exclusively with whites. "There wasn't but one other black family in East Florence," Alexander told me in Cleveland. "All the kids I played with were white, and I didn't really become aware of the whole race problem until I was about eight or nine."

Harmonious or not, it was still a radical development when white R&B fanatics began hanging out with African American singers in a tiny egg-crate studio built over Florence's City Drugstore. "When we were getting started around 1959," said Florence songwriter Donnie Fritts, "I had people asking me why we were foolin' with niggers— heard that all the time. And we were so visible, right in the middle of Florence, with people like Arthur and his friends coming in and out all day. The whole town hated it."

"I still have a ticket to a Hank Williams show at the Sheffield Community Center," remembered drummer Jerry Carrigan. "It says: 'Admit one white child.' That's the way it was, but it didn't stop guys like Arthur hanging around. It seemed like music maybe bridged that gap a little."

The very first record to come out of Muscle Shoals (or even out of Alabama itself) was actually a country song, "A Fallen Star," recorded on Tune Records in 1956 by future senator Bobby Denton. Covered by Jimmy C. Newman in Nashville, it was one of the first big crossover hits in the pop-country style. "Before the '50s," recalled Tune owner James Joiner, "you had your basic country music, and then you had your Frank Sinatra/Nat King Cole type of music. Maybe the first big country-pop crossover was Ferlin Husky's 'Gone,' and then came 'A Fallen Star.'"

The latter was a pretty twee waxing, all things considered, but it had the effect of crystallizing the fragments of a music scene in the Muscle Shoals area. "Mainly I've been involved in music as a hobby," said Joiner, who ran the family bus depot for most of his life and saw the impact of desegregation at close hand. "I go back to the very crude, raw music we were doing in the South then. We didn't know it, but we were doing a part of the black music. The young boys here were imitating Elvis, but they had their own feel for it. One of the guys I still get requests from England for is Junior Thompson, who's deceased now. He had the second record I put out on Tune."

Joiner even remembered a young Percy Sledge coming to him in the late '50s: "He came to my door in the segregated days when blacks couldn't come into the restaurant or mix. He'd call me out on the sidewalk and beg me to help him record. Well, I was honest and told him I didn't understand his music and had no connections. I had one black record on Tune by a Birmingham blues singer named Piney Brown, but it did nothing."

The success of "A Fallen Star" attracted not only Sledge but whites such as Rick Hall and Billy Sherrill, country boys with similar aspirations to pop-crossover success. Hall hailed from the area of north Mississippi that produced Bill Cantrell and Quinton Claunch, raised dirt-poor in Freedom Hills, Alabama, by a sharecropper father who loved bluegrass mandolin and the shape-note country-gospel songbooks of the Stamps-Baxter company.

"My dad taught the old Fa-So-La type of singing, the early country church music," Hall told me. "He had my sister and I singing duets and harmonies. Then I started banging around on an old mandolin my uncle had given me, and as I got older I began playing with some other kids in the community. These were just little jam sessions, doing hard country like Bill Monroe, the Louvin Brothers, Roy Acuff."

Not far away in Winston County, Alabama, the chronically shy Sherrill was growing up in the middle of the Bankhead National Forest and playing piano at his hellfire-evangelist parents' revival meetings. He and Hall finished school ten miles apart.

Drafted during the Korean War, Hall was in the Third Army Honor Guard with country singer Faron Young but was wounded and sent to San Antonio to recuperate: "In Texas I played with Western Swing bands and became heavily influenced by Hank Thompson and Spade Cooley. It was more sophisticated than the country-root music I'd been playing on this side of the Mississippi."

When he got out of service in 1955, he joined Carmol Taylor & the Country Pals as a fiddler. Playing the same local radio stations and square dances as the Pals was the more rockabilly-oriented band of Benny Cagle & the Rhythm Swingsters, featuring Sherrill on saxophone. "Billy and I started getting into the Presleys and Jerry Lees and the Chess and Atlantic stuff," Hall recalled. "I felt I'd gone as far as I could with country music, making $150 a week playing the country hoedowns and square dances."

With Sherrill and Swingsters' singer Tony Couch he formed pop-R&B combo the Fairlanes, playing weekends at the army base in Fort Campbell, Kentucky, and signing to Chess for a single entitled "If the World Don't End Tomorrow, I'm Coming After You." "There was something natural about me and black people in that we both came from poverty," Hall recalled. "I suppose you'd have termed me poor white trash, and they were considered 'niggers.' The ones I knew were good people, and I saw no reason why they should be treated any different from anyone else. I'd also spent some time in the Midwest, where they were a little more liberal toward blacks, so I had a slightly different perspective from your typical Southern farm boy."

The Fairlanes began gigging around the college circuit—especially at the University of Tennessee and the University of Alabama at Auburn—while at the same time Hall and Sherrill pursued their ambitions as songwriters. James Joiner remembered the disparate group of musicians that gathered around Tune: "Billy Sherrill played some for me, and Melba Montgomery's brother Peanut. Terry Thompson and Kelso Hurston played guitar. Ray Barger came in on bass and Eddie Goodwin of the Fairlanes played drums. Then even younger guys like David Briggs, Norbert Putnam, and Jerry Carrigan started coming around. Roger Hawkins practically learned to play drums in my studio." Another was bassist Dexter Johnson, ex-Blue Seal Pal and uncle of FAME guitarist Jimmy Johnson. Having played some of the earliest country sessions at Sun, Johnson had settled in Sheffield and built—in his garage—the very first Muscle Shoals studio.

In 1957, Joiner started Tune's publishing outlet and began taking songs by Hall and Sherrill to Nashville. "Chet Atkins told me there was something special about the people from this area that he couldn't explain, and he always looked forward to hearing the songs I'd bring him from Muscle Shoals . . . things like Rick and Billy's 'Achin' Breakin' Heart,' a hit for George Jones. 'Six Days on the Road' was a song I found here in Florence, written by Earl Green and Peanut Montgomery's brother Carl."

The following year, Joiner got a call from Tom Stafford, who managed the Princess Movie Theater in Florence and wanted to start a publishing company. Together they formed Spardus Music, which was where the story of Muscle Shoals soul really began.

Stafford was the unsung and rather tragic hero of Muscle Shoals music. To the aspiring songwriters and musicians employed by Joiner, he became a kind of guru/big brother figure. "Tom would listen to our songs," remembered Spooner Oldham, a keyboard player and Dan

Penn's most illustrious writing partner. "Most anytime day or night you could come in and express yourself to him, and he'd give you constructive criticism. He was also one of the few guys who knew any record company people."

Stafford's principal protégé was a lanky African American bellhop from the Sheffield Hotel named Arthur "June" Alexander. Born in 1940, Alexander had grown up to the sound of his father playing gospel songs on slide guitar—and to the strains of country music on the radio. He sounded like a black hillbilly and started writing with Stafford after they were introduced by the Princess Theater's ticket-collector. "Tom was a guy with big ideas," Alexander told me. "Everything revolved around this little room he had over his dad's drugstore on Tennessee Street, where he recorded songs on an Ampex two-track."

To this very primitive studio now gravitated Rick Hall, Billy Sherrill, and Donnie Fritts. "I went up to that room," Dan Penn said, "and there was Rick Hall in one bunk and Billy Sherrill in another. Well, I'd never seen a studio before, and I said to myself, 'I really like this, this is the life right here!'"

It was here, in 1958, that Stafford, Hall, and Sherrill went into partnership under the name Florence Alabama Music Enterprises, or FAME. One of the first songs they published was Alexander's "She Wanna Rock," a number Stafford took to Decca in Nashville and had covered by Canadian rockabilly singer Arnie Derkson.

The Muscle Shoals bands were entering their heyday. The daddy of them all was Hollis Dixon's Keynotes, through whose ranks nearly every Muscle Shoals musician at some point passed. "I done feel like I half-*raised* most of these kids," Dixon told me. "Just about everyone played with me, and at one time we were the hottest thing going in the colleges. We played every frat house from Tulane in Louisiana to the University of Georgia in Athens. At the beginning it was solid Jimmy Reed and John Lee Hooker. To us, there was no difference between black and white. I grew up in the cottonfields with blacks, and later I used the first two black guys in a white Muscle Shoals band, Jesse Boyce and Freeman Brown. I remember the first time Freeman came by to get his money—he wouldn't come in the house because he was worried about what our neighbors would think."

Dixon, who served in the National Guard throughout his R&B years, grew up on the hard country music of Webb Pierce but converted to black music around 1957: "The only other band at that time was the Fairlanes. My first band was Don Shrigley on guitar, Gilley Hurst on drums, and a Jerry Lee–type piano player called Charles 'Lucy' Thompson. He became the police chief in Tuscumbia. Edsel Rickard was the main bass player, though Rick Hall played bass with me a few times. Of course I didn't use horns back then—there wasn't anyone around who could play."

Bands such as the Keynotes wore matching tuxedos and played sock-hops held by girls' clubs at the Tuscumbia Armory or Sheffield's Naval Reserve Center (later Muscle Shoals Sound Studios). The wildest and greatest of them was the Mark Vs, fronted by Dan Penn and comprising David Briggs (piano), Norbert Putnam (bass), Terry Thompson (guitar), and Jerry Carrigan (drums). Penn, in Jerry Wexler's words, was "*the* great white soul singer," something only hinted at by his scant recorded output since 1958's "Crazy Over You." Onstage he would go into James Brown convulsions and roll around the floor.

"When Dan came along," recalled Jerry Carrigan, "we turned our backs on all the country stuff we'd been playing. They told us down at the air force base in Columbus, Mississippi, that we were causing too many blacks to come in the club and that we had to start playing in a different style. There *was* no other style for us, so we quit."

"At that time I considered myself primarily a singer," Penn told me, "but not long after, I had my first hit song, which was recorded by Conway Twitty. That success blew me up pretty good." The song was "Is a Bluebird Blue?," and it was Spardus Music's biggest hit. By then (1960), the FAME partnership had collapsed, with Sherrill and Stafford taking exception to the arrogance Hall had begun to demonstrate. Hall says he was the only one taking FAME seriously as anything more than a stepping-stone to Nashville, but they gave him the elbow. It was, he said, "the lowest moment of my career." Stafford kept the artists and the studio, Hall the name and some of the publishing. Sherrill headed north to Nashville.

"I remember Rick walking the streets of Florence with a piece of paper in his pocket that had "Fame Music" written on it," Penn remembered. "I thought he was kinda nuts."

"You Better Move On"

Tom Stafford retained his Spardus outlet and brought Donnie Fritts and David Briggs in as partners. In 1960 they cut Arthur Alexander on two rockabilly-tinged R&B sides, "Sally Sue Brown" and "The Girl That Radiates That Charm," which Stafford took to Memphis and leased to Judd Phillips's Judd label. Both tracks featured heavy echo on Jerry Carrigan's drums, while "Sally" used acoustic guitars and Terry Thompson tossed off a very tidy James Burton-ish solo on "The Girl . . ."

"Terry," said Briggs, "was the sort of player who hear anything once, be it Barney Kessel or the hardest R&B, then sit down and play it. He was one in a million. In fact, he'd been sort of grooming us as a studio band."[16]

Hall still had his sights set on Nashville, but despite having songs cut by Brenda Lee and Roy Orbison, he couldn't get a foot in the door. Where Billy Sherrill had followed in the steps of Shoals natives Buddy Killen and Kelso Hurston, Hall had a rougher ride: "I was kind of thought of as the guy who was hanging on to Billy's coattails in order to make it, and I was pissed about that. So I either had to do it here or not at all. I certainly had no connections in New York or L.A., where the big guns were. Finally I said, 'To hell with it, I'm gonna go home and start a little demo recording studio, get all the would-be talent together, pick the best guy from this group, and the best guy from that group, and take demos to Nashville.'"

Hall crossed over the river to Muscle Shoals, borrowed money from his car-salesman father-in-law, and turned an unused tobacco warehouse into a 4-track, egg-crate-lined recording studio. With him came Dan Penn, Peanut Montgomery, and eventually the musicians from the Spardus studio. Penn had briefly left the Mark Vs and gone to work in a Bible store in Dallas, though religion wouldn't get him properly for another twenty years. By the time he returned to Alabama, the studio was built: "Rick asked me to come and write for him, and he paid me $25 a week. I was also singing in a band called the Nomads for a while, playing joints in Birmingham and stuff." The makings of a great team were assembled.

In the summer of 1961, Tom Stafford brought Arthur Alexander down to the studio with a song he thought a potential hit. It was called

---

16 In 1993, Alexander told his biographer Richard Younger that Terry
Thompson was "the biggest racist there ever was."

"You Better Move On," and by the time it had been through Hall's hands—"we fiddled with it and fiddled with it and fiddled with it," he said—it sounded like a rural version of Ben E. King singing with the Drifters: a hillbilly "Save the Last Dance for Me." Alexander's voice suggested the Little Willie John of "Let Them Talk" gone country. The effect was gently threatening, mildly disturbing, with none of the gospel desperation that typified the Southern soul man. ("We didn"t really consider Arthur as black," Dan Penn said.)

The lineup on the record, and its equally famous flipside "A Shot of Rhythm'n'Blues," was the now entrenched Mark Vs band of Terry Thompson, David Briggs, Norbert Putnam, and Jerry Carrigan, with overdubbed backing singers Hershel Wigginton and Jeanie Greene striving desperately to sound African American. Replacing rhythm guitarist Peanut Montgomery—then touring with country band the Wilburn Brothers—was Forrest Riley, who shared the mike Alexander was singing into. "I remember sitting high up on a tall stool because Arthur was so huge," Riley told me. "Also, Tom Stafford and I had to go over and pick him up because he couldn't drive. After he was on *American Bandstand,* he bought a Lincoln Continental anyway!"

The record was a huge hit, though placing it at all took every ounce of tap-dancing persistence Hall and Stafford possessed. "At this time," Hall recalled, "there were about seven labels with a man in Nashville, and every one of them turned it down. In desperation I went to WMAK radio and played it for the music director, Noel Ball. He sent it to Randy Wood in L.A., and it came out on Dot." Hall made $10,000 and used it to build a 20' X 50' FAME studio at 603 East Avalon Avenue.

The record's success (it made No. 24 on the Hot 100 in March 1962) led to an album but resulted in Dot cutting Tom Stafford out of the action. David Briggs kept a copy of the contract in which Stafford turned over to Noel Ball the publishing rights to "You Better Move On" and other songs for a case of codeine. "Tom had gotten pretty out there on drugs," Alexander remembered. "It hurt me bad, because Tom was the R&B man . . . without him neither Rick nor Billy would have gone into R&B. Noel Ball was in it for the money; he didn't care about me or Tom. He simply wanted to capitalize on the success of 'You Better Move On,' so he picked out ten current hits for the album. I knew it wasn't gonna work. We recut 'You Better Move On' in Nashville and it sounded like shit."

The album featured stilted versions of Ketty Lester's "Love Letters," Clyde McPhatter's "Lover Please," and Dion's "The Wanderer," plus an uninvolving reading of Willie Nelson's "Funny How Time Slips Away." Better were the poppier singles that followed: Barry Mann and Cynthia Weil's "Where Have You Been" (with its very Drifters-style strings) and Alexander's own "Anna," backed by a lugubrious version of singing cowboy Gene Autry's "I Hang My Head and Cry."

In England, these records were worshipped and covered by young white bands such as the Beatles and the Rolling Stones, unaware the musicians on them were such seasoned Nashville Sound veterans as pianist Pig Robbins and bassist Henry Strzelecki. "I didn't like the Beatles' version of 'Anna,'" Alexander admitted to me. "Like Dan Penn, I thought they were little-girl shit. I preferred the Stones' version of 'You Better Move On'—they were more bluesy."

"Go Home Girl" followed in the vein of "Anna" and "You Better Move On," to be revived beautifully on Ry Cooder's 1979 *Bop Until You Drop* album. Meanwhile Noel Ball, doubtless spurred by Ray Charles's success, continued to try Alexander on country songs. The next single was Johnny Bond's "I Wonder Where You Are Tonight," which Arthur "kinda liked," while a cover of Bobby Bare's "Detroit City" (a perennial black favorite) worked well. Alexander maintained that Nashville publishers were lining Ball's pocket to ensure that their songs were used. But then, according to Alexander, pretty much everyone he ever worked with was an outright crook.[17]

Jimmy Hughes

Back in Alabama, Rick Hall was miffed at losing Alexander to Nashville. At the same time he was undecided on which musical course to take. By all accounts save his own, he preferred trite pop songs to

---

17 Not long before he died in June 1993, Alexander released the excellent *Lonely Just Like Me* on Elektra Nonesuch. Produced in Nashville by Ben Vaughn, the album featured contributions from Dan Penn, Spooner Oldham, Donnie Fritts, and versions of classic songs like "Go Home Girl," "Every Day I Have To Cry," and "In The Middle Of It All."

rhythm and blues: only the hectoring of Dan Penn and the musicians sold him on early FAME productions by the Wallace Brothers and Jimmy Hughes.

If we're to believe Penn and Jerry Carrigan, it wasn't Hughes's superb "Steal Away" that Hall favored but the unspeakable flipside "Lollipops, Lipstick, and Lace," penned by Hall himself with WLAY disc jockey Quin Ivy. Recounted Carrigan, "I distinctly remember Rick calling us into the FAME control room after we'd been demoing 'Steal Away' and sayin' 'Guys, bear with me now, 'cause I hate this R&B stuff.'" Carrigan also recalled a friend of Alexander's coming to FAME with a song called "Share Your Love with Me" and having it turned down. Later it was a smash hit for Bobby "Blue" Bland.

Whatever the truth, Florence-born Hughes was the first artist to be recorded at the new studio. Hall had met him while both worked at the Robbin Rubber Company and Hughes was performing with local gospel group the Singing Clouds. "When Jimmy started with them, we used to go and watch him rehearsing," remembered his younger cousin Percy Sledge. "I'd grown up playing ball with him and everything. He was the one that inspired all of us young people who wanted to be spiritual singers in those days."

Hughes had a high, wailing voice that conjured a chilling sense of guilt on "Steal Away," precursor of all the great country-soul ballads. The song's scenario was perfectly innocuous, but Hughes's anguished shrieks suggested he was concealing something. The fact that the title was also that of a famous "alerting" spiritual—with its hidden implication of slaves stealing away to plot a revolt—gave it added resonance. David Briggs's country piano fills—"it was 6/8, half R&B, half country," the pianist said—turned it into a kind of gospel honky-tonk song, and the follow-up (a version of James Brown's "Try Me") had much the same feel.

"We went through the same thing with 'Steal Away' that we'd had with 'You'd Better Move On,'" Hall said. "Couldn't get a deal. So I started my own label, FAME, and put it out on that. Pressed up five hundred copies, put them in the back seat of my car, and drove with Dan to Memphis, New Orleans, Mobile, Birmingham, Montgomery, Macon, Atlanta . . . the whole Southern chitlin' circuit. I did a tap dance for all the black stations. I said, 'Look, I don't have any money, but if you play the record and it's a hit, you know, I won't forget you.' Black people welcomed our involvement with their music; it was an inroad, a way for them to get ahead. I was a conduit for their talent, and word spread pretty quick. There was never any hostility or anything but good will towards me from black people all over the South. For years, most people thought I *was* black until they met me."

Hughes stayed at FAME until 1966, though he never had another "Steal Away." Other sides on the label showed Hall trying him out on feeble uptempo songs such as "Everybody Let's Dance," apparently blind to the fact that he was at his best on country-soul blues-ballads (e.g., "Why Not Tonight?," Penn and Oldham's "I Worship the Ground You Walk On"). But then Hughes, more than any other, was the artist around whom the FAME sound was constructed: stylistically, as well as technically, they were feeling their way.

"We were just guessing," Jerry Carrigan remembered. "Rick learned hands-on. We didn't have any other studios to spy on."

Dan, Spooner, and the Country-Soul Ballad

The classic Muscle Shoals ballad evolved as white writers began combining their country roots with their gospel-R&B instincts. "Our rhythm and blues," Dan Penn said, "were about white and black people intermingled. The blacks did the foreground and the whites did the background. I mean, you've got your country in there, you can't turn it, but the black singer made it go rhythm and blues. White people, you know, they just ain't as hip as blacks, never was and never are gonna be, but you put them in there and they pull some of that slick and hipness off the blacks. They put some realness in there, like real earth, and just surrounded those blacks with it."

Penn himself finally settled in Muscle Shoals in 1963, recording the second single on Fame, "Close to Me," and collaborating on songs with Donnie Fritts, Rick Hall, and David Briggs. At this time, Dewey "Spooner" Oldham was hanging around FAME as a sort of reserve keyboard player. Like Penn, he'd grown up on bluegrass, Hank Williams, and cotton-picking. In Oldham's case it was a combination of WLAC, Jerry Lee Lewis, and Dixieland jazz that weaned him off country:

"I started writing songs on a little upright piano we had in the house, must've been about sixteen. My sister sang a sort of lamenting love song I wrote, but it wasn't until I met Dan that I got serious about songwriting. I knew he'd written a hit record, and that kind of triggered my motivation. I thought two heads would be better than one, and we decided to get together at James Joiner's place. We spent about six hours and ended up writing four songs, and from then on we'd just get together occasionally and write something. I remember thinking he was one of the best singers I'd ever heard, of any color.

"How did the Southern ballad style come about? Those slow, bluesy, pitiful things? I don't know . . . sincerity, I guess. I don't know if Dan and I were equally oriented towards ballads, but I know that when I would play them and feel them, he could fall into it easily, and vice versa. He would always have his guitar, and I'd be at the piano. We probably wrote over a hundred songs."

"I always considered I was doing as much on the music as he was," Penn told me, "while he was doing as much on the lyric. As the lyricist, I had a right to dig into the melody and change that too. We'd write two or three songs in a night. Sometimes we'd write in a car or go to a park, but usually we'd drop a few pills and sit up all night in the studio."

Over the next three years, a stream of heartbreaking, achingly pure love songs poured from Penn and Oldham's combined pens—Joe Simon's "Let's Do It Over," Percy Sledge's "Out of Left Field," Mighty Sam's "In the Same Old Way," and dozens more. Their construction was simple—"part church, part hills," as Gerri Hirshey wrote—but their melodies were exquisite.

"The ballads were 6/8," said Donnie Fritts, a worthy second-stringer to Penn and Oldham. "I don't know why, but that felt so naturally good to us. It was *right there*. And I can't explain how the country feel crept into all our songs, because apart from a few guys like George Jones we didn't *like* country music. You don't hear that 6/8 thing any more—ballads have gotten real lush, with lots of chords. Those early ballads didn't have a lot of chords."

The 6/8 country-chord ballad was the apex of FAME's art. The songs sounded almost too pure, too naively pained. In a later pop age where romance became merely a subtext of urban glamour, their hurt

Top: Sun and Stax Records R&B legend Rufus Thomas in Memphis.
Below: Sun backroom boys Stan Kesler and Roland Janes outside the
Sam Phillips Recording Service building in Memphis.

Stax star William Bell in his adopted Atlanta, Georgia.

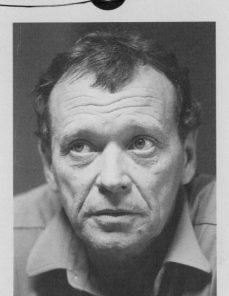

Top: Stax producer and American Studio owner Lincoln "Chips" Moman at the Peabody Hotel in Memphis.
Below: The old Stax studio on Memphis's East McLemore Avenue.

Top left: Otis Redding's former manager and Capricorn Records founder Phil Walden in his adopted Nashville.
Right: Stax cofounder Estelle Axton at home in Memphis.
Below: Stax artist-songwriter David Porter in Memphis.

Top: The old American Studio building at 827 Thomas Street, Memphis.
Below: Backing singer turned country-pop star Sandy Posey in Memphis.

Top left: Goldwax co-owner and producer Quinton Claunch outside his Memphis home.
Right: Hi Records co-owner/producer Willie Mitchell outside the Royal Recording studio in Memphis.
Below: Interior of the Royal studio, home to hits by Al Green and many more.

Top: Tune Records owner James Joiner in Florence, Alabama with the first Muscle Shoals hit.
Below: Shoals star Arthur Alexander in his adopted Cleveland.

Legendary producer and studio owner Rick Hall in his FAME office in Muscle Shoals, Alabama.

Exterior and interior of the FAME studio in Muscle Shoals, Alabama.

Top left: Producer and FAME client Bill Lowery outside his Atlanta office.
Right: FAME keyboard player David Briggs in his adopted Nashville.
Below: Percy Sledge producer turned accountant Quin Ivy in his Nashville office.

The ultimate country-soul songwriting partnership.
Top: Spooner Oldham at home in Center Star, Alabama.
Below: Dan Penn in his backyard in Nashville.

Top: Muscle Shoals and Malaco singer-songwriter George Jackson in Memphis.
Below: FAME star Clarence Carter at home in Atlanta.

Top: The old Muscle Shoals Sound studio in Sheffield, Alabama.
Bottom: David Johnson outside his Broadway Sound studio in
Sheffield, Alabama.

Top left: FAME session guitarist and producer Moses Dillard in his Nashville office.
Right: FAME keyboard player turned producer Barry Beckett outside his Nashville office.
Bottom: Singer-songwriter Donnie Fritts outside the relocated Muscle Shoals Sound studio in Sheffield, Alabama.

Fritts's old songwriting partner Eddie Hinton in Decatur, Alabama.

Top left: Monument Records boss Fred Foster.
Right: Tree Music publisher and Joe Tex producer Buddy Killen.
Bottom: R&B songwriter-producer Ted Jarrett. All pictured in Nashville.

Country-soul man Big Al Downing in Nashville.

Top: WLAC legend and Sound Stage 7 producer John "R" Richbourg, at home in Nashville three months before his death.
Below: Sound Stage 7 singer Roscoe Shelton in Nashville.

Country-soul star Dobie Gray pictured in Nashville.

Top: Songwriter and session guitarist Mac Gayden.
Below: Shreveport soul drummer turned Nashville executive James Stroud. Both pictured in Nashville.

Top: Country-soul "canary" Johnny Adams in his native New Orleans.
Below: Adams's former producer and SSS label owner Shelby Singleton in his Nashville studio.

Clockwise from top left: Producer-arranger Wardell Quezergue in New Orleans; label owner Stan Lewis outside his offices in Shreveport, Louisiana.; songwriter Jerry Strickland at home in Shreveport; and former Muscle Shoals Horns man Harrison Calloway in the Malaco Records office in Jackson, Mississippi.

Top: Producer and Sea-Saint co-founder Marshall Sehorn in New Orleans.
Below: Sehorn's old Sea-Saint partner and Crescent City legend Allen Toussaint outside his New Orleans studio.

Top: Poster for Bobby "Blue" Bland show in Memphis.
Bottom: Mighty Sam McClain performing in his adopted New Orleans.

seemed almost crude. Between Percy Sledge's "When a Man Loves a Woman" and Freddie Jackson's "You Are My Lady" lay a cultural abyss. "Man, I ain't heard Aretha in a long while," Dan Penn protested to me. "She's so slick, she's way up in the stratosphere somewhere. Black folks today are out on the street rapping and zinging, but we didn't do that, our records was just 'I love you, baby . . .'"

In the end, maybe it all came down to the age-old split of North and South. "The South's an old romantic place, no doubt about it," Penn said. "Slavery and the Civil War had a lot to do with how we are now, and especially with arts like music. People are slower and more laid-back down here, and you can feel that in the music."

The Sound

Around the country-soul ballad form Rick Hall constructed the Muscle Shoals sound—what Bill Millar described as "that distinctive Southern rhythm section of clipped guitar, sparse bass, and drums, all recorded open-miked with the amplifiers low."

It was a sound encapsulated in the name Muscle Shoals itself, rhythmically tight, dense, and compact, while melodically loose, fluid, and supple. Compared to Stax it was close, intimate, and enveloping, with precious little echo. Essential ingredients were discreet but rock-hard bass, a sharp, precise snare beat, and a variety of country-style fills on keyboard and guitar.

"The type of sound we had there was different to anywhere in the world, and people came from all over to get that bottom-bass sound," Percy Sledge said. "Muscle Shoals is where I'd go to work on all my songs. The Wilson Dam would give me the background noise, and the woods would give me my echo chamber. I'd have my fishing pole in the water and I'd just be wailing away."

"My country background had an influence," Hall told me, "because I was quite melodic-thinking, and Hank Williams records, for instance, had a lot of melodic fill on them: the arrangements would answer the vocal. I never believed in records being stock to the extent that the rhythm pattern just went along and you changed the melody without being led there by strings or voices. In other words, we used pick-up notes: I wanted to be led there and not just planted."

"Rick's country influence affected the melody lines," said Barry Beckett, a later arrival at FAME. "He would think white lines on top of black tracks. Also, instead of using the steel guitar we would use the organ. You can't bend an organ, but you've got the same transparency that steel provides in country. And you could still incorporate country piano licks into the overall form of the Muscle Shoals sound. The feel itself came from laying back behind the beat a little. Nashville would play right *on* the beat, but if you divide your beat up into, say, a hundred increments and lay back the bass drum two increments and the back beat four, it doesn't mean you're playing out of time; it means you're playing on the backside of the beat. Billy Sherrill, who came from Muscle Shoals, knew the secret about laying back, and he started incorporating that into the Charlie Rich stuff in Nashville."

"We went to a lot of trouble getting our drum sound," Hall said. "We were among the first people in the country to start miking all the parts of the kit separately. Most people just had one mike dangling over the drums so you didn't get the distinction. Plus our drummers were very conscious of the bass drum, which was always coordinated with the bass itself to give it that extra punch. At the same time, I've always tried to cut loose records. We worried that records sounded too tight or preplanned. Dan had the same philosophy. We'd overlook a mistake in a second if the groove was right. I didn't care if the guy fell off the fucking drumstool if he had the groove."

The sound took a while to develop. From the crude 1961 recording of "You Better Move On" to the supercharged beat of Wilson Pickett's "Land of a Thousand Dances" in 1966 was a technical quantum leap. For the first three years at FAME, Hall capitalized on the success of "Steal Away," which had been picked up for distribution by Vee Jay and went all out to establish the studio's name. One of the first Southerners to bring in his custom was Atlanta publisher Bill Lowery with vocal group the Tams. "A country artist of mine, Sonny James, had done some demos at FAME," Lowery remembered, "and I loved the sound on them. So I brought in the Tams, who were the original Beach Music group and very popular with white kids."

The Tams came to Muscle Shoals in the autumn of 1963 and cut several tracks, including two ("What Kind of Fool" and "You Lied to

Your Daddy") that became big pop hits in 1964. These weren't by any stretch of the imagination Southern soul—Joe Pope's gurgling voice was a pure novelty-pop instrument—but their success attracted further attention to the little studio in the back of beyond. The next year Lowery brought white pop act Tommy ("Sheila") Roe, who hit with the Rick Hall–Dan Penn song "Everybody," while Nashville DJs John Richbourg and Hoss Allen (still pumping out R&B on WLAC) came in with soul artists Joe Simon, Freddie North, and Earl Gaines.

In December 1964, the basic rhythm section of Briggs, Putnam, and Carrigan made a move to Nashville that had been on the cards for some months. "I came up here to pitch a song to Brenda Lee's producer Owen Bradley," David Briggs remembered, "and his response was that he didn't want the song but he did want the piano player. Which was me. And I found out that I'd been working three days in Muscle Shoals for what I could make in Nashville in three hours."

Back in the Shoals, Briggs spread the news and reformed the Mark Vs (under the name Dan Penn & the Pallbearers) for one last regional tour. "The Mark Vs were so popular on campuses that we knew if we cut the band down to four of us—Dan, Norbert, Jerry, and myself— we could make a killing. We didn't even use a guitar on that last tour, because Terry Thompson had become a chronic drinker and we couldn't rely on him to make gigs. The name came about because I'd found this cheap hearse to transport our equipment in!"

Penn: "I was kind of disappointed when David and Jerry and Norbert left for Nashville, 'cos we'd hung together quite a few years, but I had my job with Rick and I'd begun to engineer some. All I really cared about was the studio. I hadn't thought about cutting my own records or anything for a long time. I wanted to be a writer and a record producer. In truth, I hadn't lost anything but some good friends, and they wasn't going that far."

"Rick said we wouldn't last thirty days," Jerry Carrigan recalled. "He said we'd be back knocking on his door. But it was a perfect time to come up to Nashville, because country music needed a change— and of course we played it a whole lot different. Not everyone made us feel welcome, but we had something of a track record as a rhythm section, and that made it easier."

"We'd all made fun of Nashville records at FAME," Briggs said. "We had this little joke, because almost every record that came out of Nashville from 1960 to 1964 had a little guitar chink on it, and even funnier was the fact that it was usually played by Kelso Hurston from Muscle Shoals."

Hall was hit hard by the departure, the blow made still worse when—shortly afterwards—Terry Thompson died of a drug overdose. A new rhythm section was slowly built up from the second-string musicians who'd been biding their time at the studio. Rhythm guitarist Jimmy Johnson, a member of local band the Del-Rays, had worked as Hall's go-fer since 1961, while another Del-Rays drummer, Roger Hawkins, was a regular sideman for Grand Ole Opry comedian Cousin Wilbur. Spooner Oldham, meanwhile, had already deputized for David Briggs whenever the opportunity arose. Still around to supply the country guitar fills was Peanut Montgomery, while Albert "Junior" Lowe doubled on bass and guitar. "Junior got his roots from the country blues," Jimmy Johnson recalled. "He had some real good natural-feeling country licks that worked well for black music."

From this nucleus, Hall built his greatest band and obtained his finest sessions. The next four years were FAME's golden age, and Hall worked his musicians hard to achieve it: "We had longer hours than Nashville, where you were in trouble if you didn't get four sides in three hours. I don't believe anybody can cut four hit records in three hours. I spend a minimum of three hours per song, and I don't think *that's* enough. Another factor was the competition between the players: we'd have, say, three bass players on a session, one in the studio and two sitting out in the lobby, and whoever came up with the best riff got the gig. I'd also give the musicians pep-talks to deflate their egos, saying stuff like, "This artist has come all the way here to cut a hit record and if you don't give him one, you may never be cutting a record again." I was the total dictator of the session, and everyone was always on pins and needles with me. I was hell when I was well, and I was never sick!"

If they made him unpopular, Hall's bullying tactics paid rich dividends. Late 1964 brought Nashville producer Buddy Killen—yet another Shoals native—to FAME with a hitherto unsuccessful protégé named Joe Tex. "I came with Kelso Hurston, pianist Ronnie Wilkins, and Roger Miller's old gutstring guitar," Killen recalled. "We worked seven hours on a song called "Fresh Out of Tears," and it just wore everybody out, so I suggested to Joe that we try a couple of lines from a song he'd written called "Hold What You Got." I told the musicians I wanted straight country chords, then overdubbed the gutstring guitar doing an arpeggio with the piano. When it came time to do some harmonies, Joe said, 'Man, I don't know nuttn' about harmony!' in that real gravelly voice. But we got a couple of rough takes. It was a mess, but when I got back to Nashville I found one chorus that held together and spliced it in every time the chorus came around. That record sold 50,000 copies the first day. It was a pop smash."

"Hold What You Got" was a black country homily, a perfect vehicle for Tex's whimsical downhome preaching. Its spare, stripped arrangement was country soul at its finest. "You want to know my secret for getting a crossover hit?" Tex said shortly before his death in 1982. "I used the same formula every time: half soul musicians, half country." The blend gave Tex an enduring if limited style and led eventually to his *Soul Country,* an entire album of country songs.

Quin Ivy and Percy Sledge

The next development in Muscle Shoals music took place a few miles east of FAME in a supremely unsophisticated studio belonging to disc jockey Quin Ivy. A sharecropper's son raised in the country on fiddles and mandolins, he too had been turned on to R&B.

"One year they installed a radio station in my hometown of Oxford, Mississippi," Ivy told me. "I got to be close friends with a DJ called the Boogie Man, who played a lot of LaVern Baker and Ivory Joe Hunter. DJs like Dewey Phillips in Memphis and John R. in Nashville were big influences on me, and later John R. would come down to my studio for its echo chamber."

Ivy himself started out at the little Oxford station, then in 1957 moved up to WMPS Memphis for nine months. Four years of flitting from station to station between Nashville and Shreveport, Louisiana, finally ended in Muscle Shoals, where he joined Sam Phillips's old station WLAY. In 1963, still at WLAY, he opened the Tune Town record store on 2nd Street in Sheffield, all the while maintaining close ties with the scene at FAME.

"I'd known Rick when he was still trying to make it in Nashville," Ivy said, "so we got together and wrote a couple of songs for Jimmy Hughes. Later I had a brainstorm and suggested that I build a studio and he pass on the business he didn't want. I got a used 351 Ampex, an old burlap for a second overdub recorder, plus an RCA console from WLAY, and we built a classic spit'n'bailing-wire studio across the street from Tune Town. Total investment was $7,000."

"I called it the Hot Dog," Percy Sledge remembered. "It was just a straight, long studio—no more than twenty feet across. The echo chamber was made out of tin, and they used to tease me and say, 'Percy, you'd better hope there don't come an electrical storm, because with all that tin you're liable to come out looking like Buckwheat!' It never happened, because we'd just cut off the electricity."

Ivy tried to persuade Dan Penn to come in with him as engineer but quickly discovered how important Penn was to Hall. Instead, the latter pointed him in the direction of Marlin Greene, who'd recorded as a country-pop artist on Tune and RCA-Victor and occasionally substituted for Terry Thompson in the Mark Vs. "Marlin could do anything," Ivy recalled. "He played guitar, engineered, arranged strings, drew the logo for the business, and even designed my second studio." Ivy offered Greene 10 percent of the business, and they got to work on a session by local backing singer Donna Thatcher, later a member of the Grateful Dead.

The second session at Ivy's Norala studio produced "When a Man Loves a Woman," the biggest hit ever to come out of Muscle Shoals. "Meeting Percy was a happenstance," Ivy said. "He worked as a nurse at Colbert County Hospital, and one day he walked into the store. Someone Percy had looked after in hospital was there and said "Oh, by the way, Quin, do you know Percy sings?" And Percy came back that afternoon with his group the Esquires. I can still remember the pick-up truck corning round the comer with a Hammond B3 organ on it!"

Sledge was a country boy, born just southwest of Muscle Shoals in 1941 and raised on cotton and hillbilly music. "Percy told me he didn't know there *was* a black singer until he was twenty-one years old," said David Johnson, who took over Marlin Greene's engineering job in 1967. "He said country was all he sang in the cotton fields."

Sledge's rich, nasal baritone was the exemplary country-soul voice, clearly African American but just as clearly redolent of country singers from Lefty Frizzell to Charlie Rich. He'd begun singing in school, then joined Professor James Richards & the Esquire Combo as lead singer, playing the fraternity circuit at universities such as Ole Miss. As we know from James Joiner, he'd been trying for years to land a record deal.

At the Norala studio that afternoon, the Esquires played Ivy the germ of "When a Man Loves a Woman." "The words left a great deal to be desired, but the melody and the way Percy sang it immediately just knocked me out," Ivy remembered. "We spent two weeks rewriting the lyrics but still credited the song to bassist Cameron Lewis and organist Andrew Wright, who'd come up with the melody."

For the session itself, Ivy booked the FAME band: Roger Hawkins on drums, Junior Lowe on bass, and Spooner Oldham on "a little red Farfisa organ." Jimmy Johnson engineered while Marlin Greene played the discreet country guitar fills. "I can still hear that nasal country sound in Percy's voice," Oldham recalled. "He had it more than most *country* singers!"

"I was nervous before the session," Sledge admitted to me. "I was a little guy from the fields meeting guys in a studio with all this equipment around. But they took me under their wing and made me feel comfortable. Marlin and Jeanie were super; Quin and Jimmy were unbelievable. The musicians gave me some kind of *spunk* and took all the nervousness away from me. They made me feel like I was a *singer,* which I'd always felt I wasn't, because I'd hear people like Smokey Robinson or the Temptations, and I didn't think I was nothing like them—which I'm not, but I didn't think I'd be able to *get* nowhere like them. They gave me the belief."

With its descending, wavelike chords, the song was so ingenuously simple it defied dissection. While by no means Sledge's greatest moment, even if he'd recorded nothing else, it would stand as one of the eternal country-soul anthems. "When I did 'When A Man Loves

A Woman,'" Sledge said, "I knew then that I had my own thing. I didn't need to worry about singing like Pickett or Otis or James Brown or nobody else. And my own thing was expressing myself deeply from within my heart. Every song I ever did, that's the way I did it."

Thanks to Rick Hall, "When a Man Loves a Woman" was released on Atlantic and sealed Jerry Wexler's ties to Muscle Shoals. "I was sitting with this distributor in Atlanta," Hall recalled, "and suddenly he asks if I want to speak with Wexler, who to me was like God or something. Next thing I'm on the phone stammering out something to my idol, and he says to let him know if I have any product that excites me. Well, it wasn't but two weeks before Dan came to me and said they had a hit record over at Quin's studio if they didn't screw it up. The minute I heard it, I knew it was a No. 1 record. Both Jerry and Quin gave me 1 percent as a finder's fee, and that started the whole Atlantic thing for us."

For Sledge it was instant stardom, with the record making No. 1 on both R&B and pop charts in April 1966. A hastily assembled album featured ballads by Dan Penn ("Success" and "You Fooled Me") and Peanut Montgomery ("Love Me All the Way") but failed to capture Sledge's style in the way "Warm and Tender Love," the follow-up single, did. A straight country song acquired backstage at New York's Apollo Theater from Bobby Robinson of Fire & Fury Records, "Warm and Tender Love" suited Sledge's humble wooing technique perfectly. (And dig the whiter-than-white backing vocals of Sandy Posey, Hershel Wigginton, and Marlin Greene's wife Jeanie.) Recorded on the same session was the even better "It Tears Me Up," first of two sublime Penn/Oldham ballads Percy hit with in 1967. "I see him kiss your lips/Squeeze your fingertips/ It tears me up . . ." ached the simple, heartbroken lyric, as spare an expression of pain as any in Southern soul.

The Sledge style, richly plaintive, was established. Right up until 1970 he recorded a succession of country-soul ballads that conveyed not the wracked torment of a James Carr (a version of "Dark End of the Street" was tame by comparison) but an indulgent kind of grief: Donnie Fritts and David Briggs's "High Cost of Leaving," Nashville writer Steve Davis's "Take Time to Know Her," and Bobby Russell's

"Sudden Stop" were some of the best. Marlin Greene teamed up with guitarist Eddie Hinton to write hauntingly delicate songs like "Cover Me" and "You're All Around Me," while Penn and Oldham's hushed, intricate "Out of Left Field" may be his greatest side of all. "I think we always felt that song was ahead of its time," said Quin Ivy. "The audience out there just wasn't ready for it."

As Gerri Hirshey noted in *Nowhere to Run,* Sledge was a country foil to the urban boisterousness of the Wilson Pickett-style Soul Man. "I believe there's a distinct difference between soul singing and simple sock-it-to-me funk music," Sledge said in 1970. "Soul lies generally in the lyrics. The singer surely has to feel what the lyric is trying to explain to the listener. He has to believe in it and not just sing like a parrot. I would certainly describe myself as a soul singer rather than a funk man. I find it much harder to whoop it up because that's not my way. Most artists judge their success by how much noise and excitement they create, but I prefer my audience to be quiet."

"The interesting thing about Percy," Quin Ivy told me, "is that not many blacks bought his records after 'When a Man Loves a Woman.' I used to tell Atlantic, you should see the people who come to his shows—they're white country people, almost exclusively." David Johnson, who produced an unreleased country album by Sledge, maintained this was still the case in 1985: "For the last year, I've been booking Percy into Texas beer joints and honky-tonks, real redneck dives, and we've been selling out; the people have been going *nuts.* And that's people from nineteen to fifty, people who were making out to 'When a Man Loves a Woman' and people who were conceived to it!"[18]

Atlantic at FAME

The success of humble Percy Sledge inaugurated the Atlantic era at Muscle Shoals. Jerry Wexler had already been to Memphis and experienced the informal style of Southern "head arrangements": "I'd go down there and watch Steve and Duck and Booker come in every

---

18 The unreleased country album did eventually make it into the record stores. Released by Demon in 1989, *Wanted Again* featured cozy, cornball versions of George Jones's "She Thinks I Still Care," Jim Reeves's "He'll Have To Go," and Charley Pride's "Kiss An Angel Good Morning."

morning, hang up their coats, and start playing whether they had a song to rehearse or not. Compared to what we were doing in New York it was very fresh." He'd taken Wilson Pickett down there and come away with "In the Midnight Hour" and "634–5789," only to have the singer aggravate everyone involved and receive polite marching orders. Then, in 1966, Jim Stewart and Steve Cropper closed the door to outside producers who'd been exploiting Stax's policy of charging for completed sessions rather than by the hour.

"How was I accepted in Memphis?" Wexler said to me. "Very nicely. Okay, let me put it this way—there was a big ambivalence, like a love-hate relationship. I was like a father, with all the pluses and minuses which go with that franchise. They felt I was bringing something to them and opening things up, but they also felt they were being patronized by me, like they were children. So there was affection and resentment. It took me far too many years to get their unguarded friendship. I was always on trial, on approval. Carpetbagger New York Jew—that's a heavy load to carry down there."

With the doors shut at Stax, Wexler had the bright idea of taking Pickett to FAME, where three enormous hits—"Land of a Thousand Dances," "Mustang Sally" and "Funky Broadway"—were recorded in swift succession in the summer of 1966. Big-city Pickett was somewhat out of place in Muscle Shoals—he claimed he nearly got back on the plane after touching down at the town's tiny airport and seeing African Americans picking cotton—but actually he'd been born in Alabama himself and twenty-odd years in Detroit had done little to erase his Southern gospel roots. Rick Hall (whom Pickett had assumed was black) pulled out all the stops for the session, applying his customary pressure on the musicians. "On 'Land of a Thousand Dances,' we had three bass players trying to play that riff," he said. "While Junior Lowe was in the studio, Tommy Cogbill was sitting in the lobby reading *Billboard!*"

The lead guitarist was none other than Chips Moman (brought down by Wexler himself), who had a knack of coming up with licks that, in Hall's words, "you'd damn near have to build the whole session around." Brass was the Memphis horns of Wayne Jackson, Floyd Newman, Gene "Bowlegs" Miller, and Willie Mitchell's brother

James. The result was a pummelling dance-floor beat whose crossover appeal had little to do with the country soul of Joe Tex or Percy Sledge but did result in FAME playing host to the superb debut Atlantic session by Aretha Franklin.

"I was the only person that knew who Aretha was," Dan Penn told me. "I kept close tabs on the black folks back then, and I knew from her Columbia records that she was good. I knew her family background. I kept telling everyone, 'This girl is gonna kill y'all.'" In February 1967, accompanied by her husband Ted White, Franklin flew to Muscle Shoals and cut the two songs that would make her a superstar. For six years Columbia had been dolling her up as a supper-club torch singer when all the time what she needed was some Southern home cooking. Like Pickett, she was from Detroit but born in the South (in Memphis). All the FAME band really did that day was bring the uptown diva back to her Southern gospel roots.

"There was a sadness in her, and you couldn't define it," Wexler said of Franklin. "It was ungraspable, like quicksilver. But it was my job to furnish the most nurturing context for the music, to get the kind of players who were alert to the little changes or improvisations that she might throw in there."

The tight, humid-sounding "I Never Loved a Man (the Way I Love You)" was the most perfect record Franklin ever made. From the deep bass, crisp beat, and watery electric piano of its opening bars, the record was a magnificently understated blues, a tour de force of sultry intelligence. The components—Spooner Oldham's Fender Rhodes interlocking with Aretha's own grand piano, the economical interjections from the horn section, Chips Moman's brilliantly spiky guitar fills—were all exquisite, all exactly in place. Almost as good, too, was a song only completed in New York, Moman's and Penn's country-soul masterpiece "Do Right Woman—Do Right Man." Never again would Franklin sing against such a sparse, downhome backcloth: just piano, bass, drums, and Moman's acoustic guitar.

Sadly, she would never again record at FAME at all, thanks to an incident that showed just how easily racial tensions between North and South could flare up. "Somebody pinched Aretha's butt," Oldham recalled, "and later in the hotel Ted White and Rick Hall got in a drunken fight." (The "somebody" in question was white trumpeter Ken Laxton, who'd never played on a Muscle Shoals session before.) It was a classic confrontation between Southern white and Northern African American, with a paranoid White anticipating trouble at every turn and a belligerent Hall doing incalculable damage to his relationship with Wexler. Leaving without even finishing her "Do Right Woman" vocal, Franklin vowed she would never return.

A Florida Connection

Some of the greatest country soul sides cut in Muscle Shoals were recorded in 1966 by Florida DJ Papa Don Schroeder's first act, Mighty Sam. Born Sam McLain near Monroe, Louisiana, in 1941, he sounded like a cross between Brook Benton and Bobby "Blue" Bland. He had moved out of gospel to sing with such R&B groups as Shreveport's Elgie Brown & the Soul Brothers.

Winding up in Pensacola, Florida, on a live date, he joined the Dothan Sextet and sang with them at the 8506 club. There he was heard by country DJ and booking agent Schroeder, who persuaded him to leave the Sextet and make records. "I can remember going home to think about it," McClain told me, "and Papa Don sitting outside my house all night waiting for me to make up my mind."

McClain, not inappropriately dubbed "Mighty" in Pensacola, travelled up to Muscle Shoals to record a song called "Georgia Pines," only to be persuaded by Dan Penn to try a version of Don Gibson's "Sweet Dreams" instead. The result was another immaculate fusion of country melody and horn-blasted gospel passion, a triumph followed up by equally fine Penn/Oldham-composed ballads like "I'm a Man" and "In the Same Old Way." Even more countrified was the Schroeder/ Oldham song "Just Like Old Times." "In the mid '60s," Oldham told me, "I had a lot of strong feelings about country and R&B being interrelated. I thought many of the songs Dan and I wrote should have been done country, but we weren't in Nashville and it would have been difficult to press those songs on people."

Before McClain could start building a career he made the mistake of introducing Schroeder to James Purify, the singer who'd replaced him in the Dothan Sextet. Schroeder paired Purify with Sextet guitarist

Robert Dickey and turned them into another of the classic '60s male duos, James & Bobby Purify, who hit almost immediately with Penn and Oldham's pop classic "I'm Your Puppet."

"Suddenly everything started happening for Don," McClain remembered, "and I could hardly get in touch with him. I took him Oscar Toney as well—he was James Purify's replacement in the Sextet—and his first thing ('For Your Precious Love') boomed too! So it was like, one minute I had this guy sitting outside my house and the next I had to send him a telegram saying, 'Hey! Remember me?'"

On their Muscle Shoals ballads "Blame Me" and "I've Got Everything I Need," the Purifys were like a country soul version of Sam Cooke's proteges the Simms Twins. (In Memphis, they even recorded a version of Tennessee Ernie Ford's "Sixteen Tons.") Ultimately, however, Schroeder couldn't give them a style distinct from the other duos who'd sprang up in the wake of Sam & Dave. Bell Records built him his own studio in Pensacola, but it made little difference. The best thing recorded there was an uptempo version of Charlie Rich's "My Elusive Dreams" by Moses & Joshua Dillard, who came to Florida from Greenville, South Carolina.

Dillard had led a band in Greenville called the Dynamic Showmen, backing up the soul acts that came through town. When Otis Redding played there, he invited Dillard to play guitar on Arthur Conley's "Sweet Soul Music" session at FAME. "Papa Don was recording Mighty Sam there at the same time," Dillard recalled, "and he accepted one of my songs for Sam. We got together and my band became his studio band in Pensacola."

Dillard was an interesting case of an African American who briefly penetrated the white session world of Muscle Shoals and felt less than happy about the scarcity of "brothers" on the scene. "It was the road musicians who had to put it on fire, and those white guys couldn't go out on the road," he told me. "The difference between the blacks and the whites was that the whites knew how to write it down. Now I'm one of those blacks who's been in all-white situations all my life, so I'm comfortable, but at the same time I know where my roots are. And when it was all said and done, I had to go back to the black community."

"It wasn't because we didn't *want* black musicians," Dan Penn countered. "As a matter of fact we'd have liked some, but they just weren't walking the streets in Muscle Shoals. We had to get our black horn players from Memphis and Nashville."

Clarence Carter

Before his huge "Sweet Soul Music" hit in April 1967, Otis Redding's protégé Arthur Conley had recorded for Redding's own Jotis label (e.g., the sublime "Let Nothing Separate Us") and for FAME. On Rick Hall's label he cut two Penn/Oldham classics, "In the Same Old Way" and "(Take Me) Just As I Am," then signed to Atco. Another arrival at this time was the blind Alabaman Clarence Carter, whose first FAME side coupled the uptempo "Tell Daddy" with the country-soul "I Stayed Away Too Long" in January 1967.

Carter had a ragged, rural feel that went back to his stepfather's country-blues records and to the hillbilly artists he'd heard on the radio as a pupil at the Taladega School for the Blind. "We'd listen to country music all the time, mainly because our whole faculty was white," he told me. "Every morning at 11.30 the teacher would turn on his radio and let us listen to James & Martha Carson, who broadcast from WSB in Atlanta. Then he'd test us on which Christian song James and Martha had sung. I can also remember Roy Acuff and Ernest Tubb, and George Morgan's 'Candy Kisses.' Later I met some blues guys that used to play around Montgomery, and they told me how Hank Williams used to come over and sit in with them. They said he was a pretty nice dude. I even wanted to cut a country album myself, but Rick didn't think it was a good idea. I don't think we'll ever get as many blacks into country music as whites are into soul, but I happen to like country for the stories it tells. A blues song can ramble on and contradict itself within the lyric, but a country song never does that. It has a complete story from beginning to end."

Carter first came up to FAME as one half of Clarence & Calvin, a duo who'd been dropped by Duke and were looking for a deal. With Hall they cut one side, "Step By Step," which came out on Atco in 1965. Hall signed them as a duo but was left with a solo Clarence Carter when Calvin Scott (also blind) suffered an accident. "Rick decided to go ahead with me when he learned that I wrote songs," Carter remembered. "He was really trying to build up his publishing catalog." Atlanta duo the Wallace Brothers did his "I Stayed Away Too Long" on Jewel (produced by Junior Lowe and Barry Beckett), while Etta James turned his "Tell Daddy" into the powerhouse "Tell Mama." "I was very influenced by Clarence," Hall said. "He had a real knack for little licks that were offbeat. 'Tell Mama' was a good example."

Carter's best records were the hard, punchy hits that followed in the "Tell Mama" vein—"Slip Away," "Too Weak to Fight," and "Snatching It Back"—but his latent country feel came out in ballads like "I'd Rather Go Blind" and a ribald adaptation of "Dark End of the Street." His biggest hit was the hokey "Patches," a General Johnson song that Hall decided told his own life story:

> *My poppa was a great old man*
> *I can see him now with a shovel in his hand*
> *Education he never had*
> *But he did wonders when the times got bad*
> *The little money from the crops he raised*
> *Barely paid the bills we made . . .*
>
> (© Heath-Levy Music Ltd, 1970)

"At Muscle Shoals," Carter said, "they knew how to change a song completely with one lick. Rick showed me I didn't have to holler into the microphone to be picked up, and I was really surprised by how I sounded singing soft. Rick's suggestions always made the record sound better, always. Mind you, he insisted things were done the way he thought they should be done. The only way you got him to do it the way *you* thought it should be done was to make him think *he* thought of it! And see, I learned how to do that."

Chess

1967 brought new customers to the studio in search of the "hard, gutty" sound Hall and staff had patented. Ted Taylor, a melismatic falsetto wailer in the Jimmy Hughes mould, came from Shreveport's Ronn label to record the excellent *You Can Dig It* album, featuring versions of Percy Sledge's "Cover Me," Clarence Carter's "Road of Love," and Kip Anderson's "Without a Woman" (a Dan Penn/Quin Ivy song whose Anderson original on Checker was another FAME masterwork).

Chess in Chicago got interested in the studio after snapping up Montgomery combo Bobby Moore & the Rhythm Aces' FAME-recorded "Searching for My Love" in late 1966. The following year they brought soul queens Etta James, Irma Thomas, and Laura Lee (plus yet another male duo, Maurice & Mac) down to Muscle Shoals.

James's hit run on Chess's Argo subsidiary—from "All I Could Do Was Cry" to "Pushover"—had dried up in 1963. Like Esther Phillips, another product of the Johnny Otis revue, she was also heavily into heroin. Hits were desperately needed; the FAME team duly obliged. Sessions in August and November delivered the darkly brooding "I'd Rather Go Blind" and the beefy "Tell Mama," together with an album's worth of Southern gems: Jimmy Hughes's "Steal Away," Otis Redding's "Security," the Wallace Brothers' "My Mother-in-Law."

"I'd never been down to that part of the South," James told me, "and it was really a relaxed atmosphere. Rick was a cool Southern cat. He didn't tell you what to do exactly; he'd just stop you if you over-did something or he'd give you an idea or two. 'I'd Rather Go Blind' would never have sounded like it did if Rick hadn't produced it, 'cause he was on the brink of losing his wife, and he had that survivor kind of thing. There was just something I liked about him." In his 2015 autobiography *The Man from Muscle Shoals,* Hall wrote that James was "a real hell-raiser, but I cut right through all that B.S. because I knew who she was and where she was coming from."

New Orleans beauty Irma Thomas was similarly pleased with her FAME sessions, which served her breathy, sensual vocals beautifully. Ballads such as "Somewhere Crying," "Yours Until Tomorrow," and "A Woman Will Do Wrong" were divine, while an entrancing cover of Otis Redding's "Good to Me" paid Redding back for his 1963 theft of "Ruler of My Heart." On these sides the FAME sound reached perhaps its purest form.

Laura Lee, finally, was more worldly and haughty than either Etta or Irma: a forerunner of Millie Jackson who wasn't going to let any no-good cheatin' man walk over her any more. Thus she took a broom and swept her "Dirty Man" out of the house with his woman "and yer dog too." To replace him she advertised "Wanted: Lover, No Experience Necessary," though later she specified that her needs required "A Man With Some Backbone." Not that she was incapable of old-fashioned country-soul romance, as she showed on splendid versions of Penn and Oldham's "Uptight Good (Wo) Man" and Curtis Mayfield's "I Need to Belong." Or, come to that, of old-fashioned country-soul guilt, as two Marlin Greene/Eddie Hinton songs, "Sure As Sin" and "It's All Wrong (But It's All Right)," demonstrated.

In these deep soul chanteuses lay the seeds of later Shoals waxings by Candi Staton, Bettye Swann, and Millie Jackson. Meanwhile, Maurice & Mac became FAME's very own Sam & Dave, scoring with Penn and Oldham's irresistibly funky "You Left the Water Running."

Candi Staton

Atlantic continued to use the FAME studio, booking in artists such as Don Covay, King Curtis, and (on its new Cotillion subsidiary) Brook Benton and Lou Johnson.

Covay, a country-influenced singer who'd been down to Stax for "See-Saw" in 1965, cut the brilliant "Stole Some Love" at FAME in 1968. Benton, a kind of country-soul Billy Eckstine, recorded such fine Arif Mardin–produced sides as "She Knows What to Do for Me" and "A Woman Without Love." Lou Johnson's *Sweet Southern Soul* LP, featuring songs by Don Covay and Eddie Hinton, as well as a version of the George Jones hit "She Thinks I Still Care," was one of the last visits Jerry Wexler made to FAME before Atlantic ceased distributing Rick Hall's label in 1968.

The first signing to the new Capitol-distributed label was Candi Staton, a downhome Gladys Knight with an irresistibly hoarse, hurt voice who'd been raised on gospel and the Grand Ole Opry in the cottonfields of Hanceville, Alabama.

"It was peas and beans, barefoot and overalls," she told me. Very quaint, except that the KKK had a training camp twenty miles away and a habit of planting burning crosses in the family garden. Musical schooling was the local Baptist church and a battery radio from which she learned the songs of such country stars as Ernest Tubb. As a child she sang in the Jewel Gospel Trio and toured the Southern states; when later she wanted to follow the secular route of Sam Cooke and Aretha Franklin, her mother forbade her. "Since I wasn't allowed to sing, I got married, and by the time I decided to leave my husband I had four kids."

Staton had one last row with her husband in 1967, then accompanied her brother to the 27–28 Club in Birmingham, Alabama, where she was made to go onstage and sing the only secular song she knew, "Do Right Woman—Do Right Man." The club owner hired her on the spot. The following week, the headliner at 27–28 happened to be Clarence Carter, who was so taken with twenty-five-year-old Candi that he not only made her accompany him to Muscle Shoals but later married her.

"I figured I was over the hill," Staton recalled, "but Rick Hall didn't have any female singers, and he was willing to try me out. I remember driving to Muscle Shoals and finding a hotel suite with a piano in it and a whole bunch of songs by George Jackson. Rick was knocked out by my voice. Next day we went in the studio."

Staton's first single was the propulsive "I'd Rather Be an Old Man's Sweetheart," a record so dynamically punchy it made even Aretha's "Chain of Fools" sound restrained. On this and "I'm Just a Prisoner," Hall achieved his most inspired blend of rhythmic crunch and blasting brass to date. New assets in the FAME team were bassist David Hood (from Shoals band the Mystics) and the nucleus of a horn section from Nashville comprising Harrison Calloway (trumpet), Harvey Thompson (tenor sax), and Ronnie Eades (baritone).

Also new around the studio was George Jackson, like O.B. McClinton, an ex-Goldwax Memphis writer whom Hall was using to fill the void left by the departures of Dan Penn and Spooner Oldham. "Jerry Wexler suggested Rick try using some black writers," Jackson told me. "He took us down to Muscle Shoals. Rick was very impressed with my material. I started writing for Clarence Carter, and later I had five songs on Wilson Pickett's *Hey Jude* album." With Carter, Jackson wrote Candi's "Sweetheart" (an instant hit) and Carter's own "Snatching It Back" and "I Can't Leave Your Love Alone."

If the funky Memphis feel Jackson brought to FAME was symptomatic of Southern soul's gradual move away from the country-ballad sound of Percy Sledge, Staton herself epitomized the country-soul marriage. A lovely version of "That's How Strong My Love Is" on her 1969 *I'm Just a Prisoner* album showed just how rawly intimate she could be on a ballad. "Rick was never mean, but he would make me sing a song over and over again until I was hoarse," she said. "He wanted to work up the emotions out of me so that I got a hoarse kind of Wilson Pickett sound."

Hall began recording Staton on country ballads like "Another Man's Woman" (sung first by Laura Lee), while an inspired soul translation of Tammy Wynette's Billy Sherrill–produced "Stand By Your Man" was a big hit in 1970. "We weren't even thinking of a hit record, just a filler," Staton said. "Clarence said to put it in the groove of Ben E. King's 'Stand By Me.'"

"They put the bird in my lap," Carter recalled. "I thought about it all night and couldn't think of any way of changing it from country. Next morning in the studio I suddenly remembered "Stand By Me," so I went over to the organ and started playing it, and everybody just started chiming in. Finally, Rick decided it was about time to turn on the machine. It was practically a first take."

The subsequent album featured further country-soul gems in "Mr. & Mrs. Untrue," "How Can I Put Out the Flame," and "That Would Mean Everything to Me," while the follow-up was Harlan Howard's "He Called Me Baby," a hit the previous year for Ella Washington.

By this time, Hall had once again been abandoned by a rhythm section—Johnson, Beckett, Hood, and Hawkins—who in April 1969 split to form Muscle Shoals Sound over in Sheffield. Though the move had been planned for some time, it was kept under wraps to avoid friction with Hall. In Barry Beckett's words, "we moved because after the Capitol deal Rick wanted us to work exclusively for him on salaries that would have given us a third of what we'd been making with outside work. We figured he had us over a barrel, so it was either open a new studio or move to Nashville. It made for a dirty parting that we'd hoped to avoid. We were bitter enemies there for a while."

The blow was doubly hard on Hall when Atlantic turned their acts over to Muscle Shoals Sound, Jerry Wexler having advanced Jimmy and Roger $19,000 to overhaul the unused Fred Bevis studio on Jackson Highway. Along with other developments in Memphis, Nashville, New Orleans, and Atlanta, the split marked the beginning of the end of the South's country-influenced soul sound. Like Chips Moman, both Hall and the Muscle Shoals Sound crew would, as the decade turned, begin moving into new areas of pop, rock and—significantly—country. There were still great soul records to come, but the sense of missionary R&B fervour embodied in a man like Dan Penn seemed to have gone forever.

4 Nashville Blue

That black music came out of Nashville at all was remarkable enough. Never had any city been so identified with white country music—or with one dominant musical style, come to that. Indeed, the R&B and soul records that *did* come out of Nashville were not infrequently tinged with that dominant style. Country musicians played on them, and country writers often penned the songs. At the same time, however, the very first independent label to be established in Nashville—Bullett—had recorded such R&B stars as B.B. King and Cecil Gant.

Other indies recording R&B followed in the '50s: Republic cut African American singers such as Louis Brooks and Christine Kittrell, while Randy Wood's Dot enjoyed the R&B hits "Little Red Rooster" and "Weepin' or Cryin'" by the local Griffin Brothers. At Champion, Ted Jarrett produced Kittrell and leased successful Gene Allison sides to Vee Jay in Chicago. And then there was Excello.

Jarrett was one of the few African Americans to achieve any success as a Nashville producer. Born in rural Tennessee near Murfreesboro, he began writing songs at an early age and eventually enrolled at Nashville's Fisk University. "In the country, we heard only country music, because black music was not exposed on the radio in those days," he told me. "Blues was only played in joints where you went to drink, and blacks couldn't afford records or record players."

While at Fisk in 1955, Jarrett wrote "It's Love Baby (24 Hours a Day)" and saw it become a hit not only for Excello's Louis Brooks &

117

the Hi-Toppers but for Ruth Brown on Atlantic and Hank Ballard & the Midnighters on King. Other winners included "Love, Love, Love," a country hit for Webb Pierce and a pop one for Johnnie Ray, plus Christine Kittrell's "Sittin' Here Drinkin'." The biggest success came with "You Can Make It If You Try," a churchy ballad cut in 1958 by gospel singer Gene Allison. Other Allison sides, such as "Everybody But Me," showed an even more pronounced gospel-country leaning.

Jarrett could not escape the influence of white Nashville, especially when he later worked on country and western "soundalike" records with Bob Holmes, another independent black producer: "Bob and I did those records for a company called Spar. He'd do the arrangements, and I'd get the singers and rehearse the songs. We had a black singer called Herbert Hunter, who did all those songs like 'Your Cheatin' Heart.' He was on the Ray Charles kick, but he could imitate all the male country artists."

Holmes himself had graduated from a more jazz-oriented background, growing up in Memphis and working with Hank Crawford. As a pianist, though, he'd played on Nashville sessions for Marty Robbins and Jimmy Dean. "The situation for black music in Nashville was bad," he told me. "The musicians' union really discouraged you from joining, and the president of the local told me they weren't gonna give me any work. Once Bobby Bland came to town [to record 'Stormy Monday' and 'Turn On Your Lovelight'] and they called a white piano player."

In the early '60s, Holmes worked in the R&B division of Bill Justis's Tuneville company, where many of the new Nashville cats—songwriters such as Kris Kristofferson and ex-Cricket Buzz Cason—were hanging out. Soul sides by Sandra King, the Hy-Tones, and the Charmettes were leased to Amy/Mala/Bell, and Holmes persuaded Justis to set up the gospel label Chalice. Here he produced the Gospel Chords, the Sounds of Nashville, and Lucille Jones's Travelling Notes before moving on to update the rosters at Nashboro and Excello.

Another African American to play country sessions in Nashville in the '60s was pianist Benny Latimore, later a Miami-based R&B star. "I learned how to play Floyd Cramer's things," he told me *Living Blues,* "and I played on sessions with Jerry Reed, Ray Stevens, and Boots

Randolph. Those dudes were incredible, man. They could play blues, country, pop, whatever you wanted."

Fred Foster and Sound Stage 7

In the late '50s, white men such as Fred Foster at Monument and Shelby Singleton at Mercury began to experiment with the poppier end of the R&B market. Singleton brought Brook Benton and Clyde McPhatter to Nashville. Foster hit with vocal group the Velvets. Both were country boys, Singleton hailing from the Texas/Louisiana border near Shreveport, Foster from Rutherford County, North Carolina.

"I was born at the base of where the Blue Ridge and Appalachian mountains meet," Foster told me. "I didn't know there *was* any difference between black and white music early in my life. When you're out in the middle of a cotton patch and some guy's singing, you don't look up to see what color he is. My father was not a prejudiced man. I used to go to the black church rather than the white Methodist one. Then there were the brush arbor meetings, which white and blacks both attended. That meant going out into the woods and making a clearing, then building a roof out of pine and cedar and other evergreen brush. When it was finished, itinerant preachers would come and preach at revival meetings. Then you heard some *real* soul music."

Foster continued: "I have to believe there's no real difference between a white man and a black man expressing their hard times. In retrospect, of course, I can see that the black man had an additional cross to bear, so his blues were maybe a little deeper. But the difference between the black and white country music I heard growing up was negligible. It was all three- and four-chord, all played on steel-string acoustic guitars . . . the blacks might have bent the strings a little more, for extra bluesy effect, but that was about it."

One of the first blues singers Foster remembered was "a sorta L'il Abner–lookin' fella" named Hillbilly John, who stood at 6'5" and sang with a South Carolina string band called Fisher Hendley & his Aristocratic Pigs: "He played unbelievably good guitar and sang the hell out of blues songs. I just called this stuff Home Folks Music, it wasn't either black or white."

Only with the acquisition of a radio did Foster first hear the big dance bands of the swing era and realize there was another kind of music out there. At seventeen he moved to Washington D.C., working as a carhop until a break in the music business came through country writer and fellow North Carolinan Billy Strickland: "Billy and I started writing songs: the first record by the McGuire Sisters was one of ours. After a while I got a job as promotion man for a local distributor. Finally, in about 1954, I became the second field man Mercury Records ever had, covering Maryland, part of West Virginia, and the District of Columbia."

Two years working for Mercury were followed by a further two for ABC-Paramount, where he signed Lloyd Price: "Lloyd signed because I was a Southerner. He wouldn't have signed with the New York people. The point is that he and I had the same upbringing; our backgrounds dovetailed. We both got laughed at by town kids because we didn't have corduroy knickers. And Lloyd sang country songs—he told me one time that his favorite singer was Hank Williams."

In 1958, Foster left ABC-Paramount to form Monument Records. That Christmas he had a million-selling pop hit with Billy Grammer's "Gotta Travel On," following up with Pee Wee King's "Bonaparte's Retreat." Since he was doing most of his recording in the new musical mecca of Nashville, he moved there in the summer of 1960 and quickly signed his first and greatest star, Roy Orbison. Success was immediate, with the classic "Only the Lonely" making No. 2 in July. Like future Foster artists from Arthur Alexander to Tony Joe White, Orbison was a borderline country-pop R&B artist, always utilizing too many black elements to be acceptable to country radio. "My vision of Monument," Foster said, "was that I wanted to do all kinds of music. I wanted it to be well-rounded. Just like Elvis was singing songs that were all mixed up, white and black and gospel. That's what I would have done as a singer."

Foster's great contribution to Nashville soul lay in hiring WLAC's John Richbourg to produce acts for Monument's subsidiary label Sound Stage 7. Formed in April 1963, SS7s first releases were pop ephemera concocted by the likes of Bill Justis. Most successful were Justis's Spectoresque creation the Dixiebelles, an African American girl group on the road but in the studio—with the No. 9 pop smash "Down at Papa Joe's"—a white lineup led by Shelby Singleton's country-singer wife Margie. In 1965, Foster approached Richbourg, who'd briefly had his own Rich label in the mid-'50s but more recently was leasing sides by singers such as Roscoe Shelton to the Sims label.

Ex-Excello bluesman Shelton had a high, wailing tenor voice: on his Sims hit "Strain On My Heart" he sounded a little like Jimmy Hughes. He was Richbourg's first SS7 act, starting the label's five-year run of hits with the Stax-recorded "I Know Your Heart Has Been Broken." The Stax band was also unmistakable on John R.'s second SS7 production, Sam Baker's "Sometimes You Have to Cry," a fine ballad that exemplified the country-soul cross-breed: written by the African American Allen Orange from New Orleans, arranged by white country veteran Cliff Parman from Nashville, played by whites and African Americans from Memphis.

Shelton and Baker were both extremely emotional singers specializing in slow, searing ballads. Shelton was a Nashville native who'd served an apprenticeship in gospel outfits such as the Fireside Gospel Singers and the famous Fairfield Four before going secular on Excello. Baker had grown up in Jackson, Mississippi, singing in his college glee club before forming an R&B combo and signing with Phil Walden's booking agency in Macon, Georgia.

Other early Richbourg productions included sides by Little Hank, Bobby King, and (again at Stax) Sir Lattimore Brown. "Prior to Sound Stage 7," Richbourg recalled, "black singers couldn't get a break in Nashville. Once I joined the company, there were few records we didn't cover recording expenses on, primarily because of my play at WLAC. At the same time, Nashville was not keyed for R&B, and we had a difficult time finding a rhythm section that really felt the music. Hence I initially used studios like Stax, FAME, and American."

An SS7 artist that Richbourg did *not* produce was Arthur Alexander, who came from three frustrating years with Noel Ball at Dot and was personally supervised by Fred Foster. "Noel and I had become close friends," Foster remembered, "and we used to sit around and talk about Arthur's stuff and how to do it. When Noel got ill and ultimately passed away, Arthur came to me."

A first single in January 1966 coupled "(Baby) For You" with Ray Price's hit "The Other Woman," thus following Ball's lead in adapting country material to the Alexander style. The songs might have worked, moreover, but for Bill Justis's rather overdone arrangements. "Fred was a good guy," Alexander told me, "but he didn't know what I was about. He produced me as if I was Ivory Joe Hunter or something, whereas I was an Alabama country-soul balladeer. Also, all the SS7 sides I did only went to black stations, who would have played me anyway and didn't have the power to break the records."

"Arthur was going through one of his shaky periods when he was on SS7," Foster said. "He didn't know how to handle the fame because he was basically very shy. White women went after him pretty heavily, and he didn't know how to cope with that. He was on drugs that were supposed to stabilize him but did the opposite. Really he was a sweet, gentle spirit, but he got in all kinds of trouble."

The fact that Alexander cut only five SS7 singles in four years (plus one on Monument itself) suggested something wasn't quite right. The best of them were the country songs "Another Time, Another Place" and "Set Me Free" (subsequently covered by Joe Tex, Percy Sledge, and Esther Phillips), arranged simply and sung with what Foster accurately describes as Alexander's "dry, laconic approach." The singer finally left SS7 following his cover of Neil Diamond's "Glory Road" in 1970.

By this time, Monument/SS7 had its own studio band. Tired of making trips to Memphis and Muscle Shoals, Richbourg brought bassist Tim Drummond and guitarist Troy Seals down from Cincinnati and matched them up with pianist Bob Wilson, guitarist Mac Gayden, and *Blonde on Blonde* session men Kenny Buttrey (drums), Wayne Moss (guitar), and Charlie McCoy (harmonica). "Charlie had had a little high school band," Richbourg said, "and all they played was black music. Even after a lot of these guys got big in the country field, they used to listen to my show on WLAC every night. I have that straight from the horse's mouth."

"We all played soul music growing up," Gayden told me. "The black community here was stronger with younger white musicians than the country community was. I grew up playing in black bands, street groups singing *a cappella,* and I used to play with Arthur Gunter when I was in high school. Come to think of it, *he* was kind of country . . . there was a sort of country swing to 'Baby, Let's Play House.' I also worked in Ernie's Record Mart for two years—met a lot of black musicians coming through there. Right now I'm doing an album of the kind of songs I used to play when I was a kid, like John Lee Hooker's 'Boogie Chillen' and Howlin' Wolf's 'Smokestack Lightnin'. It's gonna be called *Nashville Blue*."[19]

Gayden had played in McCoy's group the Escorts, along with Wayne Moss and Kenny Buttrey. The latter also spent time in integrated band the Paramounts, featuring a young Robert Knight on vocals. In Cincinnati, Tim Drummond played bass for James Brown, while Troy Seals's checkered career encompassed gigs with a young Lonnie Mack and a stint as one half of married blue-eyed-soul duo JoAnn & Troy.

Together these musicians became loosely known as the Music City Four (or Five, as the case may have been). Like the rhythm sections at FAME and American, they had strong country roots that deeply affected the SS7 sound; unlike them, country records were what they'd principally played on. Furthermore, their country roots blended well with the songs Richbourg picked for his artists.

"Even though I was never a dyed-in-the-wool country fan," Richbourg said, "I'd been exposed to it and had come to recognize the strength of many country songs. We tailored songs by writers like Harlan Howard to the R&B market by changing the arrangements and the phrasing a little but leaving a similar feel to the tunes."

As with Memphis and Muscle Shoals—whose musicians influenced Richbourg, as his show had influenced them—Sound Stage 7 was a pure synthesis of black and white.

Joe Simon

The singer who best embodied SS7's country-soul fusion was Louisiana-born Joe Simon, who'd grown up in the country near New Orleans and sung in the choir at Simmesport's Pilgrim Rest Baptist Church.

---

19 To my knowledge, *Nashville Blue* never saw the light of day, though I did once see Gayden playing a set that included several blues songs at London's Bedford Arms.

At 15, Simon moved with his family to Oakland, California, forming vocal groups the Silver Stars and the Goldentones while also recording his first solo sides for the tiny Hush label. His deep, mellow baritone sounded like a Southern Jerry Butler, a backwoods version of that svelte Chicago heartbreaker. When "My Adorable One" took off regionally in 1962, Hush sold the master, together with Simon's contract, to Vee-Jay.

Passing through Nashville as a Vee-Jay artist in 1964, Simon stopped by WLAC and met with John Richbourg. "John was the first guy I ever met who could swing that much weight and yet be so nice," he remembered. "He asked me to give him a chance with my career and we shook hands." Richbourg's first move was to take Simon down to FAME in Muscle Shoals and cut the Dan Penn/Spooner Oldham song "Let's Do It Over," a Vee-Jay hit before the company's collapse in 1965. It was a perfect mid-tempo outing with a fluent and graceful vocal by Simon, whose velvety shading and relaxed timing had the feel of a soulful Lefty Frizzell.

After Vee-Jay folded, Richbourg signed Simon to Sound Stage 7, where he began with "Teenager's Prayer" in early 1966. Both the uptown, Ben E. King–style "My Lover's Prayer" and the pumping "Put Your Trust in Me" followed before Simon found his true country-gospel niche at American with Dan Penn and Wayne Carson Thompson's sombre "Nine Pound Steel." "No Sad Songs," insisted his next, uptempo-paced hit, but sad songs were his element, as the 1969 version of Harlan Howard's "The Chokin' Kind" attested. "John introduced me to the Nashville lyrics," Simon said. "I've written some good songs, some hit songs, myself, but to this day I can feel the country songs so much better." (He did, however, tell *R&B World* magazine that in order to be successful in country he'd "have to change my color.")

Along with Hank Cochran, Curly Putnam, and Mickey Newbury, Harlan Howard was one of the Nashville country writers most favored by Southern soul singers. Born in Kentucky in 1929, he gravitated to the West Coast and was discovered there by Johnny Bond and Tex Ritter in the '50s. They helped get his songs published, and hits for Wynn Stewart ("You Took Her Off My Hands") and Charlie Walker ("Pick Me Up on Your Way Down") followed.

Moving to Nashville in 1960, Howard continued to score with "Mommy for a Day" (Kitty Wells), "Heartaches by the Number" (Ray Price), and "Busted" (Johnny Cash and Ray Charles). The lyric twists in his songs made them fresh and unusual, and his melodies worked well for soul. Signed to Monument as a singer in 1966, it was only a matter of time before John Richbourg began to notice the possibilities of his songs. "The Chokin' Kind" had been a hit for Waylon Jennings before Richbourg gave it to arranger Bergen White, who based the new version around a chugging bass riff.

Like all his subsequent SS7 material, "The Chokin' Kind" was recorded at Music City Recorders, the studio opened behind Monument's offices by Elvis Presley's old guitarist Scotty Moore. Moore had all but forsaken the guitar, selling his old Gibson Super 400 to Chips Moman, and now concentrated on engineering sessions at the studio. He recorded the entire *Chokin' Kind* album there, overseeing further Harlan Howard songs—"Yours Love," "Baby Don't Be Looking in My Mind"—together with versions of Glen Campbell's "Wichita Lineman" and Bobby Bland's "Too Far Gone to Turn Around." The sound of the Music City rhythm section was a little weak compared to those at FAME, Stax, or American, but it served Simon well on sides like "Farther On Down the Road" and on such pure country songs as "Rainbow Road" and the *Nashville Skyline–flavored* "Straight Down to Heaven."

Simon continued recording country songs into the '70s, including the first of many soul versions of Bob Montgomery's "Misty Blue" and a nice stab at Mel Tillis's hit "Who's Julie," with its guilty scenario of the man who's said a little too much in his sleep. "Eventually I took Joe to New York," John Richbourg told me. "He wanted to get off Monument, and we signed to Polydor's Spring label. I had a good contract to produce him, $25,000 upfront, and the first thing we did on him, "Your Time to Cry," did a million. After a year, however, I agreed to let them bring in some other producers."

Spring shipped Simon off to Philadelphia maestros Kenny Gamble and Leon Huff ("Drowning in the Sea of Love") and later to disco hack Raeford Gerald, but not before Richbourg produced the 1973 *Simon Country* album, a last Southern testament before the beautiful country-soul baritone disappeared into the dancefloor morass. The album wasn't great, but Simon delivered on songs like "A Woman Without Love" and "To Get to You," against a backdrop of country instrumentation. Freddy Fender's "Before the Next Teardrop Falls" came in for the "Chokin' Kind" treatment, while Eddy Arnold's "You Don't Know Me" was transformed into an uptempo gallop.

Simon's career didn't fare too well after that. 1981 found him back in Nashville on the Posse label, for whom he recorded *Glad You Came My Way,* a post-disco soul album produced by Grand Ole Opry veteran Porter Wagoner. The record wasn't bad, but it fared poorly. 1984 had Simon reestablishing contact with his old mentor. "Joe wanted to start his own label, and he put up $20,000," Richbourg said. "It wasn't enough, but we went in the studio and cut some real good tracks . . . you know, if Joe would stick to ballads and not try uptempo stuff, he'd still be a big name today."

Tony Joe White wrote two songs, "Alone At Last" and "Stay Love," especially for the occasion—the first a throbbing mid-tempo beauty, the second a contemporary Nashville ballad. Back-to-back they trailered an album that, sadly, never materialized. Richbourg was struck down with cancer just as they began shipping the single. "Joe on his own couldn't collect from the distributors," Richbourg told me, "so we never made more than a few hundred dollars. We never even got the records back."

Happily, however, Simon was able to land a contract with Nashville's Compleat Records the following year, releasing first a Brook Benton–ish version of Lee Greenwood's country hit "It Turns Me Inside Out" and then an album, *Mr. Right,* that included Willie Nelson's even bigger hit "Always On My Mind."[20]

Besides Simon, SS7 soul men Roscoe Shelton, Sam Baker, and Lattimore Brown all continued to record until the end of the '60s. They proved to be difficult, however. "Roscoe hit the bottle, and Sam got into drugs," Richbourg said. "Lattimore, we couldn't seem to get off the ground—he wasn't that great a singer in the first place." The occasional masterpiece made up for such problems: Brown's mournful

---

20 Simon later became Associate Minister of the Cathedral of Joy Church in the Chicago suburb of Flossmoor, Illinois. "I ain't never gonna sing those songs no more," he said in the sleeve notes to *Music in My Bones,* a 1997 Rhino compilation of his country-soul and disco hits.

"It's Such a Sad, Sad World" was superb, while Shelton's "There's a Heartbreak Somewhere" was a magnificent Dan Penn–arranged fusion of gospel and country—the huge chorus half Baptist choir, half Anita Kerr Singers—with a frantic vocal redolent of Mighty Sam.

Another Roscoe on the label was Roscoe Robinson, the Arkansas-born singer who'd sung with the Five Blind Boys of Mississippi, then turned secular on Tuff in 1963. Fresh from the 1966 success of "That's Enough" on Wand, he recorded several strong country-soul ballads for Richbourg in his harsh, somewhat indistinct voice, among them "Let Me Know" and "Why Must It End."

Richbourg claimed the biggest talent he had on the label besides Joe Simon was Ella Washington, a local girl with a voice that sounded like a cross between Randy Crawford and Shirley Brown. She made her debut at American with studio guitarist Bobby Womack's "I Can't Afford to Lose Him," then had a 1968 hit with an exquisite reading of "He Called Me Baby," a Harlan Howard song set to the groove of Aretha Franklin's "Never Loved a Man." Sadly, Washington never again received such good material and failed to live up to her promise.

Richbourg's deal with Monument came to an end on the very last day of 1970, after Fred Foster signed a distribution deal with Columbia. Further singles appeared on SS7, including four by Joe Simon and two by Ella Washington, but these were from old in-the-can sessions. Richbourg himself set up a new label called Seventy Seven in 1972, issuing some fairly dreary sides by characters like Willie Hobbs, Moody Scott, and Nashville veteran Earl Gaines.

The best singers on 77 were South Carolinan Ann Sexton and the gravel-voiced Geater Davis from Conroe, Texas. Richbourg picked up Sexton's lovely 1971 Impel side "You're Letting Me Down" and co-produced her through to 1974 on ballads such as "Come Back Home," "Love, Love, Love," and Jean Wells's "Have a Little Mercy." A later album, *The Beginning,* was equal parts Bettye Swann, Betty Wright, and Margie Joseph. Davis meanwhile was a gospel-bluesman who sounded like a grief-stricken Bobby Bland. "Geater was pretty talented," Richbourg recalled. "A very good songwriter, but always in hot water financially. Car notes, rent, all that sort of thing. He'd skip his dates and create a lot of difficulty with the DJs, so we finally had a parting of the ways." Added songwriter Jerry Strickland: "Geater always seemed to have woman trouble and money trouble. He couldn't hold a woman, and he couldn't hold a dollar." Allen Orange, who'd produced several chillingly emotional sides by Davis for his own House of Orange label, now took him on to 77 for the anguished "You Made Your Bed Hard" and guilt-ridden "I'm Gonna Change."

Neither Sexton nor Davis could stop 77 going down the tubes in 1977, after which Richbourg's only involvement in the business—he'd retired from WLAC in 1973—consisted of reissuing old SS7 sides on the Sound Plus label. Southern soul was on the wane and a new inner-city funk/disco sound had taken over. "At WLAC we'd held the rural area," Richbourg said, "but towards the end of the '60s we began to lose urban blacks to the new soul stations that were starting up in cities like Atlanta. I began to lose interest in both radio and making records and took early retirement. The program director at WLAC started putting pressure on me to play certain records, and nobody had ever done that before."

A decade on, a tragically ill Richbourg reflected on contemporary "soul" music: "I don't like the modern trend of black music. It's not sincere; it doesn't represent the true feelings of blacks. It's teenage music. They've forgotten the older people." In 1985, a benefit was organized for Richbourg at the Ryman Auditorium, Nashville's original home for the Grand Ole Opry. On the bill paying tribute to him were B.B. King, James Brown, Joe Simon, Rufus and Carla Thomas, Hank Ballard, Ella Washington, the Coasters, the Tams, Tony Joe White, Ruth Brown, and Charlie Daniels.

"On the last number B.B. King did, I think everybody in the audience was crying," Richbourg recalled of the night, "and when I think about it now I want to cry. It was Ivory Joe Hunter's 'Guess Who,' and it went 'somebody loves you/guess who . . .,' and I was sitting onstage in a wheelchair 'cause I'd broken a hip. B.B. passed the mic to Rufus and it went round everybody. It was a very, very wonderful thing . . . just a complete turn-on."

"The first time I realized black people thought John R. was black," Fred Foster told me, "was when I was living on a lake outside Nashville. I had this wonderful black lady who took care of the house and my kids. One day I told her John R. was coming out to the house the next day. She just looked at me and said, 'Lord have mercy, John R. is comin' *here?*' So I said yes and thought no more about it. Well, when I got up the next morning, I didn't recognize her. I didn't know who she was. She looked like she'd just stepped out of a fashion window. I said 'Jenny, what in the world . . .,' and she just replied, real quiet, 'My man's comin,' honey.' Of course, when he walked in, you never saw such a look of disappointment in your life! She yelled 'Lord, you're *white!*' John just yelled back 'Yeah, baby, but I got a black heart!'"[21]

Shelby Singleton and S.S.S. International

Like Foster and Richbourg, Shelby Singleton pioneered the Nashville recording of black music in the early '60s. Raised on the country music of Shreveport's Louisiana Hayride, he became an area promotion man for Mercury in the mid–'50s, later graduating to sales manager for the entire South.

A born salesman—"the guy'll hype a stop sign," quipped his colleague Jerry Kennedy—Singleton moved into production purely by accident. "A country artist called Rusty Draper was in Nashville to record," he told me, "but his producer had gotten snowbound in Chicago. Mercury called me to do the session, though I didn't know the first thing about recording. The first song we cut was Hank Locklin's 'Please Help Me I'm Falling,' and it was a fairly decent-sized hit. I'd had three years' experience of going into radio stations and trying to make them play records, so I kind of knew what they would play and what they wouldn't play."

Having signed such successful Mercury rock'n'roll artists as Johnny Preston and the Big Bopper, Singleton's credentials were good enough for the Chicago company to entrust further productions to him. In 1962, he brought Brook Benton and Clyde McPhatter down to Nashville, producing big hits on both of them. Benton was a crooner whose phrasing had influenced the country-soulful Solomon Burke and who would himself go on to record such country-soul classics as "Rainy Night in Georgia." With Singleton's wife Margie, Benton wrote the fine "Lie to Me," following up in 1963 with poppier, Bill Justis–arranged hits

---

21 John Richbourg succumbed to cancer on 15 February 1986, five months after Muir MacKean, and I spent a wonderful evening with him in Nashville.

like "I Got What I Wanted" and "My True Confession." Ex-Atlantic star McPhatter meanwhile smashed with "Lover Please," written by a young Missourian rockabilly called Billy Swan.

"When I first brought Brook and Clyde down here," Singleton told me, "I'd have to keep them in my home, because there were no hotels in town that would accept blacks other than fleabags. Most of the black singers were afraid to come here in the beginning, but we had no problems from the point of view of the musicians. In those days there wasn't too much publicity about who did what on record, because if a black station knew the musicians were white they might bar the record, and vice versa."

A case in point was Louisiana singer Joe Barry, whose 1961 hit "I'm a Fool to Care" was a big R&B hit until an appearance on *American Bandstand* revealed that he was white. Barry was one of the artists Singleton signed to Smash, the pop subsidiary Mercury had entrusted to him in 1961. Other Smash signings in the first half of the '60s included Bruce ("Hey Baby") Channel, James Brown, and Jerry Lee Lewis. Working with Singleton at the Nashville office was Jerry Kennedy, who'd known him since the Louisiana Hayride days and worked at the Bayou Record Store that Singleton opened in Shreveport. According to Kennedy it was Singleton who broke the Nashville clique by importing outside musicians for a Mercury session in 1962. "Shelby made it possible for other guys to do sessions," Kennedy said. "I brought in Ray Stevens and Jerry Reed from Atlanta, and Ray had a big 1962 hit with 'Ahab the Arab.'"

Kennedy went on to produce such Smash hits as Roger Miller's "King of the Road" and Jerry Lee Lewis's honky-tonk classics "What Made Milwaukee Famous" and "Another Time, Another Place." He also helped out when Singleton left Mercury to form—with the purchase of the Sun catalog in 1967—his own stable of labels. "I'd been trying to buy the catalog for Mercury for five or six years," Singleton recalled, "but Sam Phillips wouldn't sell it because Mercury wanted to convert the masters to their label. My deal with Sam was that I would continue to issue product on the Sun label."

Basing himself in a ranchlike suite of offices on Belmont Boulevard, far from the bustle of Nashville's Music Row, Singleton set about forming the additional labels Plantation (country) and S.S.S. International (soul). Plantation had immediate success with Jeanie C. Riley's immortal tale of small-town scandal "Harper Valley PTA" (as well as Terry Nelson's odiously reactionary 1971 hit "The Battle Hymn of Lt. Calley"), but the soul outlet took longer to get off the ground. Early signings included Shreveport's Margaret Lewis, Birmingham's Sam Dees, and brothers Mickey and Clarence Murray (produced by Bobby Smith in Macon, Georgia).

First to hit, however, was duo Peggy Scott & JoJo Benson, whose infectious "Lover's Holiday" was cut by the Texan Huey P. Meaux in Jackson, Mississippi. The Florida-born Scott gave it her all on the derivative but funky follow-up "Pickin' Wild Mountain Berries," later drawing on her gospel roots for a gut-wrenching solo rendition of Brenda Holloway's "Every Little Bit Hurts." Other Scott & Benson hits included "Soulshake," a dance-floor outing that featured a hilarious duel between a pedal steel guitar and Jerry Kennedy's electric sitar.

Johnny Adams

Country-soul man Johnny Adams joined S.S.S. in the same way, when his powerful cover of "Release Me" was picked up by Singleton from the New Orleans label Watch.

A Crescent City native, Adams had sung gospel in Bessie Griffin's Consolators before recording Dorothy Labostrie's "I Won't Cry" for Ric in 1959. His voice was a highly disciplined instrument, capable of amazing range but always tautly controlled. After "I Won't Cry" became a big regional hit and a minor Crescent City classic, he cut several more singles for Ric (like the haunting blues ballad "A Losing Battle"), most of them co-written and arranged by a young Mac Rebennack. In 1963, Adams joined Watch and recorded a string of local, Wardell Quezergue–arranged hits (e.g., "I Believe I'll Find Happiness," Earl King's "Part of Me") while simultaneously recording for Huey P. Meaux's Pacemaker label in Texas.

"Release Me" had something of the feel of Joe Hinton's "Funny How Time Slips Away," particularly in its use of high, shrieking falsetto. But where Hinton was a big-band balladeer, Adams's phrasing was much closer to white country, which was why Shelby Singleton decided to bring him to Nashville. After "Release Me" had hit in

Christmas 1968, Adams journeyed up to Music City and cut one of the quintessential country-soul records, "Reconsider Me," penned by Margaret Lewis and Myra Smith in Shreveport. It blatantly echoed "Release Me," but its clipped country beat was much more pronounced. Amazingly, for a record with (albeit muted) pedal steel guitar, it made No. 8 on the R&B chart and No. 28 on the Hot 100.

From then on, Singleton introduced bluesier elements into the country structure: "I Can't Be All Bad," "In a Moment of Weakness," and "Georgia Mountain Dew" all featured swampy slide-guitar fills, most likely inspired by Duane Allman's work down in Muscle Shoals. (Lewis and Smith's "Georgia Mountain Dew" was one of many nostalgia-for-the-South songs that focused on the state of Georgia.) A last hit on S.S.S. came in the shape of an updated "I Won't Cry," arranged in 1970 by Bergen White and distinguished by the most stratospheric vocals Adams ever recorded. Better as pure country soul were the Lewis-Smith B-sides "Real Live Livin' Hurtin' Man" and "I Want to Walk Through This Life with You."

Adams's last sides for Singleton were cut at the Valparaiso, Florida, studio of Finley Duncan, who'd produced superb sides by Big John Hamilton and Doris Allen for the S.S.S. affiliate Minaret. Despite the fine "Something Worth Leaving For," the change yielded no further hits.

Silver Fox

Another of the many labels affiliated to Singleton's corporation was Silver Fox, named after Lelan Rogers, the silver-maned Texan to whom Singleton assigned it.

Rogers had been working with Esther Phillips again but was otherwise at something of a standstill. He kicked off the new label with a deep-soul treatment of Johnny Ace's "Pledging My Love" by Laura Greene & Johnny McKinnis, following through with sides by Big Al Downing, Willie Hobbs, and Shreveport artists Eddie Giles and Reuben Bell. Downing, who'd worked with Rogers earlier in the decade, recorded "Cornbead Row," an uptempo slice of "Patches"-style nostalgia written by country writers Fred Burch and Don Hill (and featuring Jerry Kennedy's ubiquitous electric sitar). Giles cut a decent version of "That's How Strong My Love Is" and Bell a good country-flavored ballad called "Too Late," but the greatest artist on Silver Fox was the husky-voiced Betty LaVette.

Like Esther Phillips in 1962, LaVette was brought to Rogers' attention by his brother Kenny. She hailed from Michigan but sounded 100 percent Southern: her spunky, tomboyish tones suggested a chitlin'-circuit version of Lulu. Having recorded for Atlantic and Lu-Pine in the early '60s, she hit on Calla in 1965 with Tompall and Jim Glaser's "Let Me Down Easy," a dark cry of hurt and loneliness embellished with ghostly vibes and slithering strings. Three years later, her funky transposition of Mickey Newbury's "What Condition My Condition Is In" was heard by the struggling Kenny Rogers, whose First Edition had a Top 5 hit with it in 1968—and who pointed LaVette in the direction of Nashville.

For her debut Silver Fox session in September 1969, Lelan Rogers recorded her with a band groomed in Memphis by Stan Kesler. This was the future Dixie Flyers, a white unit Kesler assembled when Chips Moman walked off with the nucleus of the American band in 1965. They consisted of Charlie Freeman, the guitarist who'd formed the Mar-Keys; Jim Dickinson, a keyboard player and ex-member of Sun band the Jesters; and Mike Utley (organ), Tommy McClure (bass), and Sammy Creason (drums). On "He Made a Woman Out of Me," they cooked up the perfect country-funk brew behind LaVette's snarling vocal—a Muscle Shoals-ish melange of gritty guitar, swampy electric piano and a tight beat. Another song by Fred Burch and Don Hill, it came straight out of the late '60s Tony Joe White school (and was covered by Bobbie Gentry, to LaVette's great displeasure, on the FAME-recorded *Fancy* album):

> *I was born on the levee*
> *A little bit south of Montgomery*
> *Mama worked at the big house*
> *And Daddy worked for the county*
> *I never had no learnin'*
> *'Til I turned sixteen*
> *When Joe Henry come up the river, y'all*
> *And made a woman out of me . . .*
>
> (© Green Isle Music/Fred Burch Music
> Nashville Tennessee, USA, 1969)

Nothing else LaVette recorded for Rogers was as good, but versions of Joe South's "Games People Play" and Erma Franklin's "Piece of My Heart" (the latter on S.S.S.) worked well, and the unreleased take of Charles Hodges's "Easier to Say (Than Do)" was an explosive ballad performance. (In 1981, LaVette returned to Nashville to record the excellent *Tell Me a Lie* album for Motown.) Also on Silver Fox were Hank Ballard covering Kris Kristofferson's brilliant "Sunday Morning Coming Down," Rosalind Madison's soul version of the Bobbie Gentry hit "Fancy," and George Perkins's classic lament for Martin Luther King Jr., "Crying in the Streets," leased from the Baton Rouge label Ebb Tide.

Rogers subsequently fell out with Singleton, who shut Silver Fox down in late 1970. Picking up the pieces, Rogers established House of the Fox with a roster that included Big Al Downing, Little Johnnie Blair, Kip Anderson, and James Brown sidemen Maceo & All the King's Men. Blair cut another good version of "Easier to Say (Than Do)," while Downing recorded perhaps his greatest country-soul performance, the self-penned "I'll Be Your Fool Once More."

Singleton himself dropped out of black music in the mid-'70s, opting to concentrate on Sun reissues. "The reason I got out of black music was that promoting the product had gotten so expensive," he told me. "Also, you couldn't sell black albums. We'd sell 500,000 or 600,000 on a Peggy & JoJo single and then do 10,000 on an album."

In 1985, Singleton could still be found down on Belmont Boulevard, though the corporation's offices had rather gone to seed. An unsused studio had become part of a Music City sightseeing tour, with coach parties of country and western fans shuffling through on the hour. Singleton did not seem a terribly happy man.

Billy Sherrill

Around the time Singleton was first planning to record rhythm and blues in Nashville, Sam Phillips built a Sun studio on Music Row. Nothing much came out of it—a smattering of country sides by Jerry Lee Lewis and Charlie Rich—but in the three years it functioned it gave Billy Sherrill his first real break in Nashville.

When the studio closed down in 1964, Sherrill too began cutting black sessions, both on Epic and on Columbia's main R&B subsidiary OKeh. Among them were sides by Ted Taylor, Otis Williams, Obrey Wilson, and the Staple Singers. Falsetto wailer Taylor recalled Floyd Cramer and sax man Boots Randolph playing on his sessions. "They could play the blues, but they still sounded like *hillbillies* trying to play the blues," the singer told *Living Blues* in 1976. Sherrill gave him a fair-sized R&B hit in 1965 with "Stay Away From My Baby" and used the Oklahoman's freakish voice to fine effect on both the frantic "(Love Is Like a) Ramblin' Rose" (later covered by Detroit hard rockers the MC5) and the languid "I'll Release You," a Cliff Parman–arranged answer to Esther Phillips's "Release Me."

Obrey Wilson's high, clean tenor was heard on such Epic sides as "Love Will Be Right Here," "In a Woman's Eyes," and "I Want to Tell You About My Girl," while "She Used to Be Mine" revealed a more affecting country-soul side. Ex-Charm Otis Williams, later a black country singer on Stop, fared well on the jazzy blues ballad "Love Don't Grow on Trees." Mississippian Tommy Tate made a fleeting visit to Nashville to cut the lilting, calypso-flavored "A Lover's Reward" and an impassioned version of the country ballad "Big Blue Diamonds." Finally, the Staple Singers continued the "hillbilly harmony" style of their Vee-Jay records on such country-gospel songs as "Be Careful of Stones That You Throw" and "As an Eagle Stirreth Her Nest."

With his first country hits, however—by David Houston and Tammy Wynette—Sherrill left R&B behind for good and became head of Columbia's country division in Nashville.

Buddy Killen and Joe Tex

The other major country producer with a penchant for R&B was fellow Alabaman Buddy Killen, head of the highly successful publishing company Tree.

Killen was born in Florence and played in country bands around Muscle Shoals until, at 18, he got the chance to work as a bass player on Nashville's Grand Ole Opry. Session work took up several years (you can hear him on George Jones's "White Lightning"), after which Jack Stapp, ex-program director at WSM, founded Tree and brought Killen in as an assistant. "I said I didn't know anything about publishing, and he said he didn't either," Killen told me. "For a long time I just carried this little tape recorder around and recorded songs. We became partners around 1957."

Over the years, Tree built up a country catalog bigger even than that of Acuff-Rose, making Killen—who took over presidency of the firm when Stapp died in 1980—a wealthy man. He first entertained the idea of making R&B records in the late '50s, when country hit a slump. "Out of just trying to expand my horizons a little, I got involved in cutting some black music," he told me. "I started signing some black writers and artists and putting them on various labels. I didn't know anything about R&B. I did it because it was there. But slowly it rubbed off on me."

One day in 1961, while on honeymoon in Florida, Killen received a call from an assistant at Tree who urged him to fly home to hear a singer who'd recorded for Ace and King and went by the name of Joe Tex. When he got back he found the pixie-like Tex dressed in a cowboy outfit and knew he'd found a star. As an outlet for his discovery he established the London-distributed Dial label and, in July 1961, released Tex's first single, "The Only Girl (I've Ever Loved)." It was nothing special, a country-paced ballad lacking Joe's real stamp, but along with "Meet Me in Church" and "Someone to Take Your Place" it laid the groundwork for the country-soul style that dominated his later hits.

"Nothing really happened for a while, and we got jived around by London," Killen said. "For four years I produced Joe, and we'd sell a few records here and there, but nothing big, so he called me one day and suggested I turn him loose. Well, we'd been fighting like cats and dogs in the studio deciding which way to go, me feeling the reason he hadn't hit was that his R&B was too raw and earthy. So I said I'd let him go if just once he did it my way. And that's how 'Hold What You Got' came about."

On the strength of that classic song, which—distributed by Atlantic—became the first Southern soul record to make the pop Top 10, Tex remained with Killen until his death in August 1982. Together they perfected his whimsical style, a kind of Texan pop-country-soul that encompassed everything from agonized ballads to hilarious farmyard sermons. Tex couldn't resist preaching, while the combination of James Brown rasp and Solomon Burke slur in his voice made it an ideal instrument for the job. Often his self-penned songs were merely derivative—"Hold What You Got" was swiftly followed by the crude carbon copy of "You'd Better Get It"—but interspersed among them were minor masterpieces such as "I Want to (Do Everything for You)," "The Love You Save May Be Your Own" and "I Believe I'm Gonna Make It," the last a report from a soldier in Vietnam whose sweetheart's letter inspires him to "reach up and get me two mo' enemy."

On Tex's albums, the Nashville influence was explicit in versions of Mel Tillis's "Detroit City" and Roger Miller's "King of the Road," while in general Killen's production—using a blend of Music City veterans and American Studio players from Memphis—relied on such country ingredients as acoustic guitars and soft rimshots on the drums.

True, there were big hits with funkier sides such as the New Orleans–ish "Papa Was Too," the Staxy MGs groove of "Show Me," and the pumping, American-recorded "Skinny Legs and All," but these were novelty items Tex himself disliked. "All the things that sold for me I didn't think would," he said in 1975. "Things *I* picked did nothing, like 'The Love You Save,' 'A Woman's Hands,' or 'A Woman Can Change a Man.' 'Skinny Legs' I just didn't dig, and 'Show Me' I wrote in about three or four minutes in the studio, which is why it's so repetitious. It was just to fill up an album." B-side ballads such as "A Woman's Hands" and "The Truest Woman in the World" were perhaps the best things Tex ever did, while his last classic side was 1969's "Buying a Book," a typically wry tale of older men and women who use money to attract young lovers.

"Every so often Joe would come back with a monster," Killen said. "We'd get a little cold and he'd come back with 'Skinny Legs,' we'd get cold again and he'd come back with 'I Gotcha' or 'Ain't Gonna Bump No More.'" One of Tex's biggest-selling albums was 1968's *Soul Country*. If it wasn't the record it might have been—"Joe didn't like singing other people's songs, and he wasn't really prepared," Killen recalled—it featured fine versions of "Dark End of the Street" and Curly Putnam's "Set Me Free," plus a great set of arrangements by the American Studio band.

The adaptability of Tex's own songs to country was demonstrated by the Australian country singer Diana Trask on her *Miss Country Soul* album, produced by Killen for Dot in 1968. Consisting entirely of Tex songs and sung in a voice pitched somewhere between Patsy Cline and Gary Stewart, the transition to country was virtually seamless and worked well. Other country artists to use Tex's songs included Johnny Cash with "Look at Them Beans" and Barbara Mandrell with her Billy Sherrill–produced version of "Show Me."

Besides Tex, R&B artists produced by Killen included Paul Kelly, Bobby Marchan, Chris Harris, and Clarence "Frogman" Henry. Of all of them, Kelly established the closest relationship with Killen and came the closest to Tex's country-soul style. A veteran of vocal groups in Miami, he signed to Dial in 1965 but recorded his best country-soul sides—"If This Old House Could Talk" and "Nine Out of Ten Times"—for Phillips. Female impersonator Marchan had sung with Huey Smith & the Clowns in New Orleans and made his Dial debut in 1964 with "I've Got a Thing Goin' On"/"I Gotta Sit Down and Cry," an inane dancer backed with a country ballad sung in Marchan's campiest Don Covay falsetto. Later he had a superb, Killen-produced version of Joe Tex's "Meet Me in Church" on the Cameo label. Chris Harris cut the funky "Tell 'Em Who I Am" in 1968, while Frogman Henry did his best Fats Domino impression on songs such as Chips Moman's "This Time" (1967).

Bobby Hebb, Robert Knight, and Dobie Gray

Two African Americans who emerged from Nashville in the '60s were Bobby Hebb and Robert Knight. Hebb, born in 1941, played spoons as a twelve-year-old in Roy Acuff's Smokey Mountain Boys and appeared regularly on the Grand Ole Opry. His first record was "Night Train to Memphis," released on John Richbourg's Rich label in 1960. Six years later he recorded with Sweet Inspiration Sylvia Shemwell as Bobby & Sylvia.

Signed to Phillips in the spring of 1966, Hebb cut his self-penned "Sunny" at New York's Bell Sound. A bland and lightweight piece of MOR fluff, its success was surprising but suggested how flexible regional tastes already were by the mid-'60s. Preferable was the version of Porter Wagoner's 1955 hit "A Satisfied Mind" at the end of the year.

Knight was born in 1945 and formed the Paramounts at sixteen with white drummer Kenny Buttrey. Around the same time as Arthur Alexander, the group was signed to Dot by Noel Ball, who produced two pop singles—one the minor hit "Free Me," under the name simply of Robert Knight. Their lack of success caused Knight to throw in the towel and commence a career in chemical research at Tennessee State University, where his trumpeter father had taught music. Six years later, however, Mac Gayden heard Knight sing at a fraternity party and signed him to the Monument-distributed Rising Sons label he'd formed with Buzz Cason. Cason had earlier worked for Noel Ball and then led Brenda Lee's backing band the Casuals. The first song he and Gayden wrote for Knight was the pop classic "Everlasting Love," covered in Britain by the Love Affair but an American million-seller for Knight in 1967.

Knight wasn't a terribly soulful singer, and the material Cason and Gayden selected for him—like Ray Stevens's "Isn't It Lonely Together" or their own "Love on a Mountain Top"—was closer to Motown than to Sound Stage 7. But the success of "Everlasting Love" did lead to more satisfying productions by Cason and Gayden for country writer Bobby Russell's Elf label. Ex-Excello artist Clifford Curry was a sock-it-to-'em, Pickett-style soul man whose eight singles on Elf commenced with the Chicago-style dancer "She Shot a Hole in My Soul," while in among country-pop releases by both Cason and Bobby Russell themselves were more releases by Knight and a sublime classic of the male-duo genre, Van & Titus's "Cry Baby Cry."

The singer who perhaps best illustrated Nashville's marriage of country and soul was comparatively late arrival Dobie Gray, whose string of early '70s hits on MCA included such gems of Southern-rock-styled soul as "Drift Away," "Hey Dixie," and "Watch Out for Lucy." "I don't know what you'd call them," he told me. "Country boogie-woogie, maybe?" Gray had been raised on gospel and country music in a little Texan town near Houston, his grandfather a Baptist minister who forbade the playing of blues in the house. The Grand Ole Opry, however, was permitted.

"It was pretty common to hear blacks singing a popular country tune when I was a kid," Gray said. "We experienced all the things country music sang about—plowing the ground, fishing on the bayou—and they just became a part of my life. Two guys that black people regarded as great singers were Hank Williams and Red Foley, who was influenced by black gospel music. To me, George Jones and Dolly Parton are country-soul singers—it's the way they bend notes. Patti Page would never have dared do that; it was just too black."

Gray's first-ever stage appearance was as a boy in his hometown of Brookshire, dressed in a cowboy costume and singing a Roy Rogers song. "It was me and a little girl named Erline Jackson, and I was so scared that nothing came out. Everybody laughed." A cowboy he wasn't destined to be: at the age of eleven he moved to Houston and discovered the R&B of T-Bone Walker and Bobby "Blue" Bland. Some years later in California, his taste began to incline more towards the crooning style of Nat King Cole and Johnny Mathis: "I decided I wanted to be a pop star, not realizing that country was *inside* me. I auditioned for Sonny Bono by singing "Unchained Melody" *a cappella,* and he thought I had potential as a ballad singer. Only later did I realize I wanted to sing country songs on my albums, and I got into terrible arguments with my producers over things like Bob Wills's 'My Shoes Keep Walking Back to You.'"

Gray's first hit was the bluesy, uptempo "Look at Me" on Cor Dak, though he's best known for the perennial dancefloor classics "The In-Crowd" (1965) and "Out on the Floor" (1966). Little happened after those—when Gray first met producer Mentor Williams, he was appearing in the Los Angeles production of *Hair.* Williams brought him to Nashville in 1973, recording him with a crack Memphis/Music City band at David Briggs's and Norbert Putnam's Quadrafonic Sound Studio. In addition to Briggs on piano were Mike Leech (bass), Kenny Malone (drums), Charlie McCoy (harmonica), and Reggie Young and Troy Seals on guitars. Together they provided the perfect understated backdrop to Gray's good-natured, laid-back style: part country, part soul ballad, part bar-band R&B.

"Drift Away" was an instant classic—a breezy eulogy to the power of rock'n'roll, highly evocative of the patched-denim spirit of that time. The country element was stronger still in "Loving Arms" and Troy Seals's "There's a Honky Tonk Angel (Who'll Take Me Back In)." "I remember reading a review of *Loving Arms* that said, 'His affinity with Nashville tends to make him hokey!'" Gray told me.

It's true there was something a little cozy about this Dixie chicken, something summed up in the wicker-chair-and-mint-julep plantation pose on the cover of *Hey Dixie* (1974). But this was the highwater mark of the self-conscious Southernizing of the early '70s. Far more than, say, Charley Pride, Gray represented a new breed of hip country African American. "I never wanted to *be* in the in-crowd!" he said, "And I never felt like a soul singer—I'd be standing there singing 'My Girl' or 'Ain't Too Proud to Beg' and not feeling it." A decade later he cut a pure country album with Alabama producer Harold Shedd.[22]

Otis Williams

A greater if less successful singer than Gray was Otis Williams, who recorded superb country-soul sides on Power Pak and Stop and formed what may have been the first all-black country and western band, the Midnight Cowboys.

Williams had started out at King/DeLuxe with his group the Charms, notching up mid-'50s million-sellers "Hearts of Stone" and "Ivory Tower" while at the same time singing harmony on King country sessions by Cowboy Copas, Hawkshaw Hawkins, and others. Unable to persuade Syd Nathan or Henry Glover to record him on solo country material, he went to Epic in 1960 and cut a bluesy version of Patsy Cline's "I Fall to Pieces." Though Billy Sherrill later took over production duties, not even he could be persuaded to try Williams singing country.

Only in Pete Drake, a steel guitar player who'd come to Nashville from Atlanta in 1959, did Williams find a sympathetic country ear. Both on Stop and Power Pak, Drake co-produced countryish sides that did full justice to Williams's pleading, elastic voice. "Ivory Tower" was reinterpreted beautifully, while the gospelly "To Make a Woman Feel Like a Woman" was rooted in Percy Sledge's "When a Man Loves a Woman." Best of all was Williams's agonized reading of Marty Robbins's "Begging to You" on Stop.

---

22 Gray remained in Nashville through the late '80s and the '90s, recording 1986's *From Where I Stand* for Capitol and making occasional appearances on TV station The Nashville Network. In 1996 he released *Dobie Gray: Diamond Cuts* on his own label. He also wrote songs for such country artists as David Lee Murphy.

For the *Otis Williams and the Midnight Cowboys* album, Williams assembled an all-black band from a pool of musicians who'd backed country artists in and around Cincinnati. "I wanted something a little different, more than just another black country singer," Pete Drake wrote in his sleeve note, indicating, if nothing else, just how blasé people had become about the subgenre. If it really *was* an African American band playing, they did a remarkable job with the classic piano/fiddle/steel line-up of honky-tonk. "Well I can see what happened to Jerry Lee/And I want the same thing for me/I know exactly what I wanna do/Conway did it and I can too," Williams sang on the opening "I Wanna Go Country," establishing a parallel between the conversion to country of rock'n'rollers on the one hand and that of African Americans on the other. Standout tracks on the album were Tom T. Hall's "Do It to Someone You Love" and Conway Twitty's "Hello Darlin'," while Jimmie Rodgers's "Mule Skinner Blues" was turned into a frenzied stampede of yodels, wolf whistles, and sawing fiddles. Engineered by Scotty Moore at Music City Recorders, the LP remains something of a lost classic.

"While one wonders if it helps on a personal level," Bill Millar wrote in a 1974 piece on Nashville, "the country/soul interchange certainly creates some nice music. Earl Gaines sings Jerry Reed, Jerry Jaye sings Bobby Bland, Otis Williams sings Tom T. Hall, Bobby Lee Trammell sings Bert Berns, and Bob Luman sings Spooner Oldham. *Everybody* sings Dallas Frazier."

It was extraordinary how much interchange *did* occur, especially in Nashville. However formally distinct black and white cultures seemed, music always revealed a hidden common ground of shared values and emotions. When Bobby Braddock's "I Believe the South Is Gonna Rise Again" became a hit for Tanya Tucker in the mid-'70s, many doubtless heard it as an implicit anthem of reactionary redneckism. Within months it had been covered by the African American singer Mariane Love.

5 The Deeper South

We've toured the main country-soul belt of Tennessee and northern Alabama and seen how close black and white styles came in that area during the '60s. We now briefly turn our attention to the deeper South of Mississippi, Louisiana, and Texas, where—despite its being perhaps the most bigoted of areas—we again find myriad examples of cross-influence and integration.

Swamp Pop

Of the three states, Louisiana was without doubt the most fertile breeding ground of country soul. Even in New Orleans, where white country music had never been strong, singers such as Fats Domino, Earl King, and Johnny Adams all tapped into hillbilly songs. Aaron Neville claimed his first vocal influence was the yodelling of singing cowboys the Sons of the Pioneers.

"Country and western was maybe the least obvious strand in the New Orleans fabric," said Cosimo Matassa, who engineered many of the city's legendary '50s sessions, "but it was there nonetheless. North of Baton Rouge, country music was all you'd hear, and that inevitably carried through to the city. Of course, the subject matter of R&B and country was all the same anyway—lost love, anticipated love; lost money, anticipated money—and both involved simple melodies and progressions. In south Louisiana generally, there was a major cross-influence, because just as white guys picked up on R&B, so black guys picked up on white subject matter and style, sometimes because

143

it was a natural thing to do, sometimes because that was the way to get the job."

Country surfaced most strongly in the slow, rolling, two-chord ballads that came to be known in south Louisiana as "swamp pop." Virtually indigenous to the area, they were recorded by whites and African Americans alike and drew heavily on the plaintive, unaffected music of French-speaking Cajuns. Fats Domino was godfather to the sound, but it was Earl King's 1955 "Those Lonely, Lonely Nights" that defined it. "'Lonely, Lonely Nights' was R&B," King told *Living Blues*, "but it was originally designed as a country-type tune. Huey Smith's piano solo is completely country and western, and Smiley Lewis's 'I Hear You Knocking' is in the same kind of idiom. Many other songs came from that seed thing. It was like a root, a little germ emanating out there."

Although the biggest swamp-pop hits were by whites—Rod Bernard's "This Should Go On Forever" (1959), Joe Barry's "I'm a Fool to Care" (1961)—African Americans such as Phil Phillips, Cookie & his Cupcakes, and Elton Anderson all had success with the style.

Behind the south Louisiana sound lay several independent producers, most notably Floyd Soileau in Ville Platte, Eddie Shuler in Lake Charles, and Huey P. Meaux in Texas. Shuler was a typical case: a country singer who'd formed the Goldband label as an outlet for his own group the Reveliers, then given up performing to record Cajun, blues, and rockabilly. With no centralized country music industry this far south, local producers were obliged to record anything that would sell, hence the considerable cross-pollination between the various styles of music. The result was singers such as Johnnie Allan, whose eclectic repertoire embraced both country (Merle Haggard, Bobby Bare) and R&B (Percy Sledge, Little Willie John), as well as such rock'n'roll outings as his classic version of Chuck Berry's "Promised Land"—and archetypal swamp-pop ballads—delivered in a lovely, rich slur of a voice.

Black-influenced whites like Allan came a dime a dozen in New Orleans itself. "There were more white cats here who'd lived around black people than anywhere else," recalled Harold Battiste, who headed up Specialty's New Orleans office in the late '50s. Mac Rebennack,

Frankie Ford, Jimmy Clanton, Jerry Byrne, and Bobby Charles were just the most well-known of the breed. "We were a novelty to black people, and they accepted us because we played their music so well," said pianist Ronnie Barron, a second-stringer to Rebennack and his later incarnation, Dr. John.

In a sense, the New Orleans studios reversed the situation in Memphis and Muscle Shoals: here, African Americans wrote and produced records by white frontmen. But south Louisiana was also home to zydeco, the African American counterpart to Cajun fiddle-accordion music, with country and western songs long playing a significant part in that delightful hybrid. Initially using the waltz and two-step forms of Louisiana's European immigrants, African Americans in towns such as Mamou and Lafayette followed the Cajun lead in the '60s by adapting Nashville songs to their swampy backwoods style. As Tony Russell noted, "Although zydeco is not the striking instance of interaction it may seem to be—for its exponents are usually doing no more than reproducing an inherited collection of tunes and songs—it is an outstanding example of a common stock."

Huey P. Meaux

Country and R&B came closer still in nearby East Texas, where the swamp-pop ballad took on added Mexican resonance in Huey Meaux's productions on Freddy Fender, Sunny & the Sunglows, and others. This was the style summarized amusingly by writer Richard Parker as "Country-Texan-Mexican-Louisiana-Black-White-Rhythm 'n' Blues-Western-Rock'n'Roll-Slow Dancin'-Jukebox songs."

Meaux's background suited him perfectly to such eclecticism. Born to rice-growing Cajun parents in Kaplan, Louisiana, at the end of the '20s, he moved as a child to Winnie in southeast Texas, where his father played accordion in Cajun bands and raised him on a broad spectrum of Texas-Louisiana country music. After military service in the '50s, Meaux opened a barbershop in Winnie but played drums in local bands as a sideline, landing himself a regular spot on KPAC Port Arthur.

Primitive tapes made in the barbershop found their way to Floyd Soileau of Jin Records, who was impressed enough to record Meaux's

"'73 Special" in 1959 and to lease from him the big swamp-pop hit "Breakin' Up Is Hard To Do" by Jivin' Gene. With that success under his belt, Meaux bowed out of barbering and began scouting around for local talent. Joe Barry's Domino-inspired "I'm A Fool To Care," leased by Soileau to Mercury's Smash subsidiary, proved an even bigger hit than "Breakin' Up" when it made No. 24 on the Hot 100 in May 1961. "With a lot of records," Cosimo Matassa remarked in John Broven's *Walking to New Orleans,* "you didn't know if they were black or white when they first hit the street. Jivin' Gene and Joe Barry were cases in point."

Meaux established his own set-up in the Houston suburb of Pasadena, forming a complex of labels that included Crazy Cajun, Tribe, Teardrop, and Jetstream and building a studio next door to the one where George Jones had recorded several '50s hits for Starday. On Crazy Cajun he produced various crazy Cajuns—Marc Savoy, Link Davis, and his own good self—before cutting the first of many sides by ex-rockabilly singer Baldemar Huerta, aka Freddy Fender. Swampers Joe Barry, Tommy McLain, and Warren Storm followed in succession, as did the wonderful Jimmy Donley, who killed himself in 1963 after recording the heartbreaking "Think It Over" and other gems.

On other labels, the prolific Meaux issued an array of artists that spanned the entire spectrum of Southern music in the early '60s: country singers Floyd Tillman and Jimmy Heap; blues men T-Bone Walker and Johnny Copeland; blue-eyed Texan soulboys Roy Head, Doug Sahm, and Johnny Winter. R&B-wise, his only real competition was Don Robey in Houston and Major Bill Smith in Fort Worth. (For Robey's Back Beat subsidiary he in any case produced Roy Head's big 1965 hit "Treat Her Right.")

Meaux's greatest soul artist was undoubtedly Barbara Lynn, born in Beaumont in 1942. She possessed one of the finest voices in all of Southern soul, a warm, velvety-smooth alto (not unlike that of Irma Thomas) that worked magic with the countrified ballads and swamp-pop numbers in which she specialized. Discovering her singing backup on sessions at Goldband, Meaux took Lynn first to Cosimo Matassa's studio, an appropriate location for her breezily melancholic style, and the session delivered the 1962 Top Ten hit "You'll Lose a Good

Thing," first of eight singles leased to the Jamie label in Philadelphia. The Matassa band provided a classic New Orleans underpinning of piano triplets and dipping horns, and follow-ups "Give Me a Break" and "I'm Sorry I Met You" fell into the same languorous bag. Lynn was also a dab hand at Jimmy Reed blues (e.g., "You Don't Have to Go"), providing her own choppy guitar work. Meaux, always keen to mix up the various musical styles he juggled, even got her to duet with ex-Crown Lee Mayes on the country song "Careless Hands."

When the Jamie deal expired in 1965, Lynn signed to Meaux's own Tribe label, on which a version of Maurice & Mac's "You Left the Water Running" was a minor hit in 1967. A year later, Meaux signed a lease-deal with Atlantic and farmed her out to the production team of Cliff and Ed Thomas and Bob McRee in Jackson, Mississippi, where he'd built a studio called Grits'n'Gravy. The Thomases had been minor rockabilly artists on Phillips International in Memphis, while McRee was already recording local African Americans in west Jackson as early as 1956. The trio began collaborating on songs in the early '60s and found black girl group the Poppies—Patsy McEwen, Fern Kinney, and Dorothy Moore—at Jackson State University.

"Billy Sherrill got to hear one of our demo tapes," McRee told me. "He loved the soul sound we were getting here. He signed me as a staff producer for CBS, and I began recording acts for the old OKeh label. Eventually we went to Nashville and recorded the Poppies on a Billy Sherrill song called 'Lullaby of Love,' which was a pretty big hit. Billy would come down to Jackson about once a month. He had a tremendous ear and knew exactly what he was doing."

Sherrill signed McRee and the Thomases as writers. He also produced other Jackson artists such as Tommy Tate. The CBS contract eventually expired, however, leaving McRee free to go independent. Before linking up with Huey Meaux in 1967, he produced Earl King and Huey "Piano" Smith for Ace, plus a variety of R&B and pop acts (Billy Joe Royal, Joe Odum, the Tams, and Bobby Jay McCarthy) for Bill Lowery's 1-2-3 label in Atlanta. The Thomas brothers, still in the family shirt-manufacturing business, collaborated from time to time, making more of a commitment to McRee after Meaux offered them Grits'n'Gravy as a permanent recording base. "It was an old theater, and we had a good sound," McRee said. "It lasted until the roof was leaking so bad we had to move out . . . maybe a couple of years in all."

Using a pool of musicians that included Jerry Puckett and Mike West on guitars, James Stroud and Tommy Tate on drums, Jimmy Jones and Don Barrett on bass, Carson Whitsett and Ed Thomas himself on keyboards, McRee and the Thomases produced Grits'n'Gravy sessions for everyone from Rod Bernard to Junior Parker to Peggy Scott & JoJo Benson. "Most of the records made there say 'produced by Huey Meaux,'" said Tim Whitsett, whose integrated Imperial Showband provided the studio's horn section, "but really it was Bob and Cliff and Ed. Huey would sit there reading a comic and smoking a cigar, and every now and then he'd look up and say, 'That's it'—even if you'd just made a horrible mistake. Peggy & JoJo's 'Lover's Holiday' had a bad trumpet note at the end, but Huey just said, 'No, that's OK, we'll put it out.'"

Barbara Lynn's Grits'n'Gravy-recorded Atlantic album *Here Is Barbara Lynn* was a pleasing mixture of her old smokey ballad style (on the self-penned songs "I'll Suffer" and "You're Losing Me") and poppier, Motownish songs by McRee and the Thomases. Her best sessions, though, were produced at American in 1970 by Spooner Oldham and horn man Charles Chalmers. They include such country-soul gems as "You're Gonna See a Lot More of Me Leaving," the Penn/Oldham "He Ain't Gonna Do Right," and the Donnie Fritts masterpiece called "People Like Me." As McRee observed: "In the '60s a lot of R&B things had country lyric lines and melodies and certainly weren't the type of things being produced for the black market now. Back then there were die-hard country people buying things like Clarence Carter, but now there's a void between them."

Meaux stayed in the business of making indigenous Southern records. After his '60s successes with Joe Barry, Barbara Lynn, Roy Head, and the Sir Douglas Quintet, he served a jail sentence for conspiring to violate the Mann Act—a girl brought to a DJs' convention set up shop as a prostitute and gave the police a detailed account of the weekend's proceedings. Fourteen months behind bars did his name no good, and he waited until 1975 before tasting success again, this time with Freddy Fender's huge Tex-Mex hit "Before the Next Teardrop Falls."

Aside from Jerry Lee Lewis's fine *Southern Roots* album, Fender's were the best records Meaux produced in the '70s. If the Mexican's quavering tones were an acquired taste, the material on albums such as *Rock'n'Country* and *Swamp Gold* made a delightfully nostalgic tour of Tex-Mex/Louisiana music, from honky-tonk tears'n'beer classics through Excello blues to evergreen swamp-pop ballads such as Cookie & the Cupcakes's "Mathilda." *Swamp Gold* itself was a loving update of the south Louisiana sound featuring "Breaking Up Is Hard to Do" and Dale and Grace's "I'm Leaving It All Up to You," as well as swamp-pop treatments of R&B classics by Johnny Ace, Aaron Neville, and Otis Redding. In the same spirit of hybridization, Meaux's last big success was the 1985 country version of the Cajun "My Toot Toot" by black Rockin' Sidney, a fellow artist on Jin in the late '50s.[23]

Shreveport

A town that enjoyed a certain connection with Jackson, Mississippi, was Shreveport in northwest Louisiana—a very different Louisiana from that of New Orleans and the bayous but one that nonetheless boasted its fair share of white R&B devotees. "I used to be able to go into all the black clubs in Shreveport," drummer James Stroud, who left the city to join the Grits'n'Gravy band in Jackson, told me. "That's changed, which is sad. They don't want whites any more."

Shreveport was home to the Louisiana Hayride, second only to the Grand Ole Opry as a country radio show, but it was also a strong regional center for blues and R&B. The coexistence of the two made it a logical setting for Southern soul, something it duly became after distributor Stan Lewis formed his Jewel, Paula, and Ronn labels in the first half of the '60s.

Born, like Johnny Vincent and Cosimo Matassa, of Italian heritage, Lewis began life selling newspapers and shining shoes on Shreveport's sidewalks. Being Italian and Catholic was in itself enough to give him an affinity with the plight of African Americans in the South: it was to them that he started selling records as a sideline to his jukebox and gumball-machine business after the war. The first discs he handled

---

23 Meaux did a further stretch in jail after being convicted of trafficking in child pornography in 1995.

were Aristocrat 78s that came from the back of Leonard Chess's car: "[Chess] was the first person I ever met in the record business, and he and guys like the Bihari brothers would travel about with Ampex recorders in the back of their cars and set up in nightclubs."

In 1950, Lewis and his wife Pauline expanded their tiny record store on Texas Street into a one-stop distribution point and mail-order house, dealing principally with R&B records. For their pains they would often arrive in the morning to find KKK slogans daubed on the door. "I think I broke more black music in the South than anyone except for the three big distributors [Ernie's, Randy's, and Buckley's] in Nashville." In 1951, Lewis bought airtime on KWKH, home of the Hayride, and soon had mail-order shows in Little Rock, Arkansas, and Del Rio, Texas (Wolfman Jack on XERF). It wasn't long before both Leonard Chess and Specialty's Art Rupe approached him to act as a local talent scout in the Shreveport area. He responded by signing the Hayride performer Slim Whitman to Specialty and recording Dale ("Suzie Q") Hawkins for Chess.

"So many people came to me," Lewis told me. "Webb Pierce worked down the road at Sears-Roebuck. Johnny Horton, Kitty Wells, Jim Reeves, and Floyd Cramer were all on the Hayride. If KWKH had had the foresight to build a studio here and hire a booking agent, they'd never have lost all the talent to Nashville that they did. Jerry Lee Lewis even came to me from nearby Ferriday when he was thirteen—I turned him down!"

Other famous Hayriders included Hank Williams and Elvis Presley, the latter making some of his first in-store appearances at Stan's Record Shop. "Elvis would come in my shop and check out my stock of R&B records, which was probably the best in the world at that time." As a distributor Lewis meanwhile went from strength to strength, handling RCA and Mercury and just about every independent label in America. By the early '60s he'd found the necessary motivation to start his own label, christening it after a chain of Chicago grocery stores called Jewel.

Lewis's first artist was ex-swamp-pop singer Bobby "See You Later, Alligator" Charles, a Cajun who'd been on Chess and Imperial in the '50s and had now gone country. The first African American signings were Peppermint Harris and the Carter Brothers, though Lewis also established a Jewel gospel line. For a period, the label's blues and R&B

sides were recorded in Chicago and Los Angeles, but with the formation of two further labels (Paula and Ronn) in 1965, Lewis began using
the Robin Hood Brian studio in nearby Tyler, Texas,

Ronn became Lewis' principal R&B/soul outlet, leaving Jewel to
concentrate on blues singers such as Lightnin' Hopkins and Lowell
Fulson. The Paula label, meanwhile, focused on pop acts such as John
Fred & the Playboys and Joe Stampley & the Uniques. Most prolific
on Ronn was Ted Taylor, the spine-chilling falsetto singer who'd
been produced by Billy Sherrill in Nashville. After three releases on
Jewel (including the sobbing lament "You've Been Crying"), Taylor
switched to Ronn and trekked out to FAME in Muscle Shoals. "When
a studio gets hot," Lewis said, "it's just like when an artist gets hot.
Muscle Shoals was *the* sound, and I did quite a few sessions up there."
All the material on Taylor's *You Can Dig It* album (1967) was superlative, though later—on *Taylor Made*—Ted veered closer to the funky-
ghetto paranoia of post-Sly Stone soul: songs such as "Troubled Water"
and "Something Strange Is Going On" left behind the wistful heartache of Southern country soul.

Other R&B artists recorded by Lewis included Toussaint McCall,
Barbara West, and Little Johnny Taylor. McCall had a big 1966 hit
with the funereal ballad "Nothing Takes the Place of You," while
his deadpan renditions of "I Stand Accused" and "I Left My Heart
in San Francisco" bore an unmistakable easy-listening country feel.
The sleepy baritone he employed was ideal for the country-soul ballads "Step By Step," "Like Never Before," and "One Table Away," all
recorded at FAME. Otherwise he specialized in organ instrumentals
like "La Rea," which sounded like a cross between a late-night lounge
combo and a cremation service. Subsequently he disappeared, only to
surface in 1976 with an album on the Californian McCowan label.
West went to Muscle Shoals for the Toussaint-style "Anyone But You"
and a terrific version of Theola Kilgore's "The Love of My Man," then
promptly disappeared. Johnny Taylor's roots were in gospel but he'd
switched to R&B after moving from Memphis to L.A. and charted
with 1963's classic "Part Time Love" on Galaxy. Back in the South
he kept alive a bluesy, adulterous tradition with "Open House At My
House" and "Everybody Knows About My Good Thing."

Besides Jewel, Ronn, and Paula (on which his biggest-ever pop hit, John Fred's 1967 "Judy in Disguise," was issued), Lewis signed distribution agreements with such smaller local labels as Whit, Murco, and Soul Power. The last of these was the brainchild of three men who ran a new Shreveport studio called Sound City: administrator Stewart Madison and writers-producers Bobby Patterson and Jerry Strickland. Patterson and Strickland were the ultimate country-soul partnership—Patterson a funky African American from Dallas, Strickland a Louisiana country boy who'd penned songs for Acuff-Rose in Nashville. "I didn't hardly *see* black people until I was fourteen or fifteen," Strickland told me, "and I certainly didn't hear any music besides country."

Only after writing hits such as Hank Williams Jr.'s "The Glass" and Johnny Russell's "This Man and Woman Thing" did Strickland start tuning into soul: "It wasn't like a switch was turned on one day. You hear a little of it, you start to like it, and you start putting it together with what you know." Put together with Patterson's more urban sensibility, Jerry's Nashville-trained style produced superb songs for Little Johnny Taylor, Tommie Young, and Patterson himself: blues ballads such as "Do You Still Feel the Same Way" for the very Aretha-ish Young, classic country soul ("She Don't Have to See You") for both Young and Patterson. "With the songs we wrote," Strickland recalled, "usually the punchline would be mine. Bobby came up with the rhythm patterns."

Madison had grown up in Shreveport but was working in the municipal bonds business in Houston. In 1970, Sound City's owners asked him to come up to Shreveport and run the studio. Once installed there, he assembled a band that comprised Louis Villery (bass), Richard Meek (guitar), Ron Dilulio (keyboards), and either Roy Yeager or the prodigal James Stroud on drums. Most of them were white, though leader Villery was an African American from Florida. Ironically, the first hit on Soul Power was African Music Machine's "Blackwater Gold," written by Villery and a forerunner of the dance style that would have such disastrous consequences for Southern soul: disco.[24]

---

24 Charles Hughes makes the point that disco posed a threat to soul *and* country musicians, though he also reminds us that both Nashville and Muscle Shoals dabbled in disco. (James Brown's 1979 album *The Original Disco Man* was cut at Muscle Shoals Sound.)

Soul Power lasted about two years before winding up in a lawsuit with Lewis; Jewel's agreements with Whit and Murco didn't last much longer. Lionel Whitfield's Baton Rouge–based Whit released sides by the blind Louisiana singer Bobby Powell and by ex-Cupcake Bob Camille, while Dee Marais's Murco enjoyed regional hits on local soulmen Eddie Giles and Reuben Bell. Like Jerry Strickland, Marais had been a country writer—penning George Jones's "Poor Man's Riches"—before acquiring a taste for rhythm and blues. He worked in Shelby Singleton's Bayou Record Shop in Shreveport and bought it when Singleton moved to Nashville in 1960.

Exposed to black records as a result of the demand for R&B in the East 70th St. neighborhood, in the mid-'60s Marais booked sessions by Giles and Bell at the Texan Robin Hood studio that Stan Lewis was using. Gospel-reared Eddie's "Losin' Boy" was a delightfully ingenuous song of woe penned after his wife left him for another man: "I'm like Ray Charles/Guess I was born to lose," he wailed, answered by a beautifully inane sax phrase. Later he blamed his lack of follow-up success on being too happy. "Atlantic was interested after we sold about 10,000 copies of 'Losin' Boy' in Dallas alone, but we went with Stan," Marais recalled. "Murco lasted about four years."

Reuben Bell possessed a more affecting voice than Giles—a high, crying tenor heard at its best on his Murco ballad "You're Gonna Miss Me." "Reuben listened to country as much as to R&B," Jerry Strickland remembered. "We'd be driving in the car, and he'd wanted turn on a country station when *I* wanted an R&B station!" Some years after Murco folded, Bell was one of the Shreveport artists who recorded at Sound City, both for Allen Orange's House of Orange label and for Alarm, a label formed by Strickland, Patterson, and Madison in the wake of Soul Power's demise. "Reuben had recorded for Allen Orange," Madison said. "He had a hit on DeLuxe with a song originally meant for Geater Davis. He and Geater were practically neighbors in Shreveport and wrote a lot of songs together." Bell was Alarm's first signing, produced by New Orleans maestro Wardell Quezergue on sides like "Asking for the Truth," an exquisitely painful ballad written by Bell with Strickland, and "Kiss Tomorrow Goodbye," a 1977 version of a song Quezergue had cut with Danny White in 1962.

Also produced by Quezergue on Alarm was Ted Taylor, who returned from a bleak period with a hit version of Jimmy Hughes's "Steal Away" and an album, *Ted Taylor* (1976), that mixed songs by Strickland and Bell with ballads by such African American writers as Sam Dees and Bettye Crutcher. "Ted got kidded a lot in black clubs for having such a high voice," Strickland remembered. "He'd decided in earlier years that he'd better learn to protect himself, so he took up karate. A very disciplined person and a health food nut."[25]

Alarm went out of business in 1978, after which Strickland returned to writing country songs, and Madison became the business director of Malaco Records back in Jackson. Local boy Joe Stampley scored a big hit with Strickland's "Do You Ever Fool Around" and made No. 1 dueting with Moe Bandy on Strickland's adaptation of Carl Smith's "Hey Joe." Madison was already using Malaco to overdub horns and strings, so he simply called owner Tommy Couch to ask for a job. "When I got there," he told me, "it was just a studio rental company with a little label distributed by TK. There was plenty to do."

Bobby Patterson returned to Dallas and reemerged in 1982 with the *Storyteller* album, a strong collection of dance tracks and ballads, some held over from Sound City sessions, others recorded at Malaco and in Dallas. He remains one of the great exponents of the "deep soul" guilt'n'jealousy school.

Malaco

Malaco Records was the last of the great Southern R&B indies, a major success story after several close brushes with collapse. With Tommy Couch's company, which in 1985 bought Muscle Shoals Sound, the Southern soul story came full circle. It became the third-largest independent record company in America and—thanks to a roster of groups such as the Jackson Southernaires and the Fantastic Violinaires—the country's second largest gospel label. "We just happened to take a chance with what we liked," said Stewart Madison. "We didn't understand disco so we didn't *do* disco."

What turned the label around after twenty uncertain years was a single song called "Down Home Blues," penned by former FAME/

---

25 Tragically, Taylor was killed in a road accident in Oklahoma in October 1987.

Goldwax writer George Jackson and sung by the Texan Z.Z. Hill—a journeyman blues-soul growler who'd recorded for a hundred labels great and small and most recently been dropped by Columbia. Not even issued as a single, its airplay unleashed a vast African American audience starved for years of gritty rhythm and blues, kept the *Down Home* album in the soul charts for an unprecedented ninety-seven weeks, and attracted to the label a flock of blues-soul legends who—in co-owner Wolf Stephenson's words—"had been out there and well-known but had absolutely no place to get a record out": acts such as Denise LaSalle, Benny Latimore, Little Milton, Johnnie Taylor, and Bobby Bland. With the shrewd Madison taking care of the business end and veteran promotion man Dave Clark jetting across America to exercise his powers of persuasion on R&B disc jockeys, Malaco managed to stay afloat in the strange and unpredictable world of African American music.

It was particularly apt that Malaco should have acquired Muscle Shoals Sound and its catalog, since Couch hailed from Tuscumbia and grew up with Jimmy Johnson in the Shoals area. "I really didn't know anything about music when I was growing up," he told me, "other than what I heard on the radio. The first record I bought was Bobby Bland's *Two Steps from the Blues*. I grew up listening to WLAC like everyone else. Our first contact with live music was via Hollis Dixon and the Muscle Shoals bands. I got to know them, and when I went to Ole Miss [the University of Mississippi], I started booking them for fraternity parties."

Among the groups that made frequent trips from Muscle Shoals to the Oxford campus were Dan Penn's Mark Vs, Jimmy Johnson's Del-Rays, Hollis Dixon's Keynotes, and the black Esquires, featuring a still-unknown Percy Sledge on lead vocals. The popularity of R&B among the white students led to the booking of other African American bands, mainly acts from the Carolinas such as the Dynamics, the Red Tops, and Doug Clark's Hot Nuts.

"Even the diehard segregationalists loved the black music," recalled Wolf Stephenson, who enrolled at the university a year after Couch. "It was like two worlds: the students danced to the music but the moment the musicians left the stage, they would have nothing to do with them." (Ole Miss erupted in a frenzy of bigotry when a black student, James Meredith, enrolled there in 1962.)

Graduating in 1965, Couch moved south to Jackson and worked in a pharmacy before forming a partnership with his brother-in-law, Mitch Malouf. This was Campus Attractions, set up to continue the booking business Couch had started at Ole Miss. In the space of two years, Campus Attractions (or Malaco, as it became known) brought bands like Herman's Hermits, the Dave Clark Five, and even the Who to Jackson's 10,000-seat Coliseum, enabling Couch to quit the pharmacy and open a club whose franchise he purchased from the TV show *Hullabaloo*.

Based in an office in Johnny Vincent's building in downtown Jackson, Couch began looking at the possibilities of getting into the record business: "The first thing we ever did was engineered by Jimmy Johnson at FAME, and that was a black Mississippi band on our books called Cozy Corley & the Blue Gardenia Showband. We also brought along a country singer from Jackson, and—from Muscle Shoals itself— the Esquires and the Keynotes." Somewhat unpromisingly, the resulting sides (like the Keynotes' "Paper Boy") were released on a label called Coma.

Not long after, Couch found an unused Pepsi-Cola warehouse on the northwest outskirts of the city and set about installing a 4-track studio there. Almost the first people to drop in were white Meridian songwriters Paul Davis and George Soulé. "They were both kind of like Dan Penn," Couch told me; "country and bluesy at the same time." Meridian being close to New Orleans, as well as being the birthplace of one Jimmie Rodgers, Soulé and Davis heard as much Fats Domino as country music when they were growing up. Together with future Flying Burrito Brother Chris Ethridge, they played in makeshift R&B bands covering Ernie K. Doe's "Mother-in-Law" and Barbara George's "I Know." Later, Soulé (who remembers being conditioned to hate African Americans as a boy) worked as a DJ on a station where "the manager would jump on me about playing too much blues and not enough pop."

Davis and Soulé brought Malaco the African American singer Eddie Houston, who worked in the Soulé family foundry in Meridian. With a band made up of Davis on guitar, Steve Miller on bass, and possibly

Tommy Tate on drums, Couch recorded Houston on the Davis-Soulé song "Simon Says," leased to Capitol in 1968. "Capitol had a lot of money from the Beatles," Soulé said. "I guess we were part of their tax deduction scheme." By this time, Wolf Stephenson, a Mississippi country boy who'd followed Couch down to Jackson, was handling most of the engineering chores in the studio. It was his idea to record country bluesman Mississippi Fred McDowell for a fine but unsuccessful album, also on Capitol. Following Stephenson was guitarist Jerry Puckett, fresh from West Coast stints with Ricky Nelson and the Champs.

"We did anything to keep the studio going in those days," Couch told me. "I remember saying we could do this location recording of some big general who was coming to give a speech in Jackson, but we didn't even have a portable recorder. Well, I managed to borrow one, but when I got home and checked the tape, it turned out I'd pressed the wrong button. So I got hold of a copy of the speech and made George Soulé impersonate the general!" Soulé himself had his sights set on Muscle Shoals, and—after Jerry Wexler recorded his song "Saving It All for You" with Judy Clay—"eased on up" to the new Muscle Shoals Sound studio in December 1969. Paul Davis, meanwhile, signed to Bang in Atlanta and had a first solo hit with the old Bert Berns/Exciters song "A Little Bit of Soap."

1970 was the first golden year for Couch and Stephenson. In great part this was thanks to Wardell Quezergue, the Creole arranger-producer behind '60s hits as diverse as the Dixie Cups's "Chapel of Love" and Robert Parker's "Barefootin'." Quezergue, like Allen Toussaint a producer moving away from the old New Orleans R&B sound to a grittier funk style, came up to Malaco to record "Funky Thing" by the Unemployed, then returned one weekend with a busload of New Orleans acts that included King Floyd and Jean Knight. "In that one weekend," Stephenson remembered, "we cut records that sold about five million copies."

The megasellers were Floyd's "Groove Me" and Knight's "Mr. Big Stuff," crisp funk workouts that managed to combine the Lee Dorsey-style soul of New Orleans with the meaty Memphis beat of Stax. Stax, as it happens, was one of the companies that turned down "What Our Love Needs"/"Groove Me," prompting Couch and Stephenson to release it themselves. Forming a label called Chimneyville (after the nickname given to Jackson when Sherman reduced the town to chimneys in 1863), the pair signed a distribution agreement with Atco, then watched as DJs flipped the record over to the B-side. Crucial to the sound of "Groove Me" was the supertight powerhouse drumming of James Stroud, called over from Sound City in Shreveport.

"Mr. Big Stuff" followed in the spring of 1971, bringing to prominence a singer who'd recorded Barbara Lynn–ish sides for Huey P. Meaux. On an album of the same name, Quezergue balanced Knight perfectly between the surly punch of "Take Him" or "Don't Talk About Jody" and beautifully arranged country-soul ballads such as "A Little Bit of Something" or "Why I Keep Living These Memories." Neither Knight nor Floyd lived up to the promise of their hits, however, and the next few years for Malaco proved bleak.

One giant success saved and sustained Malaco. A background singer since leaving the Poppies in the mid-'60s, Dorothy Moore had been groomed as a solo artist by her DJ manager Joe Lewis, signing to Couch and Stephenson's label in 1975. The company was on the brink of closing down when Couch and James Stroud had the brainwave of recording their new acquisition on Bob Montgomery's song "Misty Blue," a 1966 country hit for Wilma Burgess, subsequently covered by Joe Simon. The song was perfect for Moore's yearning voice, a country lament just begging for soulful treatment. Quezergue added a gossamer film of strings; Jimmy Johnson, visiting from Muscle Shoals, provided inimitable offbeat guitar chinks. The whole thing ached and wept and proceeded to sell a million and a half copies.

As with King Floyd in 1970, Couch and Stephenson were unable to get a deal for the record and so put "Misty Blue" out themselves, securing a distribution deal with Henry Stone's TK in Miami. It was followed by an equally delicious treatment of Willie Nelson's "Funny How Time Slips Away" and—in 1977—the stunning Shoals-recorded "For Old Time's Sake." After that, Moore rather lost her direction—some pop-country songs by Jim Weatherly, a version of Bobby Goldsboro's tearjerker "With Pen in Hand"—though 1985 did reunite her with James Stroud for the Nashville-recorded "We Just Came Apart at the Dreams."

There were other good examples of country soul at Malaco. Mighty Sam came up to the studio in the early '70s and cut a superb version of Toni Wine's "Mr. and Mrs. Untrue," an adultery ballad that epitomized the country connection with deep soul:

> *Keep your shades on, Janie*
> *The hotel is kinda crowded tonight*
> *And oh I'd hate to meet someone we knew*
> *And force a smile when we don't even wanna be polite*
> (© Carlin Music)

The equally powerful McKinley Mitchell came to Jackson to record an eponymous album for Chimneyville. A native Mississippian, Mitchell had grown up singing gospel and listening to country music. He moved north, however, first to Massachusetts with gospel quartet the Hearts of Harmony and then to Chicago, where he recorded two Willie Dixon–produced albums for Spoonful. The '60s found him on the Leanor brothers' One-Der-Ful label, for which he cut sides clearly inspired by Ben E. King and Clyde McPhatter.

Only when Mitchell returned to his Mississippi roots in 1978 did the latent country bent reveal itself. *McKinley Mitchell* was a blend of blues ("Run to Love," Little Johnny Taylor's "Open House At My House") and pure country-soul ballads ("Same Old Dream," "End of the Rainbow") sung in a voice that coupled blood-curdling squalls with a timbre that was almost white-sounding. The album's closing track, "Follow the Wind," was nothing less than a Wild West cowboy canter.

Even Z.Z. Hill, standard bearer for Malaco's nostalgic fetishizing of the blues, started out on the label singing country soul (Bobby Marchan's "Separate Ways," Hank Williams's "I'm So Lonesome I Could Cry"). After his "Down Home Blues" (1981), however, Malaco stuck close to their winning formula, mining a seam everyone had presumed was exhausted. Before his death in 1984, Hill followed up *Down Home* with *The Rhythm and the Blues, I'm a Blues Man,* and *Bluesmaster,* each more formulaic than the last. "I'm a Blues Man" (1983) wrapped up every blues cliché in one neat stanza:

I was raised up on Jimmy Reed,
Combread, collard greens, and black-eyed peas,
Took my first bath in muddy waters,
All you mamas better look out for your daughters
I'm a blues man . . .

(© Malaco Music Co., 1983)

In fact, Hill had been a pretty standard kind of Soul Man for most of his career, but that was easily overlooked. In any case, the salient point is that he'd broken through to a lost African American audience in the rural South and that it was now opened up to other veterans of R&B's chitlin' circuit. Malaco also provided a continuity from Stax's "blues" line of the '70s: Albert King, Little Milton, and, to a lesser extent, Johnnie Taylor.

Milton was the exemplary blues-soulman, a singer who combined the chesty growl of B.B. King with the cavernous resonance of Bobby Bland—and was a sucker for a good country tune into the bargain. (At Stax he'd recorded a roaring version of Charlie Rich's "Behind Closed Doors," while the Malaco album *Playing for Keeps* featured yet another soulful reading of "Misty Blue.") At Malaco he distilled a fusion of the King and Bland styles that synched perfectly with Couch and Stephenson's homogenous '80s R&B sound. Bland himself joined the Malaco roster in 1985, making his debut with *Members Only,* which followed the Z.Z. Hill/Little Milton pattern of mixing uptempo R&B with sweet soul ballads. It found Bland in better voice than he'd been in for years.

"When ABC got put over to MCA, I got kind of put on the shelf," Bland told me when Couch brought a Malaco live revue to London in the summer of 1989. "They weren't behind me, and I thought it was best for me to make a move as soon as possible. Dave Clark was a friend of mine, and we had worked together for a lot of years. He asked if I had a record company, and I said, 'No.' He said, 'Are you *thinking* about a record company?' I said, 'No.' So he said, 'Well, how about coming to Malaco?' So I said, 'Okay, Dave, let's give it a shot.' And so here I am. And Malaco has been very nice."

"I think our sound still has that flavor of early Chips Moman or Rick Hall," Couch said to me. "The sound is technically better today;

everything is a little more sophisticated, but that's still what we do best." Added Stewart Madison: "Muscle Shoals was the real country-black sound. We're blacker than that, yet our rhythm section is still three whites and two blacks."

Very occasionally Malaco came close to the country-soul sound of old: Tennessean Denise LaSalle wrote her Millie Jackson–ish vignettes country before turning them into R&B, while her 1984 duet with Benny Latimore, "Right Place, Right Time," could have been adapted by Nashville with no trouble at all. Essentially, though, Couch and Stephenson had settled for a rather sterile if lucrative approach to R&B. Compared to, say, Dan Penn and Spooner Oldham, Malaco's pool of "downhome" writers—George Jackson, Frank Johnson, Jimi "Count" Hughes—seemed to write from the head rather than the heart. Their blues lacked soul.

Goin' Back to Louisiana

Back down in Louisiana, so strong were indigenous musical styles that Muscle Shoals–style soul had a tough job taking root there. When Lee Lavergne of the Lanor label in Church Point wanted to break into soul, the only Louisiana singer he could find was Phil ("Sea of Love") Phillips, whom he took to Muscle Shoals in 1969. Otherwise, all his soul artists in the period 1966–72 hailed from Georgia, the last and best being Ella Brown, later of Maconites Wet Willie. Brown's Capricorn-recorded version of Dan Penn's "A Woman Left Lonely" (1972) was a minor country-soul gem.

In New Orleans, Allen Toussaint came under the influence of Stax and FAME on the one hand and Motown on the other. Along with the city's second-line rhythms and Mardi Gras party traditions, Toussaint was exposed to gospel and even country music. "Gospel influenced me at least as much as Professor Longhair and Fats Domino," he told me. "And yes, I listened to hillbilly music too, guys like Red Foley, Ernest Tubb, Jimmy Dickens, and Hank Thompson. All this stuff was on the airwaves."

The result was that Toussaint could move from such purely New Orleans recordings as Lee Dorsey's "Ya Ya" and Jessie Hill's "Ooh Pooh Pah Doo" to more gospel-based sessions on Sansu by Betty Harris and Zilla Mayes. "See, Betty was from Alabama," said Toussaint's long-time partner Marshall Schorn, a country boy from North Carolina. "She brought her gospel bag with her and was much closer to the soulful, pleading sound of Muscle Shoals than she was to New Orleans." Harris's biggest Sansu hit, "Nearer to You," could almost have been a secularization of "Nearer My God to Thee." Together with such wracked ballads as "What'd I Do Wrong" and "I Can't Last Much Longer," it revealed a singer of incredibly raw intensity, working against a Toussaint backdrop that was looser and quirkier than Stax but used the same mournful wall-of-horns effect. If black country and western was virtually nonexistent in New Orleans, even the late Lee Dorsey—whose "Working in the Coalmine" defined Toussaint's use of second-line Crescent City rhythm in the '60s—was a fan of hillbilly music. As a boy he'd learned to yodel like Jimmie Rodgers; later he completed tracks for a country album at Sea-Saint.[26] Johnny Adams, too, continued to dabble in the country field, applying his tight, careful phrasing to a selection of songs released on Hep' Me as *The Sweet Country Voice of Johnny Adams*. Fiddles and steel guitars filled out songs by Toussaint and Sehorn and versions of "Love Me Tender" and Esther Phillips's "Am I That Easy to Forget." Aside from these pure country tracks, Johnny recorded such magnificent '80s country-soul songs as "Hell Yes I Cheated," Paul Kelly's "Love Me Now," and Conway Twitty's "After All the Good Is Gone."

Like Muscle Shoals pianist David Briggs stumbling upon a bunch of Motown stars singing country songs backstage at the Apollo Theater, Marshall Sehorn was another white Southerner who discovered, to his amazement, that African Americans liked the hillbilly music he'd been raised on. When he moved to Harlem in 1958 to join Bobby Robinson's Fire and Fury—he claimed he was the first white man to work for a black record company in America—he was flabberghasted to find Robinson stocking country records in his shop on 125th Street . . . and selling them.

---

26 Dorsey's country album never appeared. He died of emphysema in December 1986.

6 Can Blue Men Sing the Whites?

Up until now we've focused on the incidence of white country elements in black Southern soul. Along the way, however, we've noted examples of straight country music performed by African Americans: *Otis Williams and the Midnight Cowboys, The Sweet Country Voice of Johnny Adams,* Ray Charles's *Modern Sounds in Country 'n' Western.* As an extension of this it's worth looking at those black singers for whom country was a principal vocation. Although to date there has only been one black country superstar—Charley Pride—ever since Deford Bailey first played on the Grand Ole Opry, African Americans have sung and recorded this whitest of musics.

Ivory Joe Hunter

The genial Ivory Joe Hunter was a perfect example of someone temperamentally suited to country but obliged as a black entertainer to sing rhythm and blues. "Growing up in the backwoods of Texas, he was close to country," said his manager Bettye Berger, "but when he started recording, blacks couldn't do country, so they called him a bluesman."

Raised on gospel and spirituals around East Texas, Hunter was first recorded by Alan Lomax for the Library of Congress in the '30s. (He never forsook religion, either: even his biggest hit, "Since I Met You Baby," was written originally as "Since I Met You Jesus.") In 1942, after playing around Beaumont and Houston, Hunter followed the Texas-Oklahoma migration westwards and wound up recording songs on his own Ivory and Pacific labels in Oakland, California. These were blues ballads in the style of Charles Brown, reflecting the mellowing influence of Nat King Cole. Only when he signed to King in 1947 did Hunter's country side emerge. Songs such as "Waiting In Vain" and the 1949 cover of Jenny Lou Carson's "Jealous Heart"—recorded in Nashville—made him a pioneer of black country a decade before Ray Charles. "If I had my way I would record nothing but country songs," he later said. "Most of them have true-to-life meaning. I just can't seem to convince the recording people, though."

Moving on to MGM in late 1949, Hunter refined his country-ballad style on the divine "I Almost Lost My Mind" (an R&B No. 1) and on a fine rendering of Eddy Arnold's "It's a Sin." Over the course of his five-year stay at the company he also cut songs by Hank Williams and Ted Daffan. The next stop was Atlantic in 1954: for the New York label he recorded such country-styled numbers as "It May Sound Silly," "A Tear Fell," and (covered by the white Teresa Brewer in 1957) "Empty Arms." Even "Since I Met You Baby" (1956) was fundamentally a country song, pointing to Hunter's entwined country and gospel roots. Perhaps his best country performance was the 1959 cover of Bill Anderson's honky-tonk weeper "City Lights" on Dot, a beautiful vehicle for his velvety, sentimental voice.

The '60s were a leaner period, a process of hopping from label to label without a long-term deal. Sides were released on Capitol, Smash, Vee-Jay, Stax, Goldwax, Veep, and Sound Stage 7 without any real success. Veep had the nice country ballad "Did She Ask About Me" in 1967, while the following year saw a version of the Charms's "Ivory Tower" on SS7. Happily, the '70s rescued him from ignominious obscurity in the form of Epic's *Return of Ivory Joe Hunter* album, recorded at the Sam Phillips studio in Memphis with the aid of Isaac Hayes, Bowlegs Miller, and the backing vocals of Rhodes, Chalmers & Rhodes. Included were versions of all his great hits—"Since I Met You Baby," "Empty Arms," and "I Almost Lost My Mind" among them.

Appropriately, Hunter's final album was *I've Always Been Country* (1973), recorded at Jack Clement's and Pete Drake's studios in Nashville.

At last he had the country band he'd always wanted; that it consisted of seasoned soul sidemen like Reggie Young, Tommy Cogbill, and Charlie McCoy, as well as Buddy Spicher (fiddle) and Lloyd Green (steel), was a nice touch. Engineered by Stan Kesler, it featured a new "City Lights" plus versions of Merle Haggard's "Today I Started Loving You Again," the Glaser Brothers' "Streets of Baltimore," and (a fitting Texan choice) Bob Wills's "San Antonio Rose."

Tragically, not long after finishing the album, Hunter was struck down with lung cancer. As his condition worsened and medical bills mounted, a benefit concert was organized by the Grand Ole Opry in October 1974. It was a measure of the extent to which he brought black and white music together that the benefit united on one stage Tammy Wynette, housewife matriarch of country, and Isaac Hayes, macho godfather of soul. Others featured at the concert included George Jones and Sonny James, the latter of whom had just enjoyed a country million-seller with "Since I Met You Baby." Hunter himself was brought on in a wheelchair, only to die a month later in Memphis.

Big Al Downing

Another R&B singer who wound up in the country field was Big Al Downing, the giant Oklahoman produced by Lelan Rogers on the Carlton, Lenox, and Silver Fox labels. Born in 1940, Downing heard country and western long before he heard the blues: "I was always around farmers, hauling hay and stuff, and they'd have radios in their tractor-trailers that played nothing but country music. We also had what we called the country hoedowns, where you had harmonica, guitar, and a fiddle, and you mixed black gospel songs and old white country songs like 'Red River Valley.'"

At sixteen, Downing joined white rockabilly band the Poe-Kats, led by the Elvis-style Bobby Poe. They were a rock'n'roll party band, with a white frontman who could take off all the greased-quiff redneck rebels and a black piano player, Downing, who could mimic Little Richard and Fats Domino. (On "Just Around the Corner" and "Oh! Baby," Downing rolled them both into one.) "Fats was the biggest influence on me—he was a guy that white people liked, a white man's black man. At the time, we called rock'n'roll the black-white sound, and he commercialized that. It wasn't really blues and it wasn't really country."

With Vernon Sandusky on guitar, the Poe-Kats played beer joints and Veterans of Foreign Wars halls for "whatever they'd throw in the bucket." Adding drummer Joe Brawley, they cut the splendid "Down on the Farm" in Fort Worth and were promptly hired as a backing band for Capitol's rockabilly star Wanda Jackson. "There wasn't as much prejudice as you'd expect," Downing recalled, "even though I'd stand beside her and sing with her. There'd be times when the others would have to sneak me into a hotel with a towel over my head, but I never heard any racist remarks."

Before breaking with her, the Poe-Kats played on Jackson's "Let's Have a Party" and "Mean Mean Man" in Hollywood, then headed east to Boston. In 1959, Downing hooked up for the first time with Lelan Rogers, who took him to Cosimo Matassa's studio in New Orleans to record a very Domino-ish version of Gene Sullivan's country hit "When My Blue Moon Turns to Gold Again." While he continued to gig and record with the Poe-Kats, Downing cut another solo country song, an uptempo cover of Marty Robbins's "Story of My Life," in 1962. "I always wanted to do country but nobody else wanted me to," he told me. "They always said my voice was too heavy. When Ray Charles and Esther Phillips started singing country it gave me some hope."

In 1963, after Domino himself had recorded some of his songs (e.g., "The Land of Make Believe"), Downing was paired by Rogers with "Little" Esther Phillips. Curiously, they didn't record any country material, just two songs—"You Never Miss Your Water" and "If You Want It (I Got It)"—in a lighthearted Brook Benton/Dinah Washington vein. Rogers, however, did produce Downing on the lovely Lenox side "Mr. Hurt Walked In," which combined the Solomon Burke of "Just Out of Reach" with the Esther Phillips of "Release Me."

Like many white musicians of the time, Downing's fellow Poe-Kats decided that—with a little grooming—they could be America's Beatles. All they had to do was ditch their 250 lb black pianist, and they'd be all set for superstardom as the Chartbusters. So much for the Beatles' championing of black R&B. "They wanted the teenage female market," said Downing, who was left behind at the Washington D.C. club where they'd been working. The rest of his '60s were spent leading a seven-piece James Brown–style band around American army bases across the world. Only when he was reunited with Rogers and signed to Silver Fox at the end of the decade did he get another shot at recording. Neither "Cornbread Row" nor "Medley of Soul" (three Four Tops songs segued into one side) was as good as the self-penned "I'll Be Your Fool Once More" on Rogers's own House of the Fox label. Cut at Muscle Shoals with Maceo Parker and the King's Men (James Brown's band), this was black country soul at its understated best, a spare and simple ballad Downing revived when he finally "went country" at the end of the '70s. "I'd gotten with Gloria Gaynor's producer Tony Bongiovi and had a disco hit called 'I'll Be Holding On,'" he said. "One day when we were looking for a follow-up, I started playing some of my old country songs at the piano, and Tony said that's what we should be doing."

Signing to Warner Brothers in 1979, Downing made the country Top 20 with the twee Uncle Tom tale of "Mr. Jones," after which he scored several more hits with Warners. 1982's *Big Al Downing* album offered a taste of the man's somewhat clichéd songs: a plaintive George Jones ballad in "Just Strangers," a yee-haw redneck ball in "Beer Drinkin' People." More soulful was the 1984 single "There'll Never Be a Better Night for Bein' Wrong."

Downing made his home in country, and that's where he stayed: "When I was doing disco and that, I had to be so hip, I couldn't be myself. And country people are a lot more loyal than disco people."[27]

O.B. McClinton

Like Big Al Downing, Mississippi-born Obie Burnett McClinton started out in R&B but harbored the desire to sing country. "The only difference between them," he reflected, "is the back-up instruments. Most people think the blues is black man's music and country is white man's music, but the only difference is that the blues is performed to

---

27 Downing's most loyal audience turned out to be the rockabilly fanatics who packed out his shows in Europe. It was for such diehards that he made such albums as 1996's *Rockin' and Rollin.'*

a harmonic and heavy drum beat, while country is done with a guitar and light drums. In R&B, it's the music that's predominant; in country it's the words."

McClinton's father was a farmer and Baptist preacher who abhorred rhythm and blues but permitted his son to listen to country radio: "By the time I was old enough to realize that country singers were red-necks and that there *weren't* any black ones, I'd developed a love for the music, and my voice had developed a deep Southern twang. I got in a lot of fights at school because of it."

In 1962, the twang notwithstanding, McClinton won a choral scholarship to Rust College in Holly Springs, where he stayed for four years. It was during this time that he was discovered by Quinton Claunch and signed as "Obie" to Goldwax. Not cutting it as an R&B singer, McClinton nonetheless found success as a writer when James Carr recorded "She's Better Than You," "A Man Needs a Woman," and "You Got My Mind Messed Up." These Otis Redding–derived country-soul hits led to work at FAME in Muscle Shoals, where he penned Clarence Carter's "You Can't Miss What You Can't Measure" and Willie Hightower's "Back Road into Town." Redding himself cut "Keep Your Arms Around Me" on the *Sings Soul Ballads* album.

Still McClinton itched to sing the country music he loved, one that only intensified with the increasing success of Charley Pride. One day he was writing in the Muscle Shoals Holiday Inn when he learned that Stax A&R chief Al Bell was in the room next door. Wasting not a moment he pressed himself on Bell and played him his country songs. Bell liked them, and, in January 1971, signed McClintnon to Enterprise, the Stax subsidiary that gave the world Isaac Hayes's Barry White–style reworkings of "Walk On By" and "By the Time I Get to Phoenix."

Kicking off with "Country Music's My Thing"—and recording four albums in as many years—McClinton sounded like an African American version of Merle Haggard. His best records were country versions of soul songs (William Bell's "My Whole World Is Falling Down," Wilson Pickett's "Don't Let the Green Grass Fool You"), though he even got around to covering Haggard's notorious redneck anthem "Okie from Muskogee." After Stax's collapse in 1975, he signed to Mercury and released "Black Speck," the funky tale of an African American country singer (based on Charley Pride) performing in a smalltown club: "I did the song because I wanted blacks to know that I relate to being black. When I first went to Stax, I made it clear that if being black and proud would hinder me from succeeding, then I didn't want to succeed."

The Mercury stint didn't last long: in quick succession he moved on to ABC-Dot, Epic, and finally Sunbird. On Epic, he was produced by Buddy Killen, charting in 1978 with "Hello, This Is Anna" and the catchy "Natural Love," while Sunbird released an album distastefully titled *Chocolate Cowboy* in 1981. He died of cancer in 1987, aged just 47.

Hank and Lefty Raised His Country Soul

An older and better singer, similarly influenced by Merle Haggard, was Stoney Edwards, born to African and native-American parents in Oklahoma in 1930.

"My folks were originally from North Carolina, the kind of people referred to as 'hillbillies,'" Edwards recalled. "They played and sang country music, and I grew up around banjos and fiddles on our farm. I never heard R&B until I was a grown man, and it did nothing for me when I heard it."

Edwards grew up on Western Swing and the Texas honky-tonk of Lefty Frizzell, but in the mid-'50s—like Frizzell himself—he moved to California. With no ambitions as a singer, he worked as a cowboy, a janitor, and a pipe fitter before becoming a machinist in a Richmond shipyard. Only through a serious accident there was he forced to write and sing songs. Discovered at a benefit show for Bob Wills in Oakland, he signed to Capitol in June 1970 and released *Stoney Edwards: A Country Singer* the following year. His superb hard-country baritone was like a blend of Frizzell and Haggard, best heard on the 1973 hit "Hank and Lefty Raised My Country Soul."

Edwards stayed at Capitol six years, recording such albums as *Mississippi You're on My Mind* (1975) and *Blackbird* (1976) and doing beautiful things with songs like Kris Kristofferson's "For the Good Times" and Harlan Howard's "I Don't Believe I'll Fall In Love Today." Chip Taylor's "Blackbird" went one step beyond McClinton's "Black

Speck," de-tabooing the word "nigger" in its story of a black couple instilling race pride in their son. In 1978, Edwards signed to JMI, a label formed by ex-Sun/Charley Pride producer Jack Clement, and cut the soulful, Brook Bentonesque "If I Had It to Do All Over Again." Finally, in 1980, he wound up on the Music America label, recording such gems as Curtis Wayne's "No Way to Drown a Memory," Tommy Collins's "Because It Isn't You," and Merle Haggard's even more notorious "Fightin' Side of Me."

"I'd like to see more blacks in country," Edwards said in the '70s. "But I want them to understand it, to be aware of people like Jimmie Rodgers, Bob Wills, and the Carter Family. I want them to respect it and know what it stands for. I'm not in it for a fast buck."[28]

Charley Pride

Charley Pride may have been country music's token African American, but he was a remarkably successful token. *Cashbox* named him the top-selling male country artist of the '70s, and at one time he'd sold more records for RCA than anyone except Elvis Presley. Part of the reason for this was that he hardly sounded black at all, making his assimilation and acceptance by the country audience easier than it might have been. True, some Southern DJs initially referred to him as their "good nigra"—while his first tours in the civil rights period of the mid '60s had frequent moments of tension and nastiness—but in retrospect Pride had a surprisingly smooth ride.

He was born in 1938 in Sledge, the "Mississippi cotton-picking Delta town" commemorated in his 1974 hit of that name. Though this was blues country, Opry stars Ernest Tubb and Webb Pierce became Pride's favorites. At fourteen he began teaching himself Hank Williams songs on a cheap Sears-Roebuck guitar. Music at this point was a sideline to baseball, his major obsession: by 1961 he was playing as an outfielder for the Memphis Red Sox in the Negro American League. After a two-year stint in the army, he signed with the California Angels, working as a zinc smelter in Montana in between seasons. It was in the Montana mining town of Helena that he began singing part-time

---

28 After releasing a comeback album, 1991's *Just For Old Time's Sake,* Edwards died in April 1997.

in a country and western club, only to be heard one night by touring Nashville singer Red Sovine and persuaded to audition for Chet
Atkins in Nashville.

By 1966 Pride was signed to RCA and enjoying, with "Snakes
Crawl At Night," the first of his many hits. In November, *Country
Charley Pride* was released, and many whites learned to their amazement that they'd been buying singles by an African American. To top
it off, the following January Ernest Tubb welcomed him to the stage
of the Opry, the first black artist to play there since harmonica player
Deford Bailey in 1941.

African Americans dubbed Pride an Uncle Tom for singing "the
Man's music." *National Lampoon* even published a cartoon of him
applying blackface. Meanwhile he toured the deep South with such
liberal denizens of Nashville as Willie Nelson, who (the story goes)
once kissed him full on the mouth to stun a Louisiana audience into
overlooking his color. The '70s gave him an amazing hit run, com-
mencing with "I'm Just Me" in 1971 and taking in such huge sellers
as "Kiss an Angel Good Mornin'," "She's Too Good to Be True,"
"Amazing Love," and "Then Who Am I." Few of these were anything
but bland, predictable Nashville records—"my songs are safe, that's the
image that works best for me"—but Pride at least had a strong voice,
which was more than could be said for many Nashville stars.

In August 1985, Pride left RCA after twenty years, saying he was
unhappy with the "youth" orientation the company was pursuing.
The "token nigra" had become a pillar of the country establishment.

Blacks in the Saddle Again

These, then, were some of the African Americans who, to varying
degrees, made it as country singers. There were countless others who
tried and failed. The only black female singer to make it to the Opry
was Linda Martell, a South Carolinan who signed to Shelby Singleton's
Plantation label in 1969 and appeared on the show in August of that
year.

Originally a soul singer, Martell found she got a better response
with country when performing at the air force base outside Charleston.
Nashville beckoned and Singleton produced "Color Him Father,"

a single that made No. 22 on *Billboard*'s country chart. An album, tastelessly titled *Color Me Country,* included several songs by Margaret Lewis and Myra Smith, the Shreveport team who wrote for such S.S.S. International artists as Johnny Adams. These were rather self-consciously "country" songs like "The Wedding Cake" and "Old Letter Song," although "Bad Case of the Blues," Martell's only other success, was reasonable. She was not a particularly good singer—and certainly not much of a yodeller—and her eventual disappearance from the Nashville scene probably didn't break too many hearts.

Another female singer was the quaintly-named Ruby Falls. Born on a farm near Jackson, Tennessee, she gained most of her singing experience in the Midwest before moving to Nashville. On 50 States Charta Records, she had the *Sweet Country Lady* album and a handful of decent sides that included "Beware of the Woman," "Show Me Where," and "He Loves Me All to Pieces."

Bobbie Roberson began her career when she moved from Brewton, Alabama, to New York in 1969; after five years of singing in soul and funk groups, she returned to Alabama and cut the 1980 country album *Was Young Love Born to Die?* on her husband/manager's Bolivia label.

Oklahoman Maxine Weldon was brought up in Bakersfield, California, and exposed to the Merle Haggard/Buck Owens scene there. She sang country in Hawaii and Japan before joining the rock circus in San Francisco in the late '60s. Even *Star Trek* actress Cindy Lu embarked on a country career in a Billy Vera & Judy Clay–style duo with a white male singer. When Indiana-born Terri Adams took a job singing country at a bar outside San Diego in 1977, she became an unlikely hit with local Ku Klux Klansmen. In the gospel field, finally, the great Shirley Caesar covered such sentimental country songs as "Faded Rose" and the Wilburn Brothers' "Didn't We Papa."

Among the other male artists who made occasional black dents in the white domain of country were G. Hawl Jones, who played bass for Hank Williams Jr. before recording '70s solo sides on Dot produced by Pete Drake, and Eugene "Texas" Ray, a harmonica player from Lubbock who'd been out of the music business for twenty years when he came through Nashville in 1974 and signed to Hickory Hollow Music. Others included John Goodwine (with "Don't Treat Me Like a

Stray" on Phinal Sound in 1976), Leo Hall (a Georgian in his sixties), Welton Lane (with Dallas Frazier's "I Just Got Tired of Being Poor," produced on Epic by Kelso Hurston), organist Jimmy E. Russell, Carrol Washington, Tommy Brooks, James Allen, Howdy Glenn, Cecil Williams, Casey Anderson, and Rosie "the Midnight Cowboy" (aka Mr. Country Soul). Dwight Rucker was one half of male duo Malchak and Rucker.

This was quite apart from the many undocumented cases of rural African Americans still drawing on the old "common stock" of folk and hillbilly songs. If it hadn't been for the discovery of singers like the Virginian John Jackson in the mid-'60s, we'd never have known such a process of exchange was going on. Born in 1924, Jackson grew up in the highlands of Rappahannack County, exposed to a music that was equal parts Blind Lemon Jefferson and the Carter Family, Jimmie Rodgers, and Blind Boy Fuller. He played blues but also joined a white hillbilly band as a guitarist and even learned the banjo. When discovered by Arhoolie Records in 1965, he was still playing Jimmie Rodgers's "T. B. Blues." Two years later he recorded the Delmore Brothers' "Gonna Lay Down My Old Guitar."

Also on Arhoolie was the Texan L. C. "Good Rockin'" Robinson, a Gatemouth Brown–style bluesman who played fiddle and steel guitar and settled in Oakland in the '50s. Robinson had learned the steel guitar from Bob Wills sideman Leon McAuliffe and recorded for the Blues on Blues label as well as for Arhoolie. Two other African Americans to cut pure steel-guitar albums were Doug Quattlebaum, with 1961's *Softee Man Blues* and Freddie Roulette, with *Sweet Funky Steel* on Janus in 1975.[29]

Even the singing cowboys exerted a fascination over African Americans. Leadbelly sang "Out on the Western Plains," while Otis Blackwell—the New York songwriter who penned million-sellers like Presley's "All Shook Up" and Jerry Lee Lewis's "Great Balls of

---

29 A less rural example of the "common stock" songster was the late Ted Hawkins, who sang Hank Williams's "Your Cheatin' Heart" and Webb Pierce's "There Stands the Glass" alongside his favorite Sam Cooke songs. After being plucked from boardwalk-busking obscurity on L.A.'s Venice Beach, he released his major-label debut (*The Next Hundred Years*) in 1994 but died the following year.

Fire"—remembered his love for the genre thus: "Growing up, the blues was our thing, but my thing was cowboys. Tex Ritter was my man! Naturally, blues was always there. If it was black it was blues. But I've always cared a lot for country music. I'd go to the pictures and see three features of nothing but cowboys and cartoons."

In fact, there were African Americans in westerns long before *Blazing Saddles* and *Silverado*. In the rush of "singing cowboy" films that followed Gene Autry's success in the '30s, one series featured big-band singer Herb Jeffries.[30]

In real life, too, there were post-Emancipation black cowboys who sang and played the fiddle: Big Jim Simpson came up the Chisholm Trail and settled in Wyoming; fiddlers George Washington and Sabrien Bates rode with Billy the Kid in the bloody Lincoln County feud.

By the time the halcyon days of country soul were over in the early '70s, African American artists had begun to pay homage to country music in ever greater numbers. As we've already seen, singers other than Ray Charles had made country albums—even Nat King Cole recorded one, 1962's *Ramblin' Rose,* while baritone crooner Arthur Prysock cut a country LP on King—but few were Southern soul artists.[31]

Tina Turner changed that when she recorded *Tina Turns the Country On* (1974), recalling her childhood as little Annie Mae Bullock in the cottonfields of Tennessee. Two years later, Bobby Womack followed a succession of superb Muscle Shoals–recorded soul albums with the unfairly overlooked *B. W. Goes C'n'W,* originally entitled *Step Aside, Charley Pride, and Give Another Nigger a Try* (and then *Black in the Saddle Again*).

"I was very sincere about that album," Womack told me, "but people categorize you and they say *"What?!"* But country and western is my roots; it's deeply rooted in all my songs and lyrics. My people came

---

30 Jeffries was still going strong at the ripe old age of 80, the year after releasing his 1995 Warner Western album *The Bronze Buckaroo Rides Again.* A song from that record, "I'm A Happy Cowboy" was the final track on the *From Where I Stand* box set.

31 One of the more unlikely was the 1965 album *The Supremes Sing Country, Western and Pop.* The group's version of Floyd Tillman's "It Makes No Difference Now" was included on the second CD of *From Where I Stand.*

from the hills of Virginia and played a lot of it. I mean, Charlie Rich, he's *baaad!* You ain't gonna tell me he ain't soulful, bending the melody like he does . . ."

Womack's love for Rich showed through in the album's versions of "Behind Closed Doors" and "I Take It On Home," both turned to inimitably Womackian ends. Other tracks included Eddy Arnold's "Bouquet of Roses," Floyd Cramer's "Last Date" (with a lyric added by brother Cecil), and "Tarnished Rings," a wonderfully hoary chestnut with the first verse taken by Bobby's father Solomon. Sam Cooke's "Tired of Living in the Country" made an amusingly tongue-in-cheek inclusion. Womack had flirted with country before—"Point of No Return" and "Copper Kettle" on *Looking for a Love Again* (1974)—but *B. W. Goes C'n'W* came as a shock to his fans and sold disastrously. Despite this you could still hear the country in Womack as late as 1985, on the superb "No Matter How High I Get (I'll Still Be Looking Up to You)."

A comparatively late African American tribute to country came in 1981 from Millie Jackson, the empress of X-rated Southern soul. Country had been a part of Jackson's upbringing: raised by grandparents in rural Georgia, the only TV program she was permitted to watch was *The Tennessee Ernie Ford Show.* Twenty years later she was at Muscle Shoals Sound, recording her eternal triangle masterworks *Caught Up* and *Still Caught Up* and including on them such country songs as "Loving Arms" and "I Still Love You (You Still Love Me)."

"I think the reason some country albums by black artists haven't been successful," Jackson said in 1978, "is because they've done them *too* country. Ray Charles didn't sing 'I Can't Stop Loving You' with a nasal drawl; he sang it like he sings everything else, and so it was his most successful album." Three years later she emphasized the point by opening *Just a L'il Bit Country* with a funked-up version of that Don Gibson song, featuring James Stroud on drums and the Muscle Shoals Horns on brass. A similar job was done on Harlan Howard's "Pick Me Up On Your Way Down," a 1958 hit by Charlie Walker set to a fast disco beat. Other tracks, though, were more respectful of country tradition: Tammy Wynette's "Until I Get It Right," covered by Bettye Swann in 1973, and John Conlee's "Rose Colored Glasses."

With typical bawdiness, Jackson closed the album with "Anybody That Don't Like Millie Jackson," her personal interpretation of Hank Williams Jr.'s coarse challenge to detractors.

B.B. King's *Love Me Tender* (1982) was a great country-soul album, recorded variously in Nashville, New York and Muscle Shoals. David Briggs played keyboards and arranged the songs, which included Don Gibson's "Legend in My Own Time," Ivory Joe Hunter's "Since I Met You Baby," and the Conway Twitty–Troy Seals number "One of Those Nights." Best of all was a gentle reading of Mickey Newbury's "You've Always Got the Blues," covered back in 1975 by B.B.'s pal Bobby Bland. (In the mid-'70s, incidentally, Bland lost guitarist Mel Brown and drummer Charles Polk to Nashville rebel Tompall Glaser's Outlaw Band, in which they played for three years. Glaser called it a "hillbilly blues band," though the blues element was slight.)

That even such a symbol of black power as James Brown recorded a country album (albeit unreleased) was further evidence of the pull country music exerted on Southerners of all colors and persuasions. Among the country songs Brown recorded were the standard "Tennessee Waltz" and Roy Drusky's 1961 hit "Three Hearts in a Tangle." A minor uproar occurred when the Godfather was invited on to the Grand Ole Opry by Porter Wagoner, whose keyboard player had been a member of Brown's band for two years. Incensed Nashville artists Jean Sheperd and Justin Tubb made it known clearly and loudly just how defiled they felt the sacred stage had been by this invitation. Untroubled by such outbursts, Brown performed a medley of "Your Cheatin' Heart," "Georgia On My Mind," and "Tennessee Waltz," then followed with some funk. "I felt I got as much praise as a white man who goes into a black church and puts $100 in the collection plate," he said coolly.

Brown was that rare case of a Southerner who'd urbanized himself without losing his rural roots. For a man who, during the black riots of the '60s claimed to be a racist, appearing on the Opry was quite a step. But then inside ghetto-funky Soul Brother No. 1 had always lurked the staunch Southern patriot of "America Is My Home." Significantly, too, he'd cut many of his big '60s hits in the North Carolina country studio of Arthur "Guitar Boogie" Smith.

The future of African American involvement in country music was always going to be limited. White country singers themselves became more soulful and black sounding, leaving behind the constricted, clenched-teeth delivery of yesteryear. Coupled with this, a vast majority of the white musicians who'd helped create the Southern soul sound in Memphis, Muscle Shoals, Jackson, and Shreveport moved to Nashville. Between them they turned the Nashville Sound around.

"The old Southern soul sound became what country is today," said Rick Hall's old drummer Jerry Carrigan. "A lot of Nashville records from the last three or four years are nothing but an extension of Southern R&B. We just got people playing in different grooves."

As with the Pointer Sisters' lovely "Fairy Tale," which topped the country charts in 1974, African American artists periodically took a stab at country. Diana Ross released a 1975 country single called "Sorry Doesn't Always Make It Right"; Lionel Richie wrote songs for Kenny Rogers; Booker T. Jones produced Willie Nelson's standards album *Stardust*. Still others came home to country for good, using it as a comfortable retirement home. A new Charley Pride, however, failed to emerge from all this.[32]

---

32 The experience of Cleve Francis, who grew so frustrated after cutting three albums for Liberty in the '90s that he resumed his medical practice, didn't augur well. Then again, the music of a singer like Barrence Whitfield—whose catalog included *Hillbilly Voodoo* and *Cowboy Mambo*, '90s albums recorded with singer-songwriter Tom Russell—suggested that black-white cross-pollination was alive and well in modern-day America. More recently, former Hootie & the Blowfish frontman Darius Rucker has succeeded in making the transition from roots rock to mainstream country. Rucker was the first African American to win the New Artist Award from the Country Music Association, in 2009, and only the second to win any award at all from the CMA. He was also one of the stellar guests on 2012's *Tuskegee*, Lionel Richie's album of countrified versions of his most popular hits.\

7 Separate Ways

Around the turn of the decade—the beginning of the '70s—the country-soul sound of the South began to decline. Country and R&B parted company and went their separate ways.

Jerry Wexler: "How did the Southern sound lose its momentum? I don't know, but I just knew in my bones it was gonna happen, and quickly. I mean, we'd had Joe Tex, Arthur Conley, Wilson Pickett, Solomon Burke, the Sweet Inspirations, Sam & Dave, King Curtis, the most incredible roster . . . and in one year it was all gone. Stopped, ran into a wall."

Wexler's "wall" consisted of several factors. One was that the new black pride of the late '60s bred mistrust of whites, simultaneously fostering a funkier, more ghetto-oriented soul sound. The streets erupted in race riots and needed a soundtrack to echo them. Albums such as Sly and the Family Stone's *There's a Riot Goin' On* (1971) fitted the bill. "Soul" music had moved on from the gospel passion of Atlantic's artists: its new leaders—Sly, Curtis Mayfield, Marvin Gaye, Stevie Wonder, George Clinton—were doing startling and innovatory things with R&B. Otis Redding, moreover—"an ambassador for us all," in Joe Tex's words—was gone.

A paradox needs to be restated: in the South, where the very worst racial oppression occurred, black and white musicians were arguably closer than they were anywhere else. At the time of his death, Redding himself was still being managed by white boyhood friend Phil Walden. Yet not even the unlikely alliance of "rednecks" and

179

"niggers" in Southern soul could sustain this "country-black" sound in the '70s. "Otis would not have won a diction contest," Walden said to me. "His pronunciation was very rural compared to the sophistication of Motown artists."

Against the new giants of Motown—"artists" taking control of their own material and production—the old-fashioned gospel balladeers of the South were not in a strong position to compete. The dominant new sound was the super-slick orchestration of producers such as Norman Whitfield and Philadelphia International's Gamble & Huff, and it left the humble "head arrangements" of Memphis and Muscle Shoals trailing.

A turning point in black-white relations in the South occurred at the 1968 National Association of Television and Radio Announcers' Convention in Miami, where black militants calling themselves the Fair Play Committee made known their feelings about the white "carpetbaggers" who'd exploited their music.

"By the end of the decade," Phil Walden recalled, "a lot of the results of the civil rights era had served to urbanize black music. The Miami convention signalled the end for me, and my interest waned after that. A lot of the people we'd considered friends were suddenly calling us 'blue-eyed devils,' and several white people who'd made substantial contributions to black music were threatened or beaten up. It just really turned me off. It was shakedown time, you know, and I didn't care to be shaken down."

"There was this bullshit about preempting and co-opting us and taking over the companies and radio stations," said Wexler, whose life was threatened but who was obliged to talk like the macho intellectual he was. "It was all rhetoric, but at the same time I *was* disenchanted by some of the things that went down."

"Guys like Rap Brown were getting up and trying to scare the hell out of us," Rick Hall told me. "I wasn't scared because I'd seen black guys get drunk and go crazy in the studio, but the Wexlers and people like that hadn't experienced that kind of confrontation."

"I remember some heavyweight guys slapping Jerry and Larry Utall around," said Dan Penn, "and immediately after that white people quit signing blacks. I mean, it wasn't only just that one time, it was during the whole time when blacks were getting angry and Martin Luther King Jr. was shot. But that's when the whole Muscle Shoals era came to a screeching halt, when the NAACP told us we had to do this and that, and it very quickly began to disintegrate. There was a real lull. Didn't nobody get scared, but it came down real fast."

The changes weren't immediate—African American singers were still working with white session bands and producers in the '70s—but the heyday of Southern soul was over. Stax would soon go bust, while studios such as FAME and Muscle Shoals Sound would branch out into white pop, rock, and—inevitably—country. Already Chips Moman had recorded Elvis Presley and Neil Diamond at American, along with local pop acts the Gentrys ("Keep On Dancing") and the Box Tops. The latter group he entrusted to Dan Penn.

"I told Chips, give me someone to cut, it don't matter how good or bad they are," Penn said. "So he gave me this little group and a tape with 'The Letter' on it. My only communication with the group was to tell Alex Chilton to sing 'aeroplane' instead of 'airplane'!" A No. 1 hit in August 1967, "The Letter" was a first indication to the likes of Penn and Moman that there might be more money in black-flavored Southern pop than in soul music. The Box Tops went on to record Penn and Oldham's "Cry Like a Baby" and Fritts and Hinton's "Choo Choo Train."

While it's hard to believe Penn loved working with the Box Tops, the group afforded the opportunity for some tongue-in-cheek fun. "I Met Her in Church," for instance, was a hilarious mish-mash of pop, gospel choruses, pedal steel guitars, and bizarre Jimmy Webb–style time changes, giving the distinct impression that everyone involved was well and truly out of it.

A more obvious sign that things were changing was that Atlantic itself—the leading R&B label of 1968—started to pull out of black music, setting up Cotillion as a soul subsidiary but concentrating on white rock signings like Led Zeppelin and Crosby, Stills & Nash. "The main reason Atlantic became a power in white rock," Wexler said, "is because we took the black thing as far as it would go. We couldn't get it over the way Motown had, and here's the point: Atlantic made records for proletarian black adults, Motown made them for middle-class white teenagers. However Berry Gordy got that idea, it was one of the most brilliant things that ever happened. We never got the white market, we never crossed. I mean, Aretha never even had a platinum album."

Symbolic of the era's end was the purchase of Atlantic for over $15 million by Warner Communications, with Wexler and Ahmet Ertegun staying on as executives and producers. Larry Utall's Bell, too, began pulling back from soul, switching over to the MOR and bubblegum markets with acts such as Dawn, the 5th Dimension, and the Partridge Family.

Muscle Shoals, Miami, and Macon
1. FAME

Down in Muscle Shoals, Solomon Burke's 1969 album *Proud Mary* was one of Bell Records' last Southern outings before Larry Utall turned to pop. It was also one of the last great FAME sessions to use the Roger Hawkins/ David Hood/Jimmy Johnson/Barry Beckett band, who in April of that year broke away from Rick Hall to form Muscle Shoals Sound.

A founding father of country soul, Burke had left Adantic after eight years, the last few being less successful than the first four but still producing such superlative sides as "I Feel A Sin Comin' On," "(Take Me) Just As I Am," and Mickey Newbury's "Time Is A Thief." As it happened, Wexler had grown a little tired of his old protégé: "As soon as Solomon had some hits under his belt, he got lazy and wouldn't do his homework. He'd come in not knowing the song, and as a substitute do all this over-souling and all these fake turns, not even close to the melody."

Oversouling, though, was the last thing Solomon did at FAME. If anything, on such masterful performances as "Uptight Good Woman" and the brilliantly spare version of Chuck Willis's "What Am I Living For?," he was too restrained. Then again he could flip from the control of a Brook Benton to the roar of a John Fogerty, the Creedence Clearwater Revival frontman whose song provided the title track for the album. Claims could once again be made for Burke as one of the three or four greatest singers in the history of soul music.

Along with *Proud Mary*, the last Hawkins/Hood/Johnson/Beckett sessions at FAME were Atlantic ones by Wilson Pickett and sax man King Curtis. Pickett had been recording at American with his chum

Bobby Womack, but now came back to FAME to record such blistering ballads as "Back in Your Arms" and "Search Your Heart," penned
by George Jackson. On the session was slide guitarist Duane Allman,
recruited by Rick Hall after he'd come to FAME to cut demos in 1968.

The original Southern longhair, Allman was taunted by the Shoals's
good ole boys for not taking baths and all the other things hippies did or
didn't do. "Duane was probably more shaken after seeing *Easy Rider* than
Jack Newfield or Albert Goldman," Jerry Wexler observed in a 1969
Billboard piece entitled "What It Is—Is Swamp Music." It was Allman
who suggested Pickett cut the Beatles' "Hey Jude," a novel idea but one
rewarded by a Top 30 hit. Other great tracks on the album of the same
name were Bobby Womack's beautiful "People Make The World" and
Isaac Hayes and David Porter's insatiably funky "Toe Hold."

"Rick liked my playing a lot," Allman recalled of the late November
date that produced "Hey Jude." "He said, "Why don't you just go
home and get your gear and move up here?" So I rented me a little
cabin, lived alone on this lake, with big windows looking right out on
the water. I just sat there and played to myself and got used to living
without a bunch of jive Hollywood crap in my head." Recalled FAME
guitarist Jimmy Johnson, "Duane's whole career spun off that Pickett
session . . . it's amazing how one incident, one session, can change a
person's life."

The last hit cut at the studio before the split was King Curtis's wistful
instrumental version of "Games People Play," again featuring Allman.
It marked the end of a great five-year relationship—but the beginning
of the end for Muscle Shoals country soul. With only guitarist Junior
Lowe and the horn players remaining at FAME, Rick Hall built the studio's third rhythm section around former Papa Don Schroeder sidemen
Clayton Ivey (keyboards) and Jesse Boyce (bass), other recruits being
drummer Freeman Brown, Memphis guitar prodigy Travis Wammack,
and studio manager Al Cartee. Loosely they were known as the Fame
Gang and cut an instrumental album under that name in 1970.

"That rhythm section was such a mixture of influences," said Mickey
Buckins, who engineered many of the sessions at FAME from 1969 to
1973. "You'd have Travis playing rock'n'roll guitar, Junior doing real
simplified R&B licks, Jesse's funk feel, while Clayton was a jazz freak."

Hall continued to record soul acts on FAME until he closed down the label in 1974. Besides Candi Staton, they included Willie Hightower, Spencer Wiggins, and Bettye Swann. Hightower sounded like a cross between O.V. Wright and Arthur Conley, cutting O.B. McClinton's "Back Road into Town," Joe South's country-gospel classic "Walk a Mile in My Shoes," and the great "Time Has Brought About a Change," on which he sounded like Sam Cooke after a night on the tiles. Ex-Goldwax artist Wiggins was produced by Hall on a tortured version of "I'd Rather Go Blind," and by his old mentor Quinton Claunch on the pure country song "Love Me Tonight"—another classic juxtaposition of Nashville form with black gospel vocals.

As for Swann, no more affecting purveyor of country soul exists in the history of female R&B. Her tremulous, vibrato-tinged soprano remains one of the great black voices. Born in Shreveport, Louisiana, she made her debut in the early '60s with L.A. vocal group the Fawns, then recorded as a solo artist for Money and made the Top 30 with 1967's gorgeous "Make Me Yours." Signing her to Capitol in 1969, producer Wayne Shuler—son of Goldband's Eddie—quickly recognized how well her voice worked with country songs and cut her on a spellbinding version of Hank Cochran's "Don't Touch Me," a 1966 hit and Grammy winner for Cochran's wife Jeanie Seely. Two albums—*The Soul View Now!* and *Don't You Ever Get Tired (of Hurting Me?)*—followed, featuring between them eight more country songs: some, like "Sweet Dreams" and "Then You Can Tell Me Goodbye," already covered by soul acts, others (Merle Haggard's "Just Because You Can't Be Mine," John D. Loudermilk's "You're Up to Your Same Old Tricks Again," Ray Price's "Don't You Ever Get Tired") newly adapted. If Tank Jernigan's arrangements were a little overdone, the voice came through pure and clear.

It was through Rick Hall's Capitol connections that he came to take over Swann's production duties in 1970. Doubtless he recognized the potential she had in proper Southern surroundings. After just one spine-tingling FAME side, "I'm Just Living a Lie," he produced such Atlantic hits as the George Jackson/Mickey Buckins song "Victim of a Foolish Heart" and the Merle Haggard classic "Today I Started Loving You Again." "What a fool I was, thinkin' I'd get by/ With only these few million tears that I've cried," she wept on the latter. Equally fine was the same year's version of Tammy Wynette's hit "Til I Get It Right." "Bettye was a jewel," Mickey Buckins recalled. "We could have done a lot more with her if it hadn't been for the old story of the husband being involved in the management."

In 1975, Atlantic turned Swann over to Millie Jackson's producer Brad Shapiro at Muscle Shoals Sound. There she continued in her country-soul vein with Curly Putman and Red Lane's "All the Way In Or All the Way Out" and Phillip Mitchell's "Be Strong Enough to Hold On," perhaps her all-time masterpiece. Mitchell was a lanky African American from Kentucky, a writer and singer who combined the country form of the '60s ballad with the new "cheatin'" style of the '70s. He wrote for Millie Jackson, Bobby Womack, and others, but this aching country ballad was the greatest thing he ever put his name to. "He's one of the best writers I've ever known," Jackson stated. "He never got the recognition he deserved." With its luscious horn and string arrangement by Mike Lewis, "Be Strong Enough" was also one of the last great Shoals country-soul records:

> *She's just using your little children*
> *To try and get next to you*
> *I know that's only her excuse*
> *To come by here, to see you,*
> *And to call you on the telephone*
> *You were weak enough to love me*
> *Be strong enough to hold on.*
> (Muscle Shoals Sound Publishing Co., 1976)

Candi Staton herself continued to record with Rick Hall, right up until she switched to Miami producer Dave Crawford and hit with 1976's wonderful "Young Hearts Run Free." Few of her last FAME tracks were anything but 100 percent Southern country soul: songs such as "Someone You Use," Marlin Greene and Eddie Hinton's "Sure As Sin" (pronounced "seeyun"), and George Jackson's "I'm Gonna Hold On (to What I Got This Time)." Mac Davis's "Something's Burning" had been a 1970 hit for Kenny Rogers, while Hank Cochran's "It's Not Love (But It's Not Bad)" put Merle Haggard in the R&B charts in 1972. Less countrified were the last FAME waxings of Candi's husband Clarence Carter, though *60 Minutes with Clarence Carter* (1973) closed with "I Got Another Woman," a 6/8 ballad which could have come straight from the Penn/Oldham school circa 1965.

These productions notwithstanding, Hall followed the example of Chips Moman in Memphis and eased away from soul. Soon after losing the Muscle Shoals Sound quartet, he began recording such pop acts as Mac Davis, Bobbie Gentry, and the Osmonds. The hits were big ones: Davis's "Baby Don't Get Hooked On Me," Gentry's "Fancy," and the Osmonds' "One Bad Apple," a George Jackson song—intended for the Jackson Five—that caused a furor in the black community for its blatant white appropriation of the Jacksons' style. Davis—a kind of MOR version of Tony Joe White—had done session work at the Sam Phillips studio in Memphis before perfecting his easy listening country-soul style, while Gentry was best-known for her mythic Mississippi vignette "Ode to Billie Joe."

In 1971, Hall was named *Billboard's* Producer of the Year, due recognition for the amazing number of hits he'd chalked up. A few months later, he opened a studio in Memphis, entrusting to Mickey Buckins the task of unearthing new R&B talent there. It was mistimed. "By the time I got there," Buckins said, "Stax was looking shaky, American had wound down, and Chips was getting ready to move to Atlanta. We cut some demos in Memphis, and I did a great project on Travis Wammack, but nothing really happened." In the end, Buckins himself went to Atlanta, replaced by Chattanooga engineer Sonny Limbo, who brought to FAME Ken Bell (guitar), Roger Clark (drums), and Tim Henson (keyboards), players who filled gaps left by the departures of Junior Lowe, Freeman Brown, and Clayton Ivey.

Hall continued to cut pop, as hits such as Donny Osmond's "Go Away Little Girl" and Paul Anka's "You're Having My Baby" made clear. "After Mac Davis," remembered Candi Staton, "Rick found out there was so much more money to be made in pop. I sat there for nineteen months with this contract, and he didn't record me once. Eventually he set me free and got me signed to Warners. I think when he first heard "Young Hearts" on the radio he nearly fell off his yacht. He didn't know I could sing so clear!"

Clarence Carter left FAME around the same time. "I don't think Rick has ever learned that the only way to keep people around you is to have them making money as well as you," he told me. "I went out to L.A. to negotiate a contract with ABC, and that was that."

In 1972, a new Muscle Shoals studio, Wishbone, was built by two ex-FAME employees, keyboard player Clayton Ivey and singer-writer Terry Woodford. Ivey had followed Barry Beckett up from Florida and eventually replaced him, while Indiana-born Woodford led a band called the Mystics (with David Hood on bass) before being signed as one of FAME's few white artists of the '60s. "It was quite a shock when I moved here at twelve years old," Woodford told me. "The segregated water fountains really freaked me out! At the same time, I was called a damn Yankee, so I felt like I was on the outside myself."

Significantly, Woodford's preferred style of soul music was not the Southern kind but the poppier sound of Tamla Motown: "The kind of music Dan Penn and the others wrote was almost total gospel to me, and I couldn't relate to it." With Ivey he began producing—for Motown, no less: "We leased the first white artist to Motown, a guy from Louisiana called Reuben Howell, and as a result they signed us exclusively as producers. We did the Commodores, the Supremes, and the Temptations. Stevie Wonder once kidded me that he wanted us to produce this terrible country song on him." The Motown connection was another sign that the Southern soul sound of FAME was waning.

2. MUSCLE SHOALS SOUND

At Muscle Shoals Sound, meanwhile, success was almost instant. Jerry Wexler switched his Atlantic acts to the new studio, causing no end of friction between Rick Hall and the Hawkins/Hood/Johnson/Beckett quartet. Even here, the first sessions—Atlantic producer Arif Mardin's covers album *Glass Onion*, Cher's *3614 Jackson Highway* (the studio's address)—could hardly have been described as soul music.

Only with Ahmet Ertegun's protégé R. B. Greaves, a half-Seminole nephew of Sam Cooke who'd started life as a country singer, did Hall's old rhythm section give Atlantic a soul hit. This was "Take a Letter, Maria," a pop-soul song with a Mexican, Tony Orlando–ish feel. "I think our records had a better shot at making the pop charts than many black-produced R&B records," Jimmy Johnson told me. "I guess that's why Wexler and everyone came down, else why maroon yourself in a studio with a bunch of white Southerners. Must have been disgusting for them!" Added Barry Beckett candidly: "We wanted to get a pop sound. We didn't want to be tied in to R&B for the rest of our lives."

The first chance to do something new and fresh with a white artist came with the debut Atlantic album by Texas-born Boz Scaggs, co-produced in May 1969 by studio engineer Marlin Greene and *Rolling Stone* editor Jann Wenner. In its balance between R&B and country (there was even a version of Jimmie Rodgers's "Waiting For a Train"), *Boz Scaggs* heralded a wave of post-psychedelic Southern rock. Appropriately, Duane Allman—soon to lead the first and greatest Southern rock troupe—was in attendance alongside guitarists Jimmy Johnson and Eddie Hinton. The standout track was a 13-minute version of bluesman Fenton Robinson's "Loan Me a Dime," ancestor of every extended blues-rock epic and one of Duane's great claims to guitar-heroism.

Beckett: "We hadn't clicked with Cher or Arif Mardin—they were dressed up better echo-wise, but we didn't hit grooves—but along comes Boz with 'Loan Me a Dime' and . . . well, we'd got to the point where you normally fade and somehow we hadn't got far enough, so we just carried on building it up and kept the tape rolling. And it developed a whole new style."

The success of the Scaggs album led quickly to the recording of white Atlantic artists as diverse as bluesman John Hammond (the *Southern Fried* album) and English singer Lulu. Even the Rolling Stones—having recently signed an Atlantic distribution deal for their own label—took a rest from their 1969 American tour to record "Brown Sugar," "Wild Horses," and "You Gotta Move" at Muscle Shoals Sound, a session engineered by Jimmy Johnson and partly captured in the Maysles Brothers' *Gimme Shelter* documentary.

These were heavily R&B-influenced white acts, it's true, yet—like FAME—Muscle Shoals Sound was busy cementing a reputation as a studio that could handle pop and rock'n'roll. Even a three-year contract inked with Stax in 1972 didn't alter the fact that the customers the quartet most relished were people like Paul Simon, who recorded much of *There Goes Rhymin' Simon* at Jackson Highway in 1973. The

50 percent of Stax hits cut at Sound were not, in any case, country soul records: the Staple Singers' "Respect Yourself" (1971) and "I'll Take You There" (a 1972 No. 1) were a new kind of funky gospel-pop, promoting strong messages of black pride. "At Jackson Highway we had more freedom," said Barry Beckett. "Instead of doing strictly Rick Hall licks, I was able to do other things. It felt like home."

Only with such soul acts as Millie Jackson, Bobby Womack, and the Soul Children in the mid-'70s did a new kind of Muscle Shoals country-soul, thickly textured and sumptuously arranged, arise. Jackson's "If Loving You Is Wrong," Womack's "I Don't Wanna Be Hurt By Ya Love Again," and the Soul Children's "Love Makes It Right" were some of the greatest things ever to come out of the place. Yet for every Jackson or Womack there were three or four white acts: Leon Russell, Rod Stewart, Joe Cocker, and Bob Seger, for example. Again, they were often whites who loved R&B as much as the Muscle Shoals musicians did, but it revealed the true legacy of '60s soul: whites singing black music and getting a lot further with it than African Americans ever had.

"I think Muscle Shoals kind of lost its perspective there," horn man Harrison Calloway told me. "The Bob Segers and Glenn Freys were coming in and the R&B artists couldn't afford the studio time. I mean, what was Eddie Floyd against Bob Seger?"

The wheel came full circle for the four Alabama country boys when Jerry Wexler brought Willie Nelson—his main hope for a new Atlantic country division—down for 1974's *Phases and Stages* album. Supplementing their rhythm section with Texan fiddler Johnny Gimble, steel guitarist John Hughey, and dobro maestro Fred Carter Jr., Wexler produced a concept album by Nelson that included such classic songs as "I Still Can't Believe You're Gone." "Willie has the natural blues in him," Beckett said, "and Wexler ate him up like cake. They had a ball."

Phases and Stages even beat Rick Hall to the punch in the back-to-country stakes: "The only thing I hadn't succeeded at was country," he told me. "I began to see it might be easier to drive to Nashville and sit with Buddy Killen or Billy Sherrill than to fly to L.A. for a week and tap-dance for all the majors. I was tired of the fast lane."

When Hall's run of pop hits dried up in the mid-'70s, he was faced with the choice of disco on the one hand or country on the other.

After disastrous results with the first (Pickett, Dobie Gray, and others), he turned to the music of his roots and cut hits by Gus Hardin ("After the Last Goodbye"), the Gatlin Brothers ("Denver"), and perennial good ol' boy Jerry Reed ("The Bird" and "She Got the Goldmine").

"I don't cut country records like I wanna cut them," Hall said. "They say, 'Man, you've got to have a steel guitar in there' or '. . . the rhythm's too drastic.' And I say, 'Well, my thought has always been to lead country radio, not follow it.' I thought maybe I could offer something to country, but it's tough . . . they won't let you."

3. QUIN IVY

Of all the Muscle Shoals producers, perhaps the hardest hit by the decline of the country-soul sound was Quin Ivy. He'd only ever had one major artist, after all, and that was Percy Sledge. "I was a one-man artist/producer, and that always bothered me," he told me. "But I realized that this was as far as I was gonna go in the business, and really I was lucky that I got out of black music at the right time."

Ivy didn't get out, though, before issuing a handful of country-soul gems on his South Camp and Quinvy labels, among them sides by Z.Z. Hill, Tony Borders, Don Varner, June Edwards, and Bill Brandon. Mostly they were songs by the likes of Penn and Oldham, or Greene and Hinton—6/8-time ballads such as Hill's "Faithful and True," Borders's "Cheaters Never Win," and Varner's "Home for the Summer"—but June Edwards cut a great Spooner Oldham–produced version of Loretta Lynn's "You Ain't Woman Enough (to Take My Man)." Sadly these great sides weren't enough to keep Ivy in business—and even Sledge stopped selling.[33]

In 1973, Ivy sold the Quinvy studio to his engineer and brother-in-law David Johnson, who renamed it Broadway Sound and began—like the other Muscle Shoals producers—moving out of Southern soul. Over the ensuing years, Broadway Sound played host to such black pop acts as the Drifters, the Supremes, and the Commodores, as well as to

---

33 Four volumes of Southern soul gems on Quinvy and South Camp were compiled by Charly Records in 1989 and included all the above-mentioned sides by Hill, Borders, Varner, and Edwards. They were, in order of release, *Tear-Stained Soul, High On The Hog, You Better Believe It!,* and *"More Power To Ya!"*

Southern rockers Lynyrd Skynyrd, the Outlaws, and Mama's Pride. Only a 1974 Percy Sledge album on Phil Walden's Capricorn label, *I'll Be Your Everything,* kept the studio's country-soul flame flickering.

4. CRITERIA

Another reason why the soul sound dried up in Muscle Shoals was that Jerry Wexler decided to set up his own version of Muscle Shoals Sound in the "tropical Memphis" of Miami. "I wanted to get out of New York," he said, "so I figured I'd spend the winters in Miami and the summers on Long Island."

In 1970 he bought Criteria, a studio built by Mack Emerman in 1957. With the help of Atlantic engineer Tom Dowd, he installed a new 8-track board there. In Memphis, meanwhile, a rhythm section was put together for Criteria by James Luther "Jim" Dickinson, an ex-rockabilly piano player with strong views on the racial make-up of Southern soul. "Everyone talks about white music and black music," he said. "I defy you to show me black music. How can you hear the color? The rhythm section at Stax was split right down the middle. Chips Moman used primarily white players but black horns and voices. Willie Mitchell used black players with white horns and voices."

In Arnold Shaw's 1969 book *The World of Soul,* Dickinson was still more outspoken: "I think the young white Southern musicians are more culturally important than the Southern black musicians, except for the old men, because the young ones are denying their culture. Why would Furry Lewis mess with a 14-year-old white boy? Why, because I was the first person in ten years that came to Furry and asked him to play some songs!"

Dickinson's rhythm section, christened the Dixie Flyers by Wexler, consisted of the nucleus of Stan Kesler's band at the Sam Phillips studio, a white combo that Lelan Rogers had used for Silver Fox sessions by Betty LaVette. Alongside Dickinson himself they comprised Mike Utley (organ/piano), Tommy McClure (bass), Sammy Creason (drums), and original Mar-Keys leader Charlie Freeman (guitar). Wexler moved them down to Criteria—renamed Atlantic-South—in 1970: "Tom Dowd joined me in Miami, and Jim Stewart bought a house down here, so we started a little Florida adjunct."

Among the sessions the Dixie Flyers played were those by Aretha Franklin, Sam & Dave, Esther Phillips, and Brook Benton. Besides Aretha's churchy *Spirit in the Dark,* there were great country soul sides by Phillips and Benton. Phillips, back with Atlantic after a spell on Roulette, cut one of the best R&B versions of Curly Putnam's "Set Me Free," while Benton continued in the mellow country-pop style of his "Rainy Night in Georgia" with further songs by Tony Joe White and others by Mac Davis ("Whoever Finds This I Love You") and Joe South ("Don't It Make You Want to Go Home").

At Criteria, too, the old country-soul sound eventually lost out, both to a more sophisticated kind of R&B (Aretha's "Spanish Harlem") and to the new white rock of the South. "My rock'n'roll is Southern white rock'n'roll," Wexler told me. "Those records we did with Jim Dickinson, Ronnie Hawkins, Duane Allman, Delaney & Bonnie . . . it's called *autokthenis,* if you know the term. It means it grew there. It grew from the spot and wasn't learned off phonograph records."

The studio's golden period came with the recording of Derek & the Dominos' *Layla* and the Allman Brothers' *Eat a Peach.* This had the knock-on effect of making the Dixie Flyers superfluous. "We made a lot of good records there," Wexler reflected, "but I couldn't give them enough work. I didn't know how to make it work the way they worked it up in Memphis and Muscle Shoals. I wanted to live the full rich life, with a boat so I could go to the Bahamas and fish, you know, but it didn't work. The band was also too wild, drug-wise. When Charlie Freeman died of a smack overdose, that was really the end of it. They were the last of the great in-house rhythm sections."

"When Jerry moved to Florida, there was a natural void," Atlantic supremo Ahmet Ertegun said in 1993. "You can't move that far from the center of activity and carry on the same way. See, Jerry had been a terrific all-round record man, but after he left New York, he was only interested in A & R work. He was making the music he loved, which was great, but at a certain point you also have to make records people are going to buy."

5. CAPRICORN

Wexler's hopes for Southern soul in the '70s were pinned on Phil Walden, the R&B freak from Macon, Georgia, whose management company represented many of the great Southern soul artists of the '60s. "I was fishing with Jerry in Miami one weekend," Walden told me, "and he suggested I form a record label. I said I didn't want a label, but he really encouraged me. The name Capricorn came up when we were laughing about how girls in California would always ask what sign you were. We discovered we were both Capricorn. I thought it sounded terribly corny."

After converting an old slaughterhouse on Macon's Cotton Avenue into the Capricorn studio, Walden began signing acts to the label. He was no exception to the prevailing rule, however: despite good soul releases by Sam & Bill, Arthur Conley, and Oscar Toney Jr. (especially the pleading "Down on My Knees"), Capricorn quickly moved into Southern rock. "I don't think that when those white guys opened their studios in the South their aim was ever to stick with black music," said Clarence Carter. "Phil could just as well have carried on with R&B after Otis Redding died, but he hadn't got as far along as he wanted to be."

"I was hoping for more R&B on Capricorn," Wexler admitted, "but I didn't get it. There's not much more you can say. Black artists weren't that easy to find." Ironically it was Wexler who bought Duane Allman's contract from Rick Hall and offered him to Walden, thus acting as an inadvertent catalyst for the greatest Southern rock phenomenon of all.

With the Allman Brothers Band, Capricorn unleashed the prototype blue-eyed denim soul man: the Southern hippie, bastard offspring of all the invisible white session men behind country soul. "Most every white singer I've been involved with has strong black roots," Walden said. "To the young white Southerner, black music always appealed more than white pop music. Certainly the Beach Boys' surfing stuff never would have hacked it in the South—it was just too white and it wasn't relevant. The waves weren't too high down here!"

The Allmans were the logical culmination of country soul, balancing Gregg Allman's blues against Dickey Betts's bluegrass, with Duane acting as a kind of mediator between them. They were also integrated, with African American drummer Jaimoe Johansen playing alongside the white Butch Trucks. "We got into some close ones," Gregg told me in 2002. "There were places we'd get turned away from eating: 'What are you guys doing with a nigger in the band?'"

The Allman brothers grew up in Nashville and Florida, listening to rockabilly and blues. In the mid-'60s they formed the Allman Joys and began playing the college circuit around Alabama. After country singer John D. Loudermilk produced their psychedelic version of "Spoonful" on Buddy Killen's Dial label, the band split, and the brothers teamed up with Alabamans Johnny Sandlin (drums) and Paul Hornsby (keyboards) from rival college-circuit band the Minutes. Thus was formed the Hour Glass, a band whisked off to Hollywood, dolled up in flower-power costumes, and signed to Liberty.

"We played with all the big bands," Hornsby told me in his Muscadine studio in Macon. "Jefferson Airplane, Buffalo Springfield, the whole lot. Liberty didn't know what the hell we were: we had Gregg's bluesy voice plus a little bit of country influence, and they didn't know what to do with it. They called us a 'Motown' band just because it sounded black. They knew nothing about the Southern black R&B scene."

The first Hour Glass album, an unhappy attempt to turn them into a California pop-soul band, bore this out. Overproduced versions of Goffin-King songs jostled with covers of Deon Jackson's "Love Makes the World Go Round" and Curtis Mayfield's "I've Been Trying." Huge choirs and horn sections drowned the band out. "We wouldn't play any of those numbers on shows because they weren't us," Hornsby said. "On the second album, *The Power of Love,* we pulled a lot more material from the South."

According to Jesse "Pete" Carr, who joined the Hour Glass on bass at this point, the choice of songs by the Penn/Oldham and Greene/Hinton teams reflected the influence of Sandlin, who'd been on the periphery of the FAME scene in Muscle Shoals. Certainly these numbers, together with Solomon Burke's "Hangin' Up My Heart for You," sounded better than the Gregg-composed songs that filled out the rest of the album.

Passing through Alabama on a tour of the South in April 1968, the Hour Glass stopped in at the FAME studio and cut a session at their own expense—a blues medley—to show Liberty what they were really about.[34]

---

34 Half a century later, Gregg Allman recorded his posthumous *Southern Blood* album at FAME. Produced by Don Was, it included versions of Percy Sledge's "Out of Left Field" and Johnny Jenkins's "Blind Bats and Swamp Rats."

When the company rejected the tapes that summer, the band broke up and Duane Allman settled briefly in Muscle Shoals, adding his slide guitar sound to the soul brew at FAME. A year on, after playing for Wilson Pickett, Aretha Franklin, and others, he followed Jerry Wexler's suggestion and set about forming another band with his brother.

"Duane told us to come up to Muscle Shoals," recalled Hornsby, "and when Sandlin and I got there we found Berry Oakley, a rock'n'roll bass player, and Jaimoe, who'd played in Otis Redding's touring band. But I was sick of the road and decided to go and work in Phil Walden's studio in Macon."

While Duane and Gregg assembled the Allmans, Walden finished off the Capricorn studio with Hornsby, Sandlin, and guitarist Pete Carr. "I think Phil wanted another Stax," Carr said, "but it didn't happen because of the Allmans and all the other bands that formed. The self-contained studio thing didn't work because of all the stuff he started doing with self-contained bands."

Walden recorded Hornsby, Sandlin, and Carr at Macon—with future Crusader Pops Popwell joining on bass—but otherwise used them mainly on demos for artists such as James Taylor's brothers Alex and Livingston. Besides the few sides by Arthur Conley and Oscar Toney Jr. already mentioned, virtually the only soul sessions cut at Capricorn were those booked by the hilarious Jerry Williams, aka Swamp Dogg, one of a new breed of independent African American producers working in the South (and the first black producer to be hired, in 1968, by Atlantic Records). Williams had recorded under his own name for several labels—Roulette, Ember, and Cotillion among them—before adopting his canine alter ego in 1970 and launching a series of offbeat, vaguely conceptual soul albums: Doris Duke's *I'm a Loser,* Solomon Burke's *From the Heart,* and the producer's own *Total Destruction to Your Mind.* These hastily concocted LPs were usually recorded either at Capricorn or at Quinvy in Alabama, with David Johnson engineering and George Soulé playing drums.

"Jerry was writing with Gary U.S. Bonds down in Miami and worked out a deal with Phil to come to Macon," Pete Carr remembered.

"He'd produce those albums in a day. He didn't know what a 'sound' was: he'd hear it and that was sound enough for him!"

Born in Virginia, Williams was enough of a Southerner to pick up on the country-soul tradition: albums like *I'm a Loser,* Irma Thomas's *In Between Tears,* and Freddie North's Joe Simon-ish *Friend* stood as some of the genre's last great testaments. Doris Duke's "I Don't Care Anymore," for one, captured the mood of soul's move into the cities:

> *I came to the city from the deep south*
> *When the mills shut down*
> *I married a man who treated me*
> *Like he bought me by the pound.*
>
> (© Jerry Williams Music, 1970)

The song made a predictable equation between urban life and corruption as its protagonist sank gradually into prostitution, but its Southern homesickness was genuinely affecting. "To the Other Woman," meanwhile, could have been a guilt-trip ballad by Tammy Wynette. The Dogg himself recorded such country songs as Joe South's "Don't It Make You Wanna Go Home" and Mickey Newbury's "She Even Woke Me Up to Say Goodbye," while "She's All I Got"—a song he wrote for soul singer Freddie North—became a Billy Sherrill–produced hit for Johnny Paycheck. (Sherrill also produced a duet version of Arthur Alexander's "You Better Move On" by Paycheck and George Jones.)

One of the few R&B albums recorded at Capricorn besides Swamp Dogg's productions was *Ton-Ton Macoute* by Otis Redding's first employer, Johnny Jenkins. Interestingly, it pointed forward to Southern rock more than it recapped on Southern soul. "Johnny was supposed to have been an influence on Jimi Hendrix when he played in New York," Paul Homsby said. "I think *Ton-Ton Macoute* was his last recording, and we sort of had to pull him out of the woods to do it. Basically he was pretty content to sit around and drink moonshine."

Besides the Capricorn studio players, *Ton-Ton Macoute* featured all the Allman Brothers Band besides Gregg and Dickey Betts. Essentially it was a gumbo of swamp-rock, Delta blues, and New Orleans voo-doo. Around the nucleus of Jenkins and Duane Allman, producer

Johnny Sandlin built up a big percussive sound: congas and timbales played by Jaimoe and Muscle Shoals acolytes Eddie Hinton and Tippy Armstrong. The songs ranged from Dr. John's "Walk on Guilded Splinters" to John Loudermilk's "Bad News" and Bob Dylan's "Down Along the Cove," while Capricorn writer Jackie Avery's "Blind Bats and Swamp Rats" sounded like a heavy-metal Cream from the bayous.

Ton-Ton Macoute's rock-blues fusion was a kind of exotic, night-tripper version of the Allman Brothers Band, lacking only the country ingredient of Dickey Betts. Country itself was more obviously present in some of the groups that followed the Allmans, notably the Marshall Tucker Band. Their first album, produced at Capricorn by Paul Hornsby, was released in 1973. With founding members drawn from late '60s R&B band the Toy Factory, the Tuckers followed the Californian country-rock lead and went back to their Georgia hillbilly roots.

"Kids aren't ashamed of country anymore," rhythm guitarist George McCorkle argued. "Hillbilly Band," the second side's opening track, stated their position fairly unequivocally. "I think Phil Walden was disappointed when I played him the first Tucker album and it had fiddles and steel guitars on it," Paul Hornsby said. "I think he was expecting more blazing twin guitars, and he was surprised when it was a hit. That made him start a country division, which was how come he signed Kitty Wells and Billy Joe Shaver."

"In a sense," noted Texan music writer Joe Nick Patoski, "the evolution of Southern rock was a reactionary attempt to return rock'n'roll to its native soil. After the decline of interest in rockabilly, white rock in the South had taken a back seat to country and soul." Patoski was only half-right, because Southern rock came directly out of the twin streams of country and soul, but reactionary was certainly the only word for a song such as "Sweet Home Alabama," Lynyrd Skynyrd's 1974 retort to Neil Young's "Southern Man."

For too long the South had been unfashionable; now a new breed of longhaired redneck was standing up for it. In fact, they made longhair slobbishness a statement of traditional good-ole-boyism. A certain self-consciousness came into play. Charlie Daniels sang "Longhaired Country Boy" on *Fire on the Mountain,* while in Nashville itself Bobby Bare cut the Shel Silverstein song "Redneck Hippie Romance" and ex-convict David Allan Coe actually titled an album *Longhaired Redneck*. At his annual festival in Dripping Springs, Texas, Willie Nelson set out to bring the hippies and rednecks together, though the experiment was not initially a success.

"The phenomenon," Phil Walden said, "is that people are remaining in Southern communities to record and perform." No longer did bands have to suffer what the Hour Glass did, trekking out to California in search of gold dust. Other outfits produced by Johnny Sandlin and Paul Hornsby at Capricorn included Tulsa bluesman Elvin Bishop, ex-All-mans roadies Grinderswitch, and—funkiest of all the Southern rock bands—Wet Willie. Even Rick Hall cashed in on Southern rock when he produced Travis Wammack's 1975 Capricorn album *Not For Sale*.

Pictured on the sleeve out hunting with a slingshot and a Confederate cap, Wammack was the embodiment of the backwoods redneck rocker.[35]

At the same time, of course, he'd played with such FAME artists as Clarence Carter and Candi Staton, and *Not For Sale* featured versions of Carter's "Looking for a Fox," Brook Benton's "A Lover's Question," and Swamp Dogg's "(Shu-Doo-Pa-Poo-Poop) Love Being Your Fool," a Top 40 hit in August 1975.

Walden did not neglect the old country-soul sound completely. When Percy Sledge left Atlantic in 1973, Walden signed him to Capricorn and brought in the singer's old mentor Quin Ivy to produce *I'll Be Your Everything* in Muscle Shoals. "I am particularly proud to say 'Welcome back, Percy,'" Ivy wrote in his sleeve note, "but even more important 'Welcome home.'" With a superb title track single written by George Soulé, the album marginally updated Sledge's classic '60s style with such country-pop tracks as Dallas Frazier's "If This Is the Last Time," Mark James's "Blue Water," and the Charlie Rich hit "Behind Closed Doors." With Sledge in excellent voice, the whole LP bore the air of a reunion for singer, producer, and musicians alike.

---

35 Charles Hughes makes the point that more Southern rockers deployed Confederate imagery than any country artist ever did. What, one wonders, did Carter and Staton make of Wammack's cap on the cover of *Not for Sale?* In more recent years, southern rock has morphed into the more right-on sounds of Drive-By Truckers—led by Muscle Shoals Sound bassist David Hood's son Patterson—and the interracial Alabama Shakes.

Dobie Gray was another mid-'70s signing to Capricorn, produced by Troy Seals on the Nashville-recorded *New Ray of Sunshine* (1975). Gray hadn't progressed much beyond the good-time style of his MCA albums, but there was some nice country funk in "Drive On, Ride On" and "Comfort and Please You."

By 1978, the Southern rock phenomenon was all but over, and Capricorn had gone bust. Muscle Shoals wasn't in great shape either. The post-disco slump in the record business was hurting because, as David Hood said, "the record companies just didn't have the budgets they once had to cut records outside their own backyards." Thanks, however, to the patronage of artists like Bob Seger, Glenn Frey, Julian Lennon, and the Oak Ridge Boys, Muscle Shoals Sound survived into the '80s, shifting operations to Sheffield's huge old Naval Reserve building on the banks of the Tennessee River.

Rick Hall continued to do well in country, thanks especially to the talented local writers signed to FAME Publishing. "I was tired of going through rhythm sections," he told me. "Being in an outpost like Muscle Shoals you don't *have* 3,000 guitar players signed to the union. Every time I'd break in a group and get them really clicking, they'd move across town and start their own studio. It was heartbreaking to have to start all over again each time, so I decided I would work more in the capacity of an executive producer, breaking in young people and letting them produce. With writers and producers, you get them one of two ways: you either buy them or you train them. I think it's cheaper and more profitable to train them."

As for Phil Walden, he based himself in Nashville, where—after an abortive attempt to start a new label with Chips Moman and Buddy Killen—he reactivated Capricorn Records.[36]

Memphis
1. STAX

The downfall of Stax was the most obvious symbol of Southern soul's demise. As Gerri Hirshey noted, the company's collapse in 1975

---

36 While Muscle Shoals Sound was kept busy by Malaco, Rick Hall more or less retired, with his son administering the FAME publishing catalog.

exemplified the uncertainty of Southern careers as compared with those of, for instance, Motown stars.

Stax's golden age was effectively over by 1968, when its relationship with Atlantic came to an end. It was also then, in the year Martin Luther King Jr. was assassinated in Memphis, that the company became increasingly identified with the Black Power movement. Of all the Southern labels, Stax was the only one to assume any kind of militant role, a role reflected by the politicized *Stax Fax* magazine and rewarded in 1972 by the giant Wattstax concert in Los Angeles.

The crucial figure here was Al Bell, a DJ who joined the company as head of A&R in 1966. It was Bell who steered Stax away from the country soul of William Bell and Carla Thomas towards the grittier urban sound of Johnnie Taylor and, eventually, the proto-disco of Isaac Hayes's "Theme from *Shaft*." This was not a deliberately racial move: it merely reflected Bell's desire to compete with the Motowns of black music. "There was more of a marinating of country and soul at FAME or at Goldwax," David Porter reflected. "We had a fatter sound; we wanted Al Jackson's drum sound to be 'fat.'"

In any case, it was always a matter of pride to Al Bell that Stax remained interracial through the civil rights years. "I remember being in session the day Martin Luther King Jr. was killed," William Bell said. "We were concerned to get Steve and Duck home safely. We surrounded and protected them from rioters. We weren't militant, we just had a successful black image." ("There is no race problem in Memphis," said Isaac Hayes in 1969. "It's a tight harmony, really." Other Stax employees, however, testify to the harassment the company suffered from racist police.)

"It was a horrible time," Duck Dunn confirmed to me. "The day after it happened, I was standing out in front of Stax with Isaac and David when the police came by to ask if *I* was okay! It was just an awful situation." Added Steve Cropper: "A lot of things changed dramatically in Memphis, and musically there came this real uprising. That's why the Wattstax thing happened, and why Isaac was so successful with *Black Moses*."

Bell's desire to build Stax into a Southern Motown eventually undermined its Memphis foundations. "If they could just have gone back to using basically broken equipment and rednecks and stupid people, they'd have stood a better chance," remarked Jim Dickinson.

"I worshipped Al, as everybody there did," Duck Dunn said. "He was the one who put me and Al Jackson on salary, so he was my hero. But there were some bad decisions made. I know there was an offer to take Aretha Franklin that we turned down. And who did we get instead? Lena Zavaroni!" (Sadly, Dunn wasn't joking: Scottish singer Zavaroni's *Ma! He's Making Eyes At Me* was, unbelievably, a Stax LP in May 1974.)

"Al unfortunately wanted to do things too fast at Stax," said Estelle Axton, who left the company in 1968. "He got into movies, but no one here knew anything about movies. Al wanted Stax, and he wanted to buy my brother out for $6 million. There was something of a power struggle there. We knew we had to build the company brick by brick, but he wanted it fast."

Symptomatic of Stax's move away from the gospel economy of their Memphis sound was Bell's use of Detroit producer Don Davis for acts such as the Dramatics and Johnnie Taylor. "They wanted Don to produce 'Detroit' records," said Jim Dickinson disdainfully. Though Taylor had a massive hit with the funky "Who's Makin' Love" in late 1968, it wasn't the Stax sound. Still more removed from classic Stax were the extended orchestral arrangements of "Walk On By" and "By the Time I Get To Phoenix" on Isaac Hayes's 1969 *Hot Buttered Soul* album. These provided the missing link between Norman Whitfield's Motown productions and the heavy-breathing epics of Barry White in the '70s, even if the long monologue intro to "Phoenix" parodied the kind of Baptist sermons Isaac must have heard growing up in rural Tennessee.

In September 1970, Booker T. & the MGs split up, and Steve Cropper left the company. "I wasn't happy with the way some of the things had been going on, the way the musicians were being treated," he said. Cropper primarily blamed Bell's hiring of the Fair Play Committee's Johnnie Baylor and Dino Woodward for, in Charles Hughes' words, "destroying [Stax's] interracial camaraderie." The old "happy family" picture of Stax began to crumble, and the next four years saw a steady decline in trust, friendship, and business acumen. Bell continued to expand the company, signing white rock groups such as Southwest P.O.B. and Knowbody Else to its Hip subsidiary.

Still there were great black records on the label, or on affiliates such as Koko: Shirley Brown's "Woman to Woman," Luther Ingram's original version of "If Loving You Is Wrong (I Don't Want to Be Right)," Rance Allen's sublime gospel-soul albums. Muscle Shoals Sound took over much of Stax's rhythm section work in 1972, producing sensational records by the Staple Singers ("Respect Yourself"), Mel & Tim ("Starting All Over Again"), and the Soul Children (the *Genesis* and *Friction* albums). "The Muscle Shoals guys," said Mavis Staples, "were a rhythm section that a singer would just die for." Great writing teams like Homer Banks and Carl Hampton, and Bettye Crutcher and Sir Mack Rice, poured out classics of the '70s "cheatin" genre, reinforcing a picture of black promiscuity long held dear by whites.

But the general trend was downhill. There was no one to fill the shoes of Otis Redding or Sam & Dave, unless it was Hayes, the gold-enchained superfly Black Moses whose arrival at Wattstax was preceded by two police Harley Davidsons entering the Los Angeles Memorial Coliseum with their sirens wailing. If anyone symbolized the quantum leap from '60s country soul it was Hayes, born in the cottonfields of Tennessee but now owner of a Rolls Royce protected by armed guards as it sat in the Stax parking lot.

Unfortunately, Hayes himself added to Stax's already drastic financial problems when, two years after Wattstax, he sued the company for $5.3 million, charging breach of contract. By then a series of investigations into Bell's business practices had done untold damage to the Stax name, while its distribution agreement with CBS was on the rocks.

A year later, it was all over. Just weeks after the appalling murder of Al Jackson Jr., Bell was indicted on charges of conspiracy to obtain fraudulent loans. The company was ordered to cease operations.

2. AMERICAN

Like Stax, Chips Moman's American studio came to the end of its golden period, easing up on its R&B sessions in the process.

"I don't know whether the R&B thing started to die out," Moman reflected, "so much as that the people who were doing it got a little lazy and didn't record as much. I mean, we were like a couple of music families down here, and the two families were doing all of it. In that kind of situation, people slow down and get tired. And also, we'd been so hot that the producers were like stars. It was the old Memphis ego, and I think that played a role in us falling apart."

Perhaps it was Moman's Memphis ego that made him up sticks and leave the city in 1972. Having been twice snubbed by the annual Memphis Music Awards, he opted to move to Atlanta: "We felt Memphis didn't care about us, so we just packed up and pulled out. I built a studio in Atlanta in eight days."

The last great soul record cut at American was Arthur Alexander's eponymously-titled comeback album on Warner Brothers. "No psychedelic wah-wah guitars, no imitation church choirs or superstar ego trips here," Barry (Dr. Demento) Hansen wrote in his liner note; "just Arthur Alexander from Alabama singing his story-songs with a superb Memphis band." Produced by Moman's second-in-command Tommy Cogbill, *Arthur Alexander* was vintage country soul containing some of the singer's finest performances: the stoical, self-penned "In the Middle of It All," the semi-autobiographical "Rainbow Road" (written by his old Muscle Shoals pals Donnie Fritts and Dan Penn), and new, countrified versions of such old songs as "Go Home Girl" and "Love's Where Life Begins." Alexander's country bent was even more pronounced on "It Hurts to Want It So Bad" and "Down the Back Roads," partly written by Steve Cropper. The whole LP had a quiet, understated discipline to it. Only the uptempo songs by Dennis Linde (including the original of Elvis Presley's "Burning Love") seemed out of place.

Moman's move to Atlanta turned out to be a disaster, primarily because he couldn't find any artists there. Although there'd been an Atlanta scene of sorts, centered on publisher Bill Lowery and his stable of acts (Joe South, the Tams, Billy Joe Royal, Ray Stevens, and the Classics IV), nothing much was happening in 1972. Not even Ilene Berns's decision to move her late husband Bert's BANG label to the city made an appreciable difference. Some of the American session men bought houses in the city, but it was no good: as organist Bobby Emmons said, "We all got homesick." The only place they could rely on for work was Nashville, and it was to the city of country music that they slowly began to gravitate after only a year. "We didn't go there cold," said Emmons. "We'd all done R&B sessions for Buddy Killen and John Richbourg, so we had some kind of entrée."

The most disillusioned member of the crew was Moman himself: "The last place I wanted to go was Nashville. We'd tried so hard to avoid it. I only went there to be with my musicians, and when I arrived the head of the union came over and told me he didn't approve of us being in town. That made me determined to stay."

Thus Moman, R&B and pop hitmaker extraordinaire, finally returned to the country music of his boyhood. He built an American studio on Nashville's Music Row and began producing sessions. In 1975, he scored his first country hit with B.J. Thomas's No. 1 "Another Somebody Done Somebody Wrong Song." "The Muscle Shoals and Memphis musicians broke the Nashville clique," said Bobby Emmons. "Our music infiltrated theirs." It also meant, sadly, that such great country-soul players as Reggie Young were wasted on lame country sessions. "Sometimes people cropdust with 747s," was Moman's gnomic way of putting it. He did the next best thing to recording R&B itself when he moved in with Nashville's "outlaw" fraternity and produced albums by Willie Nelson, Waylon Jennings, and Kris Kristofferson. "The day came," he boasted, "when four out of five crossover records from Nashville were made by Memphis boys. The first platinum album out of Nashville was *Ol' Waylon,* with 'Luckenbach, Texas' on it. That was us."

American's country-soul spirit lingered on in the Joe Tex and Paul Kelly records cut for Buddy Killen—there was a country song, "Leaving You Dinner," on Tex's 1977 *Bumps and Bruises* album—while another producer who gave Moman's players a break from the diet of country was Papa Don Schroeder, who came up from Florida (as he had a decade earlier) with James & Bobby Purify.

The possibilities for black-white interchange in the Nashville of the '70s, however, were slim, and there was more of a Southern soul hangover in such Moman-produced country songs as Gary Stewart's 1980 "Staring Each Other Down" than in the later records of Joe Tex (who, in any case, had joined the Nation of Islam in 1968 and changed his name to Yusuf Hazziez).

3. HI

The one Memphis company really to prosper after the Stax débâcle was Hi Records. In fact, while Issac Hayes was blueprinting the "Shaft" disco style that eventually killed off Southern soul, Hi boss Willie Mitchell was busy grooming that music's last and perhaps most eccentric star.

Al Green's records—together with those of Ann Peebles, Syl Johnson, O.V. Wright, and others—made up the last truly individual body of Southern soul music. Once again there was more than a pinch of country in the mix. Chicago bluesman Syl Johnson cut a version of Eddy Arnold's "You Don't Know Me." Green himself recorded masterly interpretations of Hank Williams's "I'm So Lonesome I Could Cry" and Kris Kristofferson's "For the Good Times."

"We spent a lot of time softening Al's style," Mitchell told me. "Originally he wanted to sound like Sam & Dave, but I told him we had to tone him down and get his range up. I knew he could cross over. When we were big with 'Let's Stay Together,' I was up in Detroit, and I heard the Bee Gees' 'How Can You Mend a Broken Heart?' on the radio, so I brought the song back to Al in Memphis. He laughed in my face and said, 'That shit is country, man!' I told him he didn't understand what we were gonna do with it."[37]

Barry Gibbs's song was the first of Green's extended ballads, numbers that really gave him the chance to explore and test his voice. Never had a soul lead been so elastic, so narcissistically self-absorbed, the song's slow, simple melody offering ample space for his free-form, double-tracked acrobatics. "For the Good Times" was even better, a gentle Ray Price hit turned into a six-and-a-half-minute meditation on regret and love's passing.

Even on harder, more urgent songs, Mitchell's sound came close to a kind of country-funk style. Shorn of soul frills, it was

37 In the booklet accompanying the *From Where I Stand* box set, Green claimed it was the encouragement of Hank Williams's widow Audrey that led to his recording "For The Good Times" and "I'm So Lonesome I Could Cry." "You see, every R&B record you hear is not necessarily an R&B song," he said. "It might have derived from country music as well."

down-home-minimalist: tight, boxed-in, intimate. "Teenie Hodges had a country sound to his guitar," noted Denise LaSalle, who recorded such Westbound hits as "Trapped By a Thing Called Love" (1971) at Hi. The studio maintained its country connections, in any case, since it was still part-owned by ex-Blue Seal Pal Bill Cantrell. The latter even started a Hi country label in the '70s, charting with Narvel Felts's version of "Drift Away," while another country ingredient of Mitchell's productions was the white vocal trio of Rhodes, Chalmers & Rhodes, led by the niece of '50s Western Swingster Slim Rhodes.

Mitchell was fortunate to attract such magnificent voices as Peebles, Wright, and Otis Clay. Peebles's "Part Time Love," Wright's "A Nickel and a Nail," and Clay's "Trying to Live My Life Without You" were masterworks of down-home R&B that showed just how far Stax had strayed from their raw, funky base. There was less of the old country-soul feel in these singers than in Al Green, but Peebles came close. "Her hard, edgy singing is pitched somewhere between Candi Staton and Denise LaSalle," wrote Clive Anderson. The ballads "A Love Vibration" and "Trouble, Heartaches and Sadness" borrowed some of the country characteristics of both those formidable women.

Green recorded one last country song—Buck Owens's "Together Again" on *Full of Fire*—before departing the Mitchell fold in 1977. His self-produced *Belle* album of that year marked the end of Mitchell's peak period. Despite fabulous late albums by O.V. Wright, Hi petered out and was soon sold to Al Bennett's Cream organization in Los Angeles. "It just put everyone in a different place," Mitchell said. "The Southern sound got lost."

Interestingly, Green recorded one of his gospel albums, *Precious Lord,* in Nashville, using Bill Cantrell and Quinton Claunch as producers and Billy Sherrill as engineer. Mitchell, meanwhile, partnered with Albert Grossman's Bearsville label to produce albums by Jesse Winchester and Paul Butterfield, then formed his own Waylo label to launch a new clutch of R&B talent. By the mid-'80s his principal artists were Billy Always and Lynn White, the first a youthful dance-oriented performer, the second a singer who upheld the tradition of Peebles and LaSalle on albums such as *Blues in My Bedroom* (1982).

Rednecks, Whites, and the Blues

"Being black for a while will make me a better white."

—Janis Joplin

The passing of country soul led to a new sound in the white South, one that drew equally on R&B and country for its inspiration. In a way, the Southern rock period revived the achievement of Elvis Presley, mixing black and white in a vital new chemistry. Although English groups (the Stones, the Animals, et al.) and bands from Northern states (the Young Rascals, Mitch Ryder & the Detroit Wheels, the many white blues acts that sprung up in the wake of Paul Butterfield) got there first, it was the South's turn now to play at black music.

Rick Hall: "There was a phasing out of blacks because whites like Duane Allman grew up and just got funkier than a lot of the black acts. Duane could play better bottleneck guitar than any black player I ever saw. This was a new breed of young, aggressive white people."

Blue-eyed soulboys had of course been roaming the South throughout the '60s: every town had its equivalent of Dan Penn's Mark Vs in Muscle Shoals. But few of these bands could compete with black stars, and most aimed no higher than the college fraternity circuit. Perhaps for most of them R&B remained merely a hobby. Aspiring professionals seemed to gravitate towards country music.

An exception was the Texan singer Roy Head, whose wild James Brown–style shows were popular with black audiences in the South, and who had a No. 2 smash in 1965 with the Huey Meaux–produced "Treat Her Right." Head's frenzied efforts to sound black led to nodes on his vocal chords, and his offstage drinking antics didn't help. Eventually he crossed over to country, and in the '70s recorded for Shannon, ABC-Dot, and Elektra. Only a brief stint on Steve Cropper's TMI label gave him a taste of the old R&B. (A similar "white James Brown"–style performer in the '60s was Macon's flamboyant, peroxide-coiffed Wayne Cochran, who scored a sizeable R&B hit with "Last Kiss" on King.)

Another white country boy to chart with horn-driven R&B sides was Indiana-born guitarist Lonnie Mack, whose superb instrumental version of Chuck Berry's "Memphis" made No. 5 in 1963. "I think country & western and R&B are real close," Mack said in 1968. "It might not sound the same but the basic idea is the same. They seem so far apart when you're playing them, but I play a lot of blues now that have country and western runs." With a bubbly vibrato guitar style that recalled Robert Ward's playing with the Falcons, Mack recorded not only instrumentals but powerful gospel-soul songs like "Why," "Where There's a Will There's a Way," and "What Kind of World Is This," most of them found on the 1964 *Wham of That Memphis Man!* album. After a period of semi-retirement in the early '70s, he reemerged to guest on Dobie Gray's *Hey Dixie* LP and to record such country rock albums as *Home At Last* and *The Hills of Indiana*.

Whites who opted for a poppier soul sound included Steve Alaimo in Miami, who hit with Arthur Alexander's "Every Day I Have to Cry" in 1963, and the Atlanta-based Joe South, who wrote for Bill Lowery's the Tams ("Untie Me") and Billy Joe Royal ("Down in the Boondocks") before hitting with 1969's "Games People Play" in his own right. As a guitarist he played on Bob Dylan's *Blonde On Blonde* and on Atlantic sessions by Aretha Franklin and Wilson Pickett. "I couldn't believe this white guy with an old Gretsch guitar had been playing all those black licks," recalled J. R. Cobb of the Atlanta Rhythm Section. South's 1968 *Introspect* album was an unusual flower-power indictment of Southern society, though generally his songs were performed better by other artists—Johnny Rivers with "These Are Not My People," Lynn Anderson with "I Never Promised You a Rose Garden," Brook Benton with the nostalgic "Don't It Make You Want to Go Home."

By the end of the '60s, as already noted, black music had become more sophisticated and urbanized. This opened the way for R&B–influenced whites to take up where Southern soul had left off. With the success of bands such as the Allman Brothers, the psychedelic sounds of 1967 were gradually replaced by a revived form of blues and country. In San Francisco itself, Creedence Clearwater Revival cooked up a Southern swamp-rock style that sounded like Solomon Burke fronting the Carl Perkins band. Meanwhile Janis Joplin—who'd started out singing Carter Family songs in her native Texas—emerged from Big Brother & the Holding Company sounding something like a white Etta James.

Down in Los Angeles, Mississippi-born Delaney Bramlett married ex-Ikette backing singer Bonnie Lynn and formed Delaney & Bonnie, the first of a series of sub–Ike & Tina revues that included Mad Dogs & Englishmen and Don Nix's Alabama State Troupers. These sanctified hippie circuses were, as Charlie Gillett observed, like "multi-racial revivalist meetings," permitting whites to play at being black.* Delaney and Bonnie even had an album—produced by ex–Mar-Key Nix—on Stax.[38]

The early '70s were dominated by whites—from Dr. John and Leon Russell to Ry Cooder and Little Feat—playing black. Even country-rocker Gram Parsons showed his affinity with Southern soul by recording the Chips Moman/Dan Penn masterpieces "Do Right Woman—Do Right Man" and "Dark End of the Street" on the Flying Burrito Brothers' *Gilded Palace of Sin* album. Bridging the gap between these mainly L.A.–based artists and the Southern rock outfits were acts such as Doug Sahm, Delbert McClinton, and the Amazing Rhythm Aces, eclectic white Southerners who fell squarely between the twin stools of R&B and country. Multi-instrumentalist Sahm mixed country, blues, and Tex-Mex, while his fellow Texan McClinton followed up the honky-tonk country of *Victim of Life's Circumstances* (1975) with the roadhouse R&B of *Genuine Cowhide* (1976) and the sizzling Southern funk of *Love Rustler* (1977).

The Aces, perhaps more than any other '70s band, walked the fine line between country and blue-eyed soul, making No. 14 with 1975's "Third Rate Romance" and recording several fine ABC albums at the Sam Phillips studio in Memphis. "We were such a mixture of influences," the band's keyboard player Billy Earheart told me. "Half of us were from East Tennessee, so there was a strong Appalachian leaning, whereas I was more into blues and R&B, stuff I heard on John R.'s show on WLAC. One thing we were sure about was that we didn't want to be stereotyped as a country-rock band." In Nashville, country-soul session men Mac Gayden, David Briggs, and Wayne Moss formed the hybrid ensembles Area Code 615 and Barefoot Jerry.

---

38 Charles Hughes makes the point that Memphis blues man Furry Lewis's inclusion in Nix's Troopers tour—as its black "authenticator"—was as a last-minute substitution for Lonnie Mack.

If the climate had been different, blue-eyed soul men Dan Penn, George Soulé, and Eddie Hinton might have stepped out from the shadows a little earlier and become '60s stars. All three of these back-room boys possessed black voices too rarely committed to vinyl. It took Tony Joe White, a swampy Elvis lookalike and veteran of Texas R&B bands, to make the Southern singer-songwriter respectable. Signed to Phil Walden's management and Fred Foster's Monument label, White's first album was *Black and White* (1968), an appropriate title for a record that mixed soul and swamp-blues (Johnnie Taylor's "Who's Makin' Love," Slim Harpo's "Scratch My Back") with pop and country (Glen Campbell's "Wichita Lineman," Bobby Russell's "Little Green Apples").

White's own songs—"Willie and Laura Mae Jones," the Top 10 "Polk Salad Annie"—were brilliant vignettes that captured the life and idiosyncrasies of the Deep South with affection and humour. In time they were covered by everyone from Dusty Springfield and Solomon Burke to Elvis Presley. By 1972, White was being produced by Jerry Wexler at Muscle Shoals Sound, whose musicians became briefly known as the Swampers. (Monument labelmate Larry Jon Wilson borrowed from White and from Bobbie Gentry, joining the stable of songwriters—White, Billy Swan, Kris Kristofferson, et al.— at Nashville's Combine Music. This Georgia native was pure Southern Gothic—funky, slightly scary, delivering the vivid imagery of songs like "Sheldon Church Yard" in a lowdown baritone growl.)

After White perfected the white country–R&B style of the '70s, it wasn't long before Muscle Shoals veterans Dan Penn and Donnie Fritts followed his lead. Penn had cut various sides and hundreds of demos but never took himself seriously enough as an artist to cut an album. When he finally got around to recording *Nobody's Fool* for Bell in 1973, drugs had taken their toll on his voice but hadn't destroyed his melodic and lyric genius. There were great things in the Bacharach-style "Raining in Memphis," the beautiful "Time," and a marvellous throwback to his vintage country soul songs, "I Hate You," covered in due course by soulman-turned-country star Ronnie Milsap and blues-ballad godfather Bobby Bland.

Fritts followed a year later with the Atlantic *Prone to Lean* album, produced by Jerry Wexler and Kris Kristofferson at Muscle Shoals

Sound. One of the best things on it was "Winner Takes All," written with Penn, while other songs came courtesy of Tony Joe White, Eddie Hinton and Kristofferson. If Fritts wasn't the world's greatest singer, the album was nevertheless a splendid celebration of the country-soul swamp-rock sound. "I'm really indebted to Jerry for making that happen," Fritts told me. "Plus it was a nice opportunity for him to work with Kris, whose band I was playing in."[39]

Like Penn, Mississippian George Soulé was used for many of the demos at FAME. In fact, his biggest hit was a demo of George Jackson's funky "message" song "Get Involved" in 1973. When this irresistible slice of Johnnie Taylor–style exhortation made the R&B Top 20, Soulé was asked, somewhat embarrassingly, to appear on TV shows. "I just didn't feel that comfortable being a white artist giving this black message," he told me.

"George could really sing; he sounded totally black," said his one-time writing partner Terry Woodford. "A real insecure guy, but very talented. I signed him as a writer and singer and produced his first record for Bell, then *he* produced *me* on Cotillion." In addition to writing with Woodford—songs cut by everyone from Lulu to Joe Tex—Soulé drummed on sessions for Rick Hall, produced acts at Muscle Shoals Sound, and engineered country records at Al Cartee's Music Mill Studio. The one thing he never got a proper shot at was singing.

Arguably the greatest white R&B to come out of the backrooms of country soul was found on Eddie Hinton's Capricorn album *Very Extremely Dangerous,* cut at Muscle Shoals Sound in late 1977. Hinton had grown up in Tuscaloosa, Alabama, singing with such college-circuit bands as the Minutes before moving to Muscle Shoals as a session

---

39 Fritts got another shot at recording with the 1997 album *Everybody's Got A Song,* while Penn was signed by Sire/Blue Horizon in 1994 and released *Do Right Man,* featuring his reworkings of classics like "Dark End Of The Street," "It Tears Me Up," and "I'm Your Puppet." The author was among the lucky few that year to have caught a Penn show in London arranged by mega-fan Bobby Gillespie, as well as the extraordinary "Southern Songwriters" evening on London's South Bank, when Penn lined up alongside Joe South, Guy Clark, Allen Toussaint, and Vic Chesnutt to tear the heart out of "Dark End Of The Street." On the back of shows like this, American singer-songwriter Jeb Loy Nichols compiled the splendid *Country Got Soul* albums, released by Ross Allen's Casual Records.

guitarist and writing for Percy Sledge with Marlin Greene. "Eddie was thought of as a wonderboy," Jerry Wexler recalled. "We all reckoned it was only a matter of time before he became a superstar." It's Hinton's guitar work you can hear on records as different as Elvis Presley's "Merry Christmas Baby" and the Staple Singers' "I'll Take You There."

Sadly, drink and drugs reduced Hinton to a state of virtual destitution within five years; when Wexler suggested Phil Walden give him a shot at recording, the one-time wonderboy was sweeping out the Capricorn studios. After a contract was signed in July 1977, Hinton travelled up to Muscle Shoals Sound to record with his old colleagues Roger Hawkins, David Hood, Jimmy Johnson, and Barry Beckett. And what a revelation it was: a scorched white voice—"the blackest of all the white boys," in Jim Dickinson's phrase—that might almost have been Otis Redding risen from the grave. A version of "Shout Bamalama" uncannily captured Redding in his early Little Richard phase, while the heartbreakingly beautiful ballads "We Got It" and "Get Off In It" sounded like Bobby Womack at his informal, lay-preaching best.

"I believed a Caucasian singing Negro music could make a lot of money," Hinton told me in Decatur, Alabama. "But the main reason I chose it was because I liked it." Unfortunately, Capricorn went bust just as *Very Extremely Dangerous* was approaching the 20,000 sales mark, leaving Hinton to begin another slippery slide downhill. In late 1984, he was found outside the Decatur Salvation Army hostel by Shoals acolyte Johnny Wyker, who installed him in a tiny one-room apartment and encouraged him to record again. "Eddie was super-talented," Jimmy Johnson said. "He did it all . . . wrote, sang, arranged, and produced. But then the brain damage set in. Last time I saw him I had to knock him down."

"Some of us got through the drugs with part of our minds intact," says Dan Penn, who brought Hinton to American in Memphis. "Something snapped in Eddie, and he was never the same again."[40]

---

40 After recording *Cry and Moan* (1991) and *Very Blue Highway* (1993) for Bullseye Blues—and having his *Letters From Mississippi* released by the small British label Zane—Hinton died of a heart attack on July 28, 1995. The title track of 1999's posthumous *Hard Luck Guy* may be the last great Southern soul record.

Hinton's album might almost have been Southern soul's last stand. Following its 1978 release, both R&B and country became increasingly slick. As cities expanded and the countryside shrank, so people began to lose the sense of their roots. The old country-soul sound of FAME and Goldwax—a music of black and white Southerners in some kind of harmony—was too heartfelt and ingenuous to survive the onslaughts of disco and hip-hop.[41] Could pop music ever regain such innocent intensity?

---

41 Note, of course, that the South spawned its own highly distinctive style of hip-hop in the late '90s, when acts such as the Geto Boys, 2 Live Crew, OutKast, Goodie Mob, Ludacris, and Lil Wayne emerged from major cities like Miami, Houston, Atlanta, and New Orleans to challenge the entrenched power bases of the East and West Coasts. Meanwhile the likes of Field Mob, Bubba Sparxxx, and Nappy Roots came out of smaller towns in Georgia, Kentucky, and Louisiana. Simultaneously, such non-Southern acts as the Wu-Tang Clan regularly sampled '70s Southern-soul hits by Hi artists like Ann Peebles and O.V. Wright.

8 Say It One More Time

"We're a bunch of rednecks and field hands playing
unpopular music. This is not popular music."
—James Luther Dickinson

"I haven't heard an Otis Redding, an Aretha Franklin,
or a Wilson Pickett in ten years. But then I haven't heard
many black singers in ten years. Not many come."
—Rick Hall

"Back then it just seemed like everyone was more into the music.
Money came later. Maybe it was because I was so much younger."
—Jerry Carrigan

"I didn't even think of the music as being white or black. It was several
years before I realized that the whole floor was full of white boys and
one black singer. I remember turning round and going . . . 'wow.'"
—Jimmy Johnson

"I just don't feel this synthesizer music. I want to hear a
human bass player with a groove that he made up, and I
want to feel a human drummer holding it in the road."
—Buddy Killen

215

"I can't stand cutting to a click-track here in Nashville. The R&B we played rose and fell, it had hills and valleys."
—James Stroud

"Since disco wiped us out, you don't have great singers any more, and you don't have great songs. There's nothing better to me than a great ballad sung by a great singer. You might feel like dancing to a disco record, but you don't live that record."
—David Johnson

"David Johnson tells me a white man just can't get arrested with a black record anymore. The racial lines have been drawn again, and unless you're black, you can forget it."
—Quin Ivy

"As long as there are people losing jobs and losing people, as long as men and women cheat on each other, there's gonna be the need to hear someone else singing about it on the radio. Those songs will keep being written to echo the feeling of the hurt."
—Jerry Strickland

"Regarding black and white music, I don't think there could have been one without the other. Do you?"
—Fred Foster

"I have a dream . . . that one day the sons of former slaves and the sons of former slave-owners will be able to sit together at the table of brotherhood."
—Martin Luther King Jr.

40 Masterpieces of Country Soul

Ivory Joe Hunter—"City Lights" (Dot, 1959)
Solomon Burke—"Just Out of Reach" (Atlantic, 1961)
Esther Phillips—"Am I That Easy to Forget?" (Lenox, 1962)
William Bell—"You Don't Miss Your Water" (Stax, 1962)
Jimmy Hughes—"Steal Away" (FAME, 1963)
Joe Hinton—"Funny How Time Slips Away" (Back Beat, 1964)
Bobby "Blue" Bland—"Share Your Love With Me" (Duke, 1964)
Tommy Tate—"Big Blue Diamonds" (OKeh, 1964)
Ray Charles—"Together Again" (ABC-Paramount, 1966)
Ruby Johnson—"I'll Run Your Hurt Away" (Volt, 1966)
Mighty Sam—"Sweet Dreams" (Amy, 1966)
Arthur Conley—"Let Nothing Separate Us" (Jotis, 1966)
Aretha Franklin—"Do Right Woman—Do Right Man" (Atlantic, 1967)
Percy Sledge—"Out of Left Field" (Atlantic, 1967)
Joe Tex—"The Truest Woman in the World" (Dial, 1967)
Toussaint McCall—"One Table Away" (Ronn, 1967)
Irma Thomas—"Good to Me" (Chess, 1967)
Roscoe Shelton—"There's a Heartbreak Somewhere" (Sound Stage 7, 1968)
Kip Anderson—"I Went Off and Cried" (Excello, 1968)
James Carr—"That's the Way Love Turned Out for Me" (Goldwax, 1968)
Ella Washington—"He Called Me Baby" (Sound Stage 7, 1968)
Johnny Adams—"Reconsider Me" (S.S.S. International, 1969)
Joe Simon—"Straight Down to Heaven" (Sound Stage 7, 1969)
Bobby Patterson—"She Don't Have to See You" (Paula, 1970)
Candi Staton—"Stand By Your Man" (FAME, 1970)
Otis Williams—"Begging to You" (Stop, 1970)

Barbara Lynn—"People Like Me" (Atlantic, 1970)

Big Al Downing—"I'll Be Your Fool Once More" (House of the Fox, 1970)

Spencer Wiggins—"Love Me Tonight" (FAME, 1970)

Betty LaVette—"He Made a Woman Out of Me" (Silver Fox, 1970)

Arthur Alexander—"In The Middle of It All" (Warner Brothers, 1972)

Dan Penn—"I Hate You" (Bell LP, 1973)

Stoney Edwards—"Hank and Lefty Raised My Country Soul" (Capitol, 1973)

Dobie Gray—"Drift Away" (MCA, 1973)

Al Green—"I'm So Lonesome I Could Cry" (Hi, 1973)

Dorothy Moore—"Misty Blue" (Malaco, 1975)

Denise LaSalle—"Two Empty Arms" (ABC, 1976)

Bettye Swann—"Be Strong Enough to Hold On" (Atlantic, 1976)

Eddie Hinton—"We Got It" (Capricorn, 1978)

McKinley Mitchell—"End of the Rainbow" (Chimneyville, 1978)

Bibliography and Further Reading

Anderson, Clive. "Memphis and the Sounds of the South," in *The Soul Book* (New York: Dell, 1975)

Bane, Michael. *White Boy Singin' the Blues* (New York: Penguin, 1982)

Bowman, Rob. *Soulsville USA: The Story of Stax Records* (New York: Schirmer, 1997)

Broughton, Viv. *Black Gospel* (Blandford, 1985)

Broven, John. *Walking to New Orleans* (Bexhill-on-Sea: Blues Unlimited, 1974)

————*South to Louisiana: The Music of the Cajun Bayous* (Gretna: Pelican, 1983)

Brown, Mick. "Deep Soul: How Muscle Shoals Became Music's Most Unlikely Hit Factory," *The Daily Telegraph*, October 2013

Bryant, Steve, et al. "The John Richbourg Story," *Souled Out*, Nos. 5 and 6, April 1980

Carrigan, Henry. "Talking with Rick Hall: *The Man from Muscle Shoals*," *No Depression*, May, 23, 2015

Cash, Wilbur J. *The Mind of the South* (New York: Alfred A. Knopf, 1941)

Charles, Ray, with Ritz, David. *Brother Ray* (New York: Warner Books, 1978)

Cohen, John. "The Folk Music Interchange: Negro and White," *Sing Out*, XIV, No. 6, January 1964

Cosgrove, Stuart. *Memphis '68: The Tragedy of Southern Soul* (Polygon, 2017)

Cummings, Tony and Hall, Denise. "The Stax Story," *Black Music*, March-June 1975

Dawidoff, Nicholas. *In the Country of Country: People and Places in American Music* (New York: Pantheon, 1997)

Dellar, Fred, Thompson, R., and Green, Douglas, *The Illustrated Encyclopedia of Country Music* (Salamander, 1977)

Escott, Colin, and Hawkins, Martin. *Sun Records* (rev. edn, Quick Fox, 1980)

220 Say It One Time for the Brokenhearted

Frechette, Dave. "Country Music Back to Black," *Essence,* September 1977

Gaillard, Frye. *Watermelon Wine* (St. Martin's Press, 1978)

Gillett, Charlie. *The Sound of the City* (rev. edn, London: Souvenir Press, 1984)

———*Making Tracks* (Panther, 1975)

Gordon, Robert. *It Came From Memphis* (Boston: Faber, 1995)

———*Respect Yourself: Stax Records and the Soul Explosion* (New York: Bloomsbury, 2015)

———"Dan Penn: Once More with Feeling," *Mojo,* 16 March 1995

———"Jim Dickinson: Earth Father," *Mojo,* 11 October 1994

Green, Douglas. *Country Roots* (New York: Hawthorne, 1976)

Green, Douglas (with Oermann, Bob). *The Listener's Guide to Country Music* (Poole: Blandford, 1983)

Grissim, John. *Country Music: White Man's Blues* (New York: Paperback Library, 1970)

———"Nashville Cats," *Rolling Stone,* December 9, *1971*

Guralnick, Peter. *Sweet Soul Music: Rhythm and Blues and the Southern Dream of Freedom* (Virgin, 1986)

———"The Last Soul Company," *Boston Phoenix,* 23 November 1983

Hall, Rick. *The Man from Muscle Shoals: My Journey from Shame to Fame* (Monterey, CA: Heritage Builders Publishing, 2015)

Hannusch, Jeff. *I Hear You Knockin'* (Swallow, 1985)

Haralambos, Michael. *Right On: From Blues to Soul in Black America* (Eddison, 1974)

Heilbut, Tony. *Thé Gospel Sound* (rev. edn, New York: Limelight, 1985)

Hirshey, Gerri. *Nowhere to Run* (New York: Times Books, 1984)

Hoskyns, Barney. *From a Whisper to a Scream: The Great Voices of Popular Music* (London: Fontana, 1991)

———"Empress In Exile: Etta James," *New Musical Express,* April 1984

———"The Last Great Soul Man: Bobby Womack," *New Musical Express,* October 1984

———"Singing For The Soul Of It: Tommy Tate," *New Musical Express,* January 1986

———"The Grandaddy of Soul: John Richbourg," *Soul Survivor* #7, Summer 1987

———"The Clown Prince of Soul," sleeve notes for *The Very Best of Joe Tex* (Charly Records), May 1988

———"The Strange Story of Eddie Hinton," *Soul Survivor* #8, Spring 1988

———"From Hi to Waylo: the Spirit of Memphis Soul," unpublished, 1988

———Joe Simon: *Lookin' Back,* sleeve notes, Charly Records, August 1988

———"Mama Tells Us All About It: Etta James," *The Times,* July 1989

———Bobby Womack: *Womack Winners,* sleeve notes, Charly Records, 1989

———"Malaco Records: Soul's Retirement Home," *The Times,* 10 July 1989

————"Crossing The Divide: Jerry Wexler," *The Independent on Sunday*, May 1993

————"Memphis Blues Again: Elvis '69," from *Aspects of Elvis* (London: Sidgwick & Jackson), 1994

————"Various Artists: *Royal Memphis Soul—Hi Records*," *MOJO*, July 1996

————"The Good Ol' Boy: Gram Parsons," *MOJO*, July 1998

————"Lost Soul: James Carr," *MOJO*, June 2000

————"Cover Story: A Dogg with Attitude," *Rock's Backpages*, November 2000

————"The Backroom Boys: Booker T & the MGs," *MOJO*, August 2001

————"Southern Men: The Allman Brothers Band," *MOJO*, December 2002

————"Sumpn' Funky Goin' On: True Tales of Blue-Eyed Backwoods Soul" sleeve notes for *Country Got Soul*, Casual Records, July 2003

————Candi Staton Comes Home to Country Soul, sleeve notes, Honest Jon's Records, March 2006

————"The Master: Reggie Young," *Uncut Legends*, December 2008

————"Out Of Left Cotton Field: The Brokenhearted Country Soul Of Percy Sledge," sleeve notes for *The Complete Atlantic Recordings* (Rhino), 2010

————"For Members Only: Bobby Bland on Malaco," *Malaco Records*, October 2010

Jones, LeRoi. *Blues People* (New York: William Morrow, 1963)

Jones, Roben. *Memphis Boys: The Story of American Studios* (Jackson: University of Mississippi Press, 2010)

Kemp, Mark. *Dixie Lullaby: A Story of Music, Race And New Beginnings in a New South* (New York: Free Press, 2004)

Kimberley, Nick. "Paranoid Sex in '60s Soul," *Collusion*, 2, February–April 1982

Malone, Bill C. *Country Music USA* (Austin: University of Texas, 1970)

————with McCulloch, Judith (eds). *Stars of Country Music* (New York: Avon, 1975)

Millar, Bill. "Southern Soul Man: John Richbourg," *Let it Rock*, April 1975

————"Big Al Downing: The Story of His Life," *New Kommotion* 24 (1980)

————"Gatemouth Brown," *Goldmine*, March 1981

Miller, Jim (ed.). *The Rolling Stone Illustrated Encyclopedia of Rock'n'Roll* (New York: Random House, 1976)

Morthland, John. *The Best of Country Music* (New York: Doubleday, 1985)

Nix, Don, *Road Stories and Recipes* (New York: Schirmer, 1997)

Oliver, Paul. *Songsters and Saints* (Cambridge: Cambridge University Press, 1984)

Russell, Tony. *Blacks, Whites, and Blues* (New York: Stein and Day, 1970)

Shaw, Arnold. *The World of Soul* (New York: Cowles Book Co., 1970)

————*Honkers and Shouters* (New York: Macmillan, 1978)

Shelton, Robert, with Goldblatt, Burt (eds). *The Country Music Story* (New York: Bobbs-Merrill, 1966)

Southern, Eileen. *The Music of Black Americans* (New York: W.W. Norton, 1971)

Toll, Robert C. *Blacking Up* (New York: Oxford University Press, 1974)

Tosches, Nick. "Cowboys and Niggers," in *Country* (New York: Dell, 1977)

Turner, William H., and Cabell, Edward J. (eds). *Blacks in Appalachia* (Lexington: University of Kentucky Press, 1985)

Vann Woodward, C. *Origins of the New South* (Baton Rouge: Louisiana State University Press, 1951)

Wade, Dorothy and Justine Picardie. *Music Man: Ahmet Ertegun, Atlantic Records and the Triumph of Rock 'n' Roll* (New York: Norton, 1991)

Werner, Craig. *A Change is Gonna Come: Music, Race and the Soul of America* (revised edition, University of Michigan Press, 2006)

Wexler, Jerry with Ritz, David. *The Rhythm and the Blues* (New York: Knopf, 1993)

Whitley, Carla Jean. *Muscle Shoals Sound Studio: How the Swampers Changed American Music* (Charleston, SC: History Press, 2014)

Younger, Richard. "No Direction Home: Arthur Alexander," *Mojo*, 25 December 1995

———*Get a Shot of Rhythm & Blues: The Arthur Alexander Story* (Tuscaloosa: University of Alabama Press, 2000)

Index

Material in notes is indicated by an n

223